Above the Law

The United States has traditionally been a great promoter of international justice – forging the Nuremberg and Tokyo tribunals after World War II and leading the way in creating tribunals to address genocides in Yugoslavia and Rwanda after the Cold War. Yet the US views the International Criminal Court – the culmination of the tribunal-building process – as a dire threat. The US voted against its establishment, passed legislation threatening to invade The Hague, and tried to destroy the ICC with economic sanctions. Delving into the uneasy relationship between the world's superpower and one of its most prominent international institutions, *Above the Law* explains how the desire to shield American soldiers from unwanted ICC scrutiny is the ultimate source of tension. Offering a sophisticated analysis of the ICC's track record that shows how American fears are overblown, Daniel Krcmaric argues that a more cooperative US policy toward the ICC would benefit both sides.

DANIEL KRCMARIC is Associate Professor of Political Science and Law (by courtesy) at Northwestern University. He is the author of *The Justice Dilemma: Leaders and Exile in an Era of Accountability* (Cornell, 2020) and numerous articles in academic journals. His research has won awards from the American Political Science Association and the Peace Science Society.

Above the Law

The United States and the International Criminal Court

DANIEL KRCMARIC
Northwestern University

CAMBRIDGE
UNIVERSITY PRESS

CAMBRIDGE UNIVERSITY PRESS

Shaftesbury Road, Cambridge CB2 8EA, United Kingdom

One Liberty Plaza, 20th Floor, New York, NY 10006, USA

477 Williamstown Road, Port Melbourne, VIC 3207, Australia

314–321, 3rd Floor, Plot 3, Splendor Forum, Jasola District Centre, New Delhi – 110025, India

103 Penang Road, #05-06/07, Visioncrest Commercial, Singapore 238467

Cambridge University Press is part of Cambridge University Press & Assessment, a department of the University of Cambridge.

We share the University's mission to contribute to society through the pursuit of education, learning and research at the highest international levels of excellence.

www.cambridge.org
Information on this title: www.cambridge.org/9781009698801

DOI: 10.1017/9781009698764

© Daniel Krcmaric 2026

This publication is in copyright. Subject to statutory exception and to the provisions of relevant collective licensing agreements, no reproduction of any part may take place without the written permission of Cambridge University Press & Assessment.

When citing this work, please include a reference to the DOI 10.1017/9781009698764

First published 2026

(top) Alfred Gescheidt / Contributor / Getty Images; (bottom) Flag with the logo of the of the International Criminal Court (ICC) (Photo by Alex Gottschalk/DeFodi Images via Getty Images)

A catalogue record for this publication is available from the British Library

Library of Congress Cataloging-in-Publication Data
Names: Krcmaric, Daniel, 1986- author
Title: Above the law : the United States and the International Criminal Court / Daniel Krcmaric, Northwestern University, Illinois.
Description: Cambridge, United Kingdom ; New York, NY : Cambridge University Press, 2026. | Includes bibliographical references and index.
Identifiers: LCCN 2025037923 (print) | LCCN 2025037924 (ebook) | ISBN 9781009698801 hardback | ISBN 9781009698788 paperback | ISBN 9781009698764 epub
Subjects: LCSH: International Criminal Court | International criminal courts–United States | Criminal jurisdiction–United States | LCGFT: Law materials
Classification: LCC KZ7312 .K73 2026 (print) | LCC KZ7312 (ebook) | DDC 345/.01–dc23/eng/20250815
LC record available at https://lccn.loc.gov/2025037923
LC ebook record available at https://lccn.loc.gov/2025037924

ISBN 978-1-009-69880-1 Hardback
ISBN 978-1-009-69878-8 Paperback

Cambridge University Press & Assessment has no responsibility for the persistence or accuracy of URLs for external or third-party internet websites referred to in this publication and does not guarantee that any content on such websites is, or will remain, accurate or appropriate.

For EU product safety concerns, contact us at Calle de José Abascal, 56, 1°, 28003 Madrid, Spain, or email eugpsr@cambridge.org

Contents

List of Figures	*page* vi
List of Tables	vii
Acknowledgments	viii
1 Washington and The Hague	1
2 US Support for International Justice	27
3 US Opposition to the ICC: Origins	85
4 US Opposition to the ICC: Practice	131
5 The ICC's Track Record	196
6 The Future of US–ICC Relations	229
References	246
Index	273

Figures

3.1 ICC membership *page* 90
5.1 American military bases abroad 210
5.2 The negligible effects of US military presence on
   ICC investigations 222

Tables

4.1 Potential American responses to ICC investigations	*page* 133
4.2 Determinants of American strategy toward ICC investigations	139
5.1 ICC investigations	200
5.2 Correlates of ICC investigations	217

Acknowledgments

This book's origins go back to March 5, 2020. On that day, the International Criminal Court (ICC) formally opened an investigation into war crimes in Afghanistan that had the potential to implicate American troops there. The Trump administration immediately condemned the investigation and claimed that the ICC harbored anti-American biases. This criticism of the ICC was nothing new. Every US president since the late 1990s worried that the ICC might disregard its legal mandate and instead inject anti-American political biases into its work. As the drama surrounding the Afghanistan investigation unfolded in Washington and The Hague, I became curious about whether American officials had a point. I spent a lot of time thinking about how I could evaluate the extent, if any, of anti-American bias at the ICC using the tools of social science. So I collected some data, wrote an article, and ultimately concluded that American allegations of bias were overblown. The process of writing the article, however, made me realize there were too many fascinating twists and turns in the US–ICC relationship for one article to come close to doing the topic justice. I needed to write a book. You now hold it in your hands.

During the long slog of writing the book, I accumulated a lengthy list of debts to many people who helped me along the way. To start, I thank the officials from both the US government and the ICC who were willing to share their unique insider perspectives on the turbulent relationship between America and the Court. Some of them were willing to have their names used in the book, whereas others asked for anonymity. Given the fraught circumstances of the US–ICC relationship today – American sanctions on the Court are back – I decided not to use the names of any of the interviewees to avoid risking any adverse consequences to their careers. These generous officials from both sides of the relationship may not see their names in print, but they were an invaluable resource.

My intellectual home as I wrote this book was Northwestern University's Department of Political Science. Countless conversations with smart colleagues in Scott Hall helped me to write the best possible version of this book. I especially appreciate the patience of my longserving department chair, Will Reno, who supported my research as it moved from a half-baked idea to a finished product. Thanks also to my wonderful students at Northwestern for indulging my digressions on why they should care about the relationship between the US and the ICC.

I was fortunate to have the opportunity to present portions of the book to audiences at several different universities and institutions. For their helpful feedback, I thank audience participants at my presentations at the Northwestern Pritzker School of Law, the University of Chicago, George Washington University, and Bridging the Gap's Atrocity Prevention Workshop at the United States Holocaust Memorial Museum.

At Cambridge University Press, I was lucky to work with John Haslam and his team. Thanks also to the anonymous peer reviewers. Whoever you are, your constructive criticism was a perfect model of how the peer review process ought to work.

Last but not least, I thank my family. My wife, Laura, is a constant source of encouragement. Our kids, Theo and Emma, make sure there is never a dull moment in our house. The drawings and stickers they often left on "Daddy's work papers" were a bright spot in the writing process. I dedicate this book to them.

1 Washington and The Hague

In 2018, newly appointed National Security Advisor John Bolton used his first public speech to describe American efforts to combat an adversary that was "outright dangerous" to "US national security interests." As his genteel Washington audience nibbled their lunches in the grand ballroom of the Mayflower Hotel, Bolton lambasted this enemy, describing it as a "nightmare come to life."[1] Likewise, Secretary of State Mike Pompeo repeatedly warned in official statements and press interviews about "the threat" this antagonist posed to American interests.[2] Bolton and Pompeo's boss agreed with their assessments. President Donald Trump issued an executive order that labeled this foe "an unusual and extraordinary threat to the national security and foreign policy of the United States" and imposed economic sanctions against it.[3]

Who is this allegedly grave threat to the United States (US)? Is it a geopolitical rival such as Russia or China? A rogue state like North Korea? A terrorist group? Perhaps surprisingly, it is a handful of judges and prosecutors on the other side of the world: the International Criminal Court (ICC).

The ICC, the world's first permanent international tribunal with jurisdiction over atrocity crimes, was established in 1998 at a diplomatic conference in Rome, Italy. The Court itself is based in The Hague, a city in the Netherlands famous for hosting numerous international organizations. The ICC began operating in 2002 after sixty states ratified its founding treaty, the Rome Statute. Unlike many other international institutions, the ICC is not intended to resolve disputes between states. The ICC is instead designed to investigate and prosecute specific individuals for a limited set of particularly heinous

---

[1] Bolton 2018.
[2] Rick Noack, "Why Does the Trump Administration Hate the ICC So Much?" *Washington Post*, April 5, 2019.
[3] Office of the President 2020.

crimes. Specifically, the ICC can punish the individuals who plan or perpetrate genocide, war crimes, and crimes against humanity.[4]

A simple but powerful idea motivated the creation of the ICC: No person, anywhere in the world, should be above the law. Perpetrators of atrocious crimes were once able to evade justice by hiding behind the security of a national border or the authority of an official government position, but the ICC aims to end this culture of impunity. Academics and policymakers alike tend to celebrate the Court's lofty ideals and ambitious goals. Legal scholars Leila Sadat and Richard Carden anointed the ICC as "the last great international institution of the twentieth century."[5] Swedish diplomat Hans Corell proclaimed at an ICC opening ceremony that "a page in the history of humankind is being turned."[6] United Nations (UN) Secretary General Kofi Annan expressed hope that the ICC would "bring nearer the day when no ruler, no state, no junta, and no army anywhere will be able to abuse human rights with impunity."[7] The first president of the ICC's Assembly of State Parties, Jordanian diplomat Zeid Raad Al Hussein, even asserted that the ICC represented "the biggest step forward in law since the Magna Carta."[8]

The ICC is a puzzling target of American ire. In many ways, the US and the ICC seem like they should be natural allies. American policymakers often sound uncannily similar to ICC officials when they discuss the importance of ending impunity around the world. When giving a speech at the Council on Foreign Relations, ICC Prosecutor Luis Moreno-Ocampo argued, "My mission is to end impunity for these crimes in order to contribute to the prevention of future crimes."[9] During a visit to Colombia, US Secretary of State Anthony Blinken similarly asserted, "Ending impunity as we know it is one of the best ways to prevent more abuses going forward."[10] Furthermore, in the years leading up to the ICC's creation, the US appeared on track to become one of the Court's key allies. American officials embraced the

---

[4] The ICC can also exercise jurisdiction over the crime of aggression under a very limited set of circumstances, an issue I discuss later in the book.
[5] Sadat and Carden 2000, 419.
[6] Barbara Crossette, "World Court Is Ratified," *New York Times*, April 11, 2002.
[7] Marlise Simons, "Without Fanfare or Cases, International Court Sets Up," *New York Times*, July 1, 2002.
[8] Quoted in Scheffer 2012a, 437. [9] Moreno-Ocampo 2010.
[10] Simon Lewis and Luis Jaime Acosta, "Blinken, on Colombia Visit, Says Human Rights Accountability Critical," *Reuters*, October 20, 2021.

idea of creating a permanent international tribunal to prosecute heinous crimes and repeatedly voiced their support, at least in principle, for the ICC. After participating in a series of preparatory meetings, the US sent a large delegation to the Rome Conference and played a prominent role in drafting many parts of the Rome Statute. One legal advisor to the American delegation in Rome, Theodor Meron, even described the ICC's founding treaty by saying, "American fingerprints are all over this document."[11]

Yet America's openness to the ICC was ephemeral and quickly shifted toward outright hostility. The US voted against establishing the ICC, refused to join the Court after its creation, threatened to invade The Hague, cut off foreign aid to countries that supported the ICC, and eventually imposed sanctions on ICC personnel designed to destroy the Court's ability to function.

This opposition to the ICC is not a mere function of political partisanship in the US. While Republicans typically use more bombastic rhetoric to attack the ICC, many prominent Democrats – including Presidents Bill Clinton, Barack Obama, and Joe Biden as well as presidential nominees such as John Kerry and Hillary Clinton – have also supported American efforts to resist the Court. Long before the aggressive policies of the Trump administration made headlines, David Scheffer, who served as America's first Ambassador-at-Large for War Crimes Issues during the Clinton administration, aptly described the strange tension in the US approach to the ICC: "The nation that forged the Nuremberg and Tokyo military tribunals after World War II and identified itself with bringing notorious war criminals to justice found itself awkwardly conflicted with a permanent International Criminal Court that would carry on the tradition."[12]

Questions and Answers

This book addresses three questions about the uneasy relationship between the world's superpower and the twentieth century's last great international institution: Why does the US fear the ICC? When, exactly, does the US oppose the ICC? And does the ICC's track record justify American hostility?

---

[11] Weschler 2000, 109.   [12] Scheffer 2012a, 164.

In line with these questions, the book's argument and evidence are presented in three parts. The first part seeks to understand American fears of the ICC. I start by stepping back to review America's broader relationship with international justice institutions. This is an important first step because if the US is wary of international justice in general, then its hostility to the ICC is neither surprising nor particularly interesting. I show that this is not the case. Drawing on official government documents, Congressional debates, diplomatic histories, and the personal memoirs of policymakers, I demonstrate that the US has often been the world's indispensable nation when it comes to pursuing international justice. For instance, the Nuremberg Trials of the surviving Nazi leadership after World War II – which later served as an inspiration for the ICC – were an American creation. The other Allies, especially Britain and Russia, preferred summary executions of captured Nazis, but the US insisted on a judicial response. Likewise, the US led the way in creating the Tokyo Tribunal that applied the Nuremberg model to Imperial Japan. After genocides in Yugoslavia and Rwanda in the 1990s, it was once again the US that pushed for international tribunals and provided the diplomatic, financial, and military backing required to make them work. Even after the ICC was established, the US has continued to support international justice efforts around the world, aiding the pursuit of accountability for atrocity crimes in places that range from Cambodia to Chad and Syria to Sierra Leone.

America's historical support for international justice makes its hostility to the ICC all the more surprising. Indeed, the paradox of America's tumultuous relationship with the ICC is its enthusiasm for virtually every other international justice initiative. We therefore need to understand US opposition to the ICC not just in isolation but also against the background of US support for other international justice institutions both before and after the ICC's creation.

The core of US opposition to the ICC, I argue, is the fear that the Court might initiate politically biased investigations and prosecutions that target American troops scattered across the globe. This fear stems from two of the ICC's institutional design features that arose out of negotiations at the Rome Conference. The first is that the Court has automatic jurisdiction over all individuals – including those from the US and other states that never joined the ICC – when they are on the territory of an ICC member. This form of territorial liability is of little concern for most states since they do not have troops abroad.

However, it creates a special challenge for the US because it has hundreds of thousands of troops stationed around the world. Given America's global military presence, its troops are uniquely exposed to the ICC and, in the nightmare scenario for the US, "can much more readily be nabbed and whisked away to The Hague."[13]

The second is that the ICC has an independent prosecutor who can select his or her own situations to investigate. This makes the ICC fundamentally different than the tribunals that preceded it in the 1990s since those tribunals could only investigate in countries where the UN Security Council granted jurisdiction. Given US veto power on the Security Council, this practice ensured that investigations were only opened when the US approved. But this is not the case with the ICC. Because of the ICC prosecutor's high level of discretion, a litany of senior American officials have alleged that the ICC would inevitably inject anti-American biases into investigations and turn the ICC into "an instrument of political warfare."[14] In line with the frequent American accusations of a "rogue" or "kangaroo" court, American policymakers fear that US troops might get dragged into politicized ICC proceedings simply for doing their jobs. Even if American soldiers never end up in the dock at The Hague, the ICC could still jeopardize US interests by putting its military under the microscope of a high-profile and potentially embarrassing investigation.

In the book's second part, I shift the focus from *why* the US fears the ICC to *when* it opposes the ICC. The basic idea underpinning this portion of the book is that even though America's fear that the ICC might someday target its troops is a constant, US policy toward the Court is a variable. The US, as described previously, has frequently been hostile to the ICC. But at some points, the US has appeared apathetic toward the ICC, largely ignoring the Court's decisions to open investigations or issue arrest warrants. At still other times, the US has even offered arms-length support to the ICC. An example is the bipartisan American support for the ICC's investigation in Ukraine, which helps the US cast Russian President Vladimir Putin as an international pariah. As Senator Lindsey Graham wryly put it, "This is one of Putin's bigger accomplishments. I didn't think it was possible, but he

---

[13] Goldsmith 2003, 96.   [14] Kissinger 2001, 94.

did it – and that's for him to rehabilitate the ICC in the eyes of the Republican Party and the American people."[15]

What explains this sort of variation in American policy toward the ICC? I start by generating a typology of three broad strategies that the US might pursue in response to ICC investigations: opposition, assistance, and neglect. I describe what makes each strategy conceptually distinct and highlight the specific tactics associated with them. I then explain why the US might pick one strategy over the others. My theoretical framework calls attention to the interaction of two key variables: (a) whether the ICC investigation threatens US troops and (b) whether the ICC investigation advances broader American foreign policy goals.

An analysis of each US presidential administration's policies toward the ICC provides strong support for the theoretical framework. For Democratic and Republican administrations alike, the desire to protect American troops around the world from ICC scrutiny is often the driving force behind US policy. Specifically, an opposition strategy is likely when the ICC turns its gaze toward conflict zones where US soldiers are present or when the ICC asserts jurisdiction over individuals from *other* countries that never signed up for the Court because the US worries about a precedent that might be used to target American servicemembers in the future. But when ICC investigations do not implicate the US military in any way, it becomes palatable for American officials to consider less hostile approaches to the Court. The choice between strategies of neglect and assistance hinges on whether an ICC investigation aligns with broader American foreign policy objectives. The US tends to assist the Court in situations where ICC involvement advances American interests, but the US generally neglects the Court – neither helping nor hurting it – when ICC involvement does nothing to further American foreign policy goals.

In the book's third part, I pivot to the ICC side of the relationship. Specifically, I examine whether claims of anti-American bias hold up in light of the ICC's history of investigations.[16] Some believe that ICC

---

[15] Charlie Savage, "U.S. Weighs Shift to Support Hague Court as It Investigates Russian Atrocities," *New York Times*, April 11, 2022.

[16] I justify my focus on investigations – rather than, say, preliminary examinations or arrest warrants – in detail in Chapter 5. But my conclusions about the absence of anti-American bias at the ICC are similar when examining these other indicators.

bias is self-evident because the Court opened an investigation in 2020 into possible war crimes committed on the territory of Afghanistan since 2003. This investigation coincided with the US occupation of Afghanistan and put American troops, among other actors, under the Court's microscope.[17] In the eyes of many US policymakers, the decision to open this investigation offered definitive proof that the ICC is politically motivated to target the US military. As Secretary Pompeo concluded, "Our fears were warranted."[18]

But are these fears really warranted? Are ICC investigations actually biased against the American military? Bias is a tricky thing to study, but I offer a creative solution in this book. My strategy for analyzing potential ICC bias differs from how government officials and political pundits typically address the issue. The standard approach is for someone to examine the details of a specific ICC investigation and then judge whether the investigation was merited. For example, this approach might ask the following question: Based on what we know about Afghanistan, was the ICC right to open an investigation there? The shortcoming of this approach is that bias is in the eye of the beholder. In a politically charged situation like Afghanistan, American officials will surely claim the investigation is biased. ICC officials will certainly consider their investigation fair and justified. Neutral observers might very well be split in their assessments. Therefore, this approach to analyzing bias would require making difficult judgment calls on which side is correct, a task that is bound to be a source of endless controversy.

A more social scientific option – which is the approach I take in this book – is to look at the bigger picture. Instead of attempting to judge the merits of a particular investigation, I analyze whether ICC investigations are disproportionately likely when US troops are present in a country. This approach allows me to evaluate the entirety of the ICC's track record. In practical terms, this means that my analysis considers all seventeen investigations the ICC has opened to date, making it impossible to cherry-pick unrepresentative cases. It also means that

---

[17] Afghanistan joined the ICC in 2003, which gives the ICC jurisdiction over any Americans there. Not long after opening the Afghanistan investigation, the ICC decided to deprioritize alleged American abuses and focus instead on alleged Taliban and Islamic State abuses, which were more numerous and severe.
[18] Rick Noack, "Why Does the Trump Administration Hate the ICC So Much?" *Washington Post*, April 5, 2019.

my analysis considers the ICC's non-investigations. Attempting to assess bias by examining only investigations is problematic because, in scholarly terms, it "samples on the dependent variable." We now have over two decades of data on the situations the ICC decided to investigate and – equally important – the situations the ICC decided *not* to investigate. A proper analysis of potential ICC bias must include all situations where investigations were possible even if they ultimately did not occur.

I consequently assess the degree, if any, of anti-American bias at the ICC with a statistical analysis of the ICC's track record. I start with a global sample of civilian killings that approximates the universe of situations the ICC might plausibly investigate. I then use geolocated data on all US foreign military bases to examine how the presence of American troops in a country affects the likelihood of the ICC launching an investigation. Contrary to the common narrative of anti-American bias, the estimated effects of US military bases are statistically indistinguishable from zero and substantively negligible. Simply put, there is no evidence that ICC investigations target America's military. As I discuss in the book's conclusion, these results suggest that it is possible – though far from guaranteed – that a better US–ICC relationship might be on the horizon.

Why the US–ICC Relationship Matters

The state of the US–ICC relationship is a crucial issue for American policymakers. They are right to be wary of the ICC if it is, in fact, targeting the US military unfairly. A rogue international prosecutor would represent a credible threat to American foreign policy interests. But if – as my evidence shows – the ICC is not biased against the US, then it is time to rethink America's combative approach to the Court. A more cooperative US policy toward the ICC could help end impunity, save lives, and advance several other American foreign policy goals.

Ending Impunity

The ICC's supporters and critics can all agree on one thing: The ICC is unlikely to live up to its lofty goal of ending impunity without American support. For instance, John Bolton, arguably the ICC's nemesis-in-chief, once noted that "whether the ICC survives and flourishes depends in large measure on the United States."[19] Though Bolton highlighted this point to advocate for a policy of US antipathy towards the ICC, his statement just as easily could have come from a human rights activist urging greater US support for the Court. The ICC's fate is not entirely in America's hands, but the US can do as much as – if not more than – any other actor to help or hinder the ICC's quest to end impunity.

The US holds so much sway over the ICC's ability to survive and flourish because the ICC has a central weakness: enforcement. The ICC does not have its own police force. It must instead rely on states to apprehend and transfer suspects to The Hague. States sometimes are willing to help fill this enforcement gap. For instance, Belgian authorities – acting on an ICC arrest warrant – captured the exiled Congolese warlord turned vice president Jean-Pierre Bemba outside of Brussels and sent him to The Hague. At other times, however, states are reluctant to aid the ICC by tracking down fugitives from justice. For every war criminal who ends up standing trial at the ICC, there are several others who remain at large and manage to travel abroad with impunity. For example, former Sudanese leader Omar Bashir – an individual discussed in detail later in the book – traveled widely across Africa for a decade despite an outstanding ICC arrest warrant for his role in perpetrating atrocity crimes in Darfur. There was little the ICC could do as state after state simply declined to apprehend Bashir as he passed through their territories. More recently, even a few of the ICC's traditional supporters – European democracies such as Italy and Poland – have wavered on whether they would carry out the ICC arrest warrant for Israeli leader Benjamin Netanyahu if he were to set foot in their countries.[20]

Given that the ICC relies on states to provide enforcement, the antagonistic relationship between the world's superpower and the ICC limits the Court's ability to get wanted criminals in the dock.[21] Some even worry that without American backing, the ICC may "follow its spiritual cousins, the League of Nations and the

---

[19] Bolton 1998, 71.
[20] Amy Spiro, "Italy Tells Israel It Won't Arrest Netanyahu under ICC Warrant If He Visits," *Times of Israel*, January 15, 2025.
[21] On America's global policing capabilities, see Krcmaric 2022.

Kellogg-Briand Pact, to the grave."[22] A more cooperative approach from the US could change this dynamic and make the ICC a more effective institution. An example from a different tribunal, the International Criminal Tribunal for Yugoslavia (ICTY), illustrates how American military, economic, and diplomatic clout can help make international justice a reality. In 1999, the ICTY indicted Serbian leader Slobodan Milosevic, the so-called Butcher of the Balkans. Even after Milosevic lost power the following year, Serbia's successor regime was unwilling to apprehend Milosevic and extradite him to the ICTY. Milosevic was effectively allowed to hide behind Serbia's borders and evade accountability. But the US changed the calculus in Belgrade by threatening to withhold hundreds of millions of dollars of foreign aid if the new regime did not arrest Milosevic and transfer him to ICTY custody. Serbian authorities quickly capitulated to American demands regarding Milosevic's fate and defended their actions by noting that acquiring American aid was more important than sheltering an indicted war criminal.[23]

If the US applied a similar enthusiasm to tracking down ICC fugitives, it could have a transformative effect on the Court's ability to get wanted war criminals to The Hague. Despite American fears about US soldiers facing unfair investigations and prosecutions, a more cooperative relationship between the US and the ICC could benefit both sides because they share the common goal of ending impunity for war crimes. As one international judge memorably described the ICC, "This court needs some American muscle."[24]

Saving Lives

The Central African Republic began a slow descent into civil war in 2012. As the country's central government collapsed, fighting erupted between Christian and Muslim militias. A Catholic mission and hospital in the village of Bossemptele managed to anger both sides of the

---

[22] Goldsmith 2003, 104.
[23] Carlotta Gall, "Yugoslavia Stalls on Aiding War Crimes Court," *New York Times*, June 22, 2001; and Marlise Simons and Carlotta Gall, "Milosevic Is Given to U.N. for Trial in War-Crime Case," *New York Times*, June 28, 2001.
[24] Marlise Simons, "US Grows More Helpful to International Criminal Court, a Body It First Scorned," *New York Times*, April 2, 2013.

conflict by assisting anyone injured or displaced regardless of their religious affiliation. Hundreds of people were hiding inside the mission when the Antibalaka, an extremist Christian militia, showed up and started abducting Muslim refugees. A potential bloodbath was in the works. But one brave nun, Sister Josephine, confronted the militia leader and informed him "that the camp was under the jurisdiction of the International Criminal Court, and that if anything happened to his prisoners he could end up in The Hague."[25] Father Bernard, the priest who ran the mission, later recounted Sister Josephine's gambit with a smile: "When the Antibalaka leader heard that, he agreed to let them go."[26]

The example of Sister Josephine illustrates the ICC's deterrence rationale: would-be war criminals and genocidaires might think twice before committing horrific abuses. Not everyone will be deterred, of course, but the threat of prosecution may be enough to stay the hand of some criminals. As the ICC's first president, Philippe Kirsch, described it, "By putting potential perpetrators on notice that they may be tried before the Court, the ICC is intended to contribute to the deterrence of crimes."[27] Indeed, the ICC's supporters often make bold claims about the Court's deterrent effect. William Pace, the former leader of the influential Coalition for the International Criminal Court, even predicted, "The ICC will save millions of humans from suffering unspeakably horrible and inhumane deaths in the coming decades."[28]

Within the academy, there is an ongoing debate on whether the ICC and other international tribunals deter atrocity crimes. Not long after the ICC's founding, Julian Ku and Jide Nzelibe reasonably concluded that in many studies "the deterrence claim is simply asserted or rejected without much empirical or theoretical analysis."[29] But the field has come a long way since then. To be sure, deterrence is notoriously hard to prove because it relies on a counterfactual. Successful deterrence hinges on events that did *not* take place (i.e., human rights violations that never occurred but would have taken place if the ICC did not exist). Despite this challenge, scholarship on deterrence has progressed in recent years. There is now an emerging scholarly consensus that the

---

[25] Anderson 2014. [26] Anderson 2014.
[27] Quoted in Hillebrecht 2016, 616. [28] United Nations 1998, 129.
[29] Ku and Nzelibe 2006, 780.

ICC and other international courts can, under at least some conditions, deter atrocity crimes.[30]

If the ICC really does deter atrocity crimes, then the US has both normative and strategic reasons to support the ICC. Normatively, the US – which often claims to put the protection of human rights at the forefront of its foreign policy – ought to do its part to save lives in countries torn apart by civil conflict and political strife. If atrocity crimes are "an affront to our common humanity," as America's 2015 National Security Strategy insists, then the US has a responsibility to support prosecutions of those who perpetrate such crimes.[31] But even if hard-nosed American policymakers are unconcerned about atrocities in far-flung corners of the globe, there is still a strategic reason to support the ICC: It might save American lives. From Bosnia to Libya and beyond, the US military has often intervened to try to stop exactly the sort of crimes – genocide, war crimes, and crimes against humanity – that the ICC is designed to prosecute and prevent. Consequently, there may be a substitution effect: Every crime that the ICC deters is one less situation where direct American military intervention is needed. To the extent that the ICC deters, the security of American servicemembers increases because there is less need to deploy them on dangerous humanitarian missions abroad. This raises notable policy implications. Instead of the ICC jeopardizing the safety of American troops with politically biased investigations – the standard justification for US hostility toward the ICC – the opposite might be true. The ICC might actually enhance the safety of American troops by keeping them out of harm's way.

Improving American Foreign Policy

Beyond its direct effects on efforts to end impunity and save lives, US opposition to the ICC is costly in more indirect ways. First, it alienates American allies, who are almost uniformly staunch supporters of the Court. When the US voted against the creation of the ICC at the Rome

---

[30] Akhavan 2001; Gilligan 2006; Kim and Sikkink 2010; Olsen, Payne, and Reiter 2010; Sikkink 2011; Meernik 2015; Hillebrecht 2016; Jo and Simmons 2016; Dancy 2017; Appel 2018; Krcmaric 2020; McAllister 2020, 2023. For less optimistic conclusions, see Wippman 1999; Drumbl 2005; Ku and Nzelibe 2006; Cronin-Furman 2013.

[31] The White House 2015.

Conference in 1998, not even one of its North Atlantic Treaty Organization (NATO) allies was willing to join it in opposing the Court. Moreover, many European allies were outright critical of the American position. The US reciprocated with vitriol of its own. Senator Jesse Helms, the influential chairman of the Senate Committee on Foreign Relations, publicly stated that "what galls me is that we sent American personnel overseas twice in this century, along with expenditure of billions of dollars, to save the bacon of countries who voted against us in this regard [the ICC]. And I damned well resent that."[32] Helms and other senators went on to discuss the possibility of pulling all American troops out of Germany as retaliation for Germany's backing of the ICC.[33] The US never followed through on this threat, but the damage to the transatlantic relationship was done. As John Ruggie summarizes, American hostility toward the ICC risks "sabotaging what most American allies consider the crowning achievement of the postwar move toward global governance."[34]

Second, it emboldens autocrats around the world to launch their own attacks on the ICC and the rule of law more generally. After the Trump administration's offensive against the ICC, American criticisms of the Court became "talking points for the leaders of Myanmar, the leaders of North Korea, the leaders of Russia."[35] Furthermore, countries under ICC investigation in recent years have felt comfortable openly attacking the Court. After the ICC launched an investigation into potential crimes against humanity committed during the Philippines' brutal "war on drugs," Filipino officials swiftly withdrew from the ICC and made it clear they would undermine the ICC's ability to collect evidence.[36] President Rodrigo Duterte even issued an ominous warning for international investigators: "Do not fuck with me."[37] In another stranger-than-fiction case, a Russian spy attempted to infiltrate the ICC's internship program to access secret information

---

[32] Senate Committee on Foreign Relations 1998.
[33] Senate Committee on Foreign Relations 1998.
[34] Ruggie 2005, 306. On how America's ICC policies may have contributed to the transatlantic rift, see also Moravcsik 2002; Gordon 2003.
[35] Matt Apuzza and Marlise Simons, "U.S. Attack on I.C.C. Is Seen as Bolstering World's Despots," *New York Times*, September 13, 2018.
[36] "I Will Arrest You: Duterte Warns ICC Lawyer to Steer Clear of Philippines," *Reuters*, April 12, 2018.
[37] "Philippine President Duterte Needs 'Psychiatric Evaluation,' Says UN Human Rights Chief," *France 24*, March 9, 2018.

concerning the Court's investigation of Russian war crimes committed in Ukraine.[38] After the spy was caught, the Putin regime escalated its war on the ICC by suggesting that Russia might target The Hague with a hypersonic missile strike, a move that echoed prior American threats to invade The Hague.[39] While the leaders of Russia, the Philippines, and elsewhere may have pushed back against the ICC regardless of US policy, America's long-standing hostility toward the ICC created a context where they anticipated that they could attack the Court without facing major consequences.

Third, it opens the US to charges of hypocrisy. In the eyes of many, the US supports international justice for others but not for itself. Its resistance to the ICC is therefore seen as yet another form of American exceptionalism that builds resentment throughout the world.[40] Nowhere was this controversial double standard clearer than in Yugoslavia. As described earlier, the US brought tremendous diplomatic and economic pressure to bear on Serbian authorities to send Milosevic and other war criminals to the ICTY for prosecution. At virtually the same time, however, the US insisted that the new regime in Belgrade sign an agreement promising never to transfer Americans to the ICC. One journalist aptly summarized the mood in official Belgrade by noting, "Questions are now being asked in Serbia about how America can demand that Belgrade extradite all war crimes suspects to stand trial at [the ICTY], while simultaneously asking that its citizens be exempt from the same process at the ICC."[41]

Fourth, it undermines America's coercive capabilities. When President Trump made the decision to impose unilateral sanctions on ICC personnel, the US faced considerable blowback. As one former State Department official acknowledged, "It creates the reality, not just the impression, of the United States as a unilateralist bully with contempt for international laws and norms."[42] Many of America's

---

[38] Annabelle Timsit and Adam Taylor, "Alleged Russian Spy Studied at Johns Hopkins and Won Internship at ICC," *Washington Post*, June 16, 2022. The alleged Russian spy, Sergey Cherkasov, posed as a Brazilian citizen but is accused of being a deep cover "illegal" operating at the behest of Russia's military intelligence agency.

[39] Isabel van Brugen, "Russia Threatens to Blow Up ICC with Hypersonic Missile," *Newsweek*, March 20, 2023.

[40] Ignatieff 2005; Sands 2005; Zvobgo 2021a.   [41] Briza 2005.

[42] Pranshu Verma, "Trump's Sanctions on International Court May Do Little beyond Alienating Allies," *New York Times*, October 18, 2020.

traditional multilateral sanctions partners came to the ICC's defense and were furious that the US turned an economic weapon typically reserved for terrorist groups and rogue nations on an international institution made up of lawyers and judges. Indeed, Trump's 2020 executive order imposing sanctions on the ICC even parroted text from previous US sanctions against the Kim regime in North Korea and the Maduro regime in Venezuela.[43] America's sanctions crusade against the ICC was costly both in its own right and because it could cripple US efforts to generate multilateral support for economic sanctions in other situations that arise in the future. As William Burke-White argued, "Applying tough sanctions against the personnel of a legitimate and broadly supported international organization undermines the broader efficacy and legitimacy of the tool for times when sanctions could actually advance U.S. national security."[44]

It might be worth bearing these costs if the ICC really is biased against the US. But if American fears of a rogue ICC are misguided – as this book implies – then the US is needlessly alienating allies, undermining the global rule of law, breeding grievances, and weakening its coercive capabilities. A more cooperative policy toward the ICC would not only help make the Court a more effective institution but would also improve American foreign policy.

Broader Implications

Looking beyond the specifics of the US–ICC relationship, this book raises more general implications for several debates in international relations.

America's Global Military Presence

My findings touch on debates about the costs and benefits associated with maintaining a massive American military presence around the world. In this regard, the US is a fundamentally unique country. It permanently stations hundreds of thousands of troops in some 800 military bases spread across nearly 80 countries. From the islands of the Pacific to the deserts of the Middle East, and from the jungles of Central America to the frozen tundra of the Arctic Circle, the US

---

[43] Burke-White 2021.   [44] Burke-White 2021.

military is seemingly everywhere. No other country has a foreign military presence that can compare to the US, nor can any historical empire such as Britain or Rome match modern-day America.

Proponents of America's global military presence argue that it is advantageous. Maintaining a "forward deployed" military, as the strategy is often called, enjoys a strong consensus in official Washington. Even in an era of fierce partisanship, sustaining a significant global military presence is one area where most Republicans and Democrats can still find common ground. The conventional argument in favor of a global military presence is about national security: it helps the US project power abroad.[45] For example, it allows the US to respond rapidly to emerging crises – anything from wars to terrorist attacks to natural disasters – in far-flung corners of the globe. America's forward deployments also play a key role in alliance politics because military bases signal a long-term American security commitment to host nations that simultaneously reassures allies and deters adversaries. Moreover, on the occasions that the US does go to war, its network of bases provides crucial logistical support that enables American soldiers to fight quite literally on the other side of the world. Beyond these security benefits, there may be economic advantages as well. America's worldwide military dominance allows it to protect the global commons, such as strategic sea lanes and shipping corridors, which are essential for trade and the US-friendly international economic order.[46]

Critics assert that America's globe-spanning military posture creates a variety of costs. To start, maintaining a global military presence is expensive. One conservative estimate finds that the peacetime US overseas military presence often costs over $100 billion per year, a number that soars considerably higher if spending in war zones is included.[47] Overseas bases may also breed grievances. Bases are a poignant reminder that the host state has sacrificed part of its sovereignty to the US, and, in some cases, bases even become the focal point of anti-American protest movements.[48] Yet another concern is that

---

[45] For historical accounts of America's global military presence and the power-projection logic that often accompanies overseas bases, see Blaker 1990; Sandars 2000; Baker 2004; Calder 2007; Vine 2015.
[46] Brooks, Ikenberry, and Wohlforth 2012.   [47] Vine 2015, 9.
[48] Cooley 2008; Yeo 2011. On the flip side, overseas military bases sometimes have a positive effect on public opinion toward the US. See Allen et al. 2020.

overseas bases distort incentives for American allies and encourage "free riding." That is, allies spend less on their own defense because they know that the US ultimately will pick up the tab and provide for their security.[49] In addition to these costs for the US, the rest of the world pays a price as well. The construction of American overseas bases has been linked to the displacement of indigenous populations, such as when British colonial administrators forcibly removed the people of the Chagos Islands so that the US could build a base on Diego Garcia, one of the islands.[50] Finally, the environmental consequences of America's global military footprint are devastating, with the Pentagon holding the dubious title of the world's largest institutional emitter of greenhouse gases.[51]

My book contributes to the debate on the costs and benefits of the US global military presence by highlighting an additional cost. Specifically, America's status as the most forward deployed country in the world generates its fear of – and underpins its hostility toward – the ICC. This hostility, in turn, causes all the aforementioned problems for US foreign policy: allies alienated, sanctions undermined, the rule of law weakened, and American double standards exposed. The US global military presence therefore may be even more costly than previously acknowledged. To be sure, the cost that I identify – international blowback associated with US hostility toward the ICC – is not the only cost or necessarily even the important cost. But as policymakers weigh the trade-offs of maintaining America's global military presence, it may tip the balance in favor of a reduced overseas military footprint.

Great Powers and International Institutions

The book speaks to broader debates about the relationship between great powers and international institutions. The conventional wisdom is that international institutions – including but not limited to international courts like the ICC – generally reflect the wishes of powerful states.[52] In this telling, major powers take the lead in creating and supporting international organizations that advance their interests in the present and "lock in" their influence for the future. At the same

---

[49] Posen 2014.   [50] Sands 2022.   [51] Crawford 2022.
[52] Abbott and Snidal 1998; Ikenberry 2000; Koremenos, Lipson, and Snidal 2001; Stone 2011.

time, weaker states agree to go along with the plans of more powerful states because formal institutional rules limit the ability of the strong to engage in arbitrary and crude coercion toward the weak. Hence, both sides get something out of the institutional arrangement, though the benefits mostly flow to the great powers. The major post–World War II international institutions – such as the UN Security Council, the International Monetary Fund, and the World Bank – are consistent with this conventional viewpoint.[53]

The ICC, however, inverts the standard account of international institutions. Weaker states, not the great powers, largely got their way during the ICC during negotiations in Rome and have been the Court's most ardent supporters since then. Indeed, the ICC was established against the explicit wishes of the US at the very height of America's "unipolar moment."[54] Moreover, since the Court opened its doors, the world's most powerful countries – not only the US, but also China and Russia – have declined to join it.

This is no accident. One of the more remarkable aspects of the ICC is that there are no special privileges for the powerful. For example, every member of the Court gets a single vote when electing the ICC's personnel, including the all-important prosecutor. This makes the ICC an unusually egalitarian international organization. Unlike the veto power granted to the UN Security Council's permanent five members or the weighted voting shares given to larger economies at the World Bank and the International Monetary Fund, there is no special voting influence for the major powers at the ICC. Even more importantly, the ICC's founders endowed the Court with an independent prosecutor who could open investigations and issue arrest warrants without first getting the permission of the members of the Security Council or any other state.

As a result of these institutional design choices at the Rome Conference, the ICC is uniquely isolated from the typical constraints of state power. This allows the Court to do things that were once unimaginable. For instance, the ICC issued an arrest warrant in 2023 for Vladimir Putin, the "most powerful man in the world,"

---

[53] These post–World War II institutions, however, may be a poor comparison for today's international courts. In fact, the vast majority of international court activity – such as issuing opinions and rulings – has occurred since the end of the Cold War. See Alter 2014, 4.

[54] Krauthammer 1990.

according to the editors of *Forbes*, the political pundit Fareed Zakaria, and a host of other commentators.[55] If the ICC can go after the world's most powerful man – a leader with a permanent seat on the UN Security Council and the world's largest arsenal of nuclear weapons – it challenges the great power privilege that has historically characterized international politics.

The absence of special privileges for powerful states at the ICC touches on a larger debate about the relationship between state power and international institutions. One school of thought highlights the fact that powerful states typically do not like institutions that are beyond their control.[56] Independent institutions – those that do not have to cater to the wishes of one or a handful of powerful states – represent a potential threat to the influence that great powers normally wield in international affairs. As Josef Joffe colorfully summarizes, "Great powers loathe international institutions they cannot dominate; lesser nations like them the way the Lilliputians liked their ropes on Gulliver."[57]

Another school of thought calls attention to several reasons why powerful states might create and support international institutions that are not (fully) under their control.[58] First, major powers may turn to independent institutions to enhance the credibility of their commitments.[59] By working through established institutional rules, strong states can more effectively "tie their own hands" and induce other states to cooperate with them. Second, states may work through independent institutions to help adjudicate disputes that they cannot resolve on their own. Acting as a third party, international legal bodies can facilitate the peaceful resolution of disputes – even over core issues such as territorial or maritime borders – more efficiently than bilateral negotiations. Specifically, international adjudicators create focal points

---

[55] Fareed Zakaria, "Why Putin Is World's Most Powerful Man," *CNN News*, March 22, 2018. For its part, *Forbes* has named Putin the world's most powerful person four different times.

[56] There is an extensive academic literature on this subject. Some key works include Mearsheimer 1994; Goldsmith 2003; Posner 2004; Goldsmith and Posner 2005; Posner and Yoo 2005; Bosco 2014a.

[57] Joffe 2003, 158.

[58] For a more general statement of the potential benefits of international institutions, see Keohane 1984.

[59] Ikenberry 2000; Moravcsik 2000; Helfer and Slaughter 2005; Alter 2008; Guzman 2008; Simmons and Danner 2010.

for agreement, produce reputational costs for noncompliance, and generate political cover for concessions that might be unpopular with domestic audiences.[60] Third, powerful states may support institutions for normative or ideological reasons.[61] As arguably the most high-profile part of the "justice cascade,"[62] the trend in world politics toward holding individuals accountable for human rights abuses, the ICC represents an attractive set of ideals. States may feel compelled to support the ICC even if they worry about ceding authority to it.

US policy toward the ICC to date generally supports the first school of thought. American hostility to the Court is in large part due to the absence of special privileges accorded to the US. For example, instead of an independent prosecutor, the US wanted the UN Security Council – where the US wields veto power and could therefore shield its troops – to control ICC investigations. But nearly every other state rejected the American position because it would create a double standard and effectively immunize the major powers from ICC authority. More broadly, one of the key fault lines during the negotiations that created the ICC involved whether to recognize that the ICC created an unequal distribution of risk for the US or to treat all states equally in the eyes of the law. The American position was clear: The US viewed itself as an exceptional nation due to its outsized role in international security affairs and therefore believed that it deserved exceptional protection from potentially frivolous ICC investigations. As one member of the American negotiating team in Rome put it, "What the United States cannot support is an international court that fails to recognize its unique responsibilities in the world when issues of international peace and security are involved."[63] Likewise, the Pentagon believed that "massive deployments justified exceptional protection for American forces."[64] When most of the world disagreed with the idea of creating a special set of standards for the powerful, the US pulled its support for the ICC.

While my assessment of American hostility toward the ICC is largely consistent with the argument that powerful states are reluctant to support international institutions that they cannot control, my book

[60] On the politics of international adjudication, see Allee and Huth 2006; Gent and Shannon 2010; Mitchell and Powell 2011; Powell and Wiegand 2014, 2023.
[61] For a broader analysis of the relationship between ideology and international institutions, see Voeten 2021.
[62] Sikkink 2011.   [63] Lietzau 2001, 138.   [64] Scheffer 2012a, 228.

also offers a friendly amendment to this claim. One key lesson of the ICC case is that it is not exactly *power* but rather *threat* that determines whether states decide to oppose international institutions.[65] If we look beyond the US to the other permanent members of the UN Security Council, it is clear that the US position toward the ICC was unique even among powerful states. Most members of the Security Council – the UK, France, and even Russia – voted in favor of creating the ICC.[66] Like the US, these states lost control over the ICC when the decision was made to give the Court an independent prosecutor rather than have the Security Council initiate investigations, but they decided to back the ICC anyway. The other member of the Security Council, China, quietly voted against establishing the ICC but stopped well short of attacking the Court in a manner similar to the American onslaught. The different responses of the US and these other powerful states are due to their different threat perceptions of the ICC. The other members of the Security Council tend to keep their troops behind their own borders, so they have much less to fear from the ICC (unless they go to war, as Russia did in Ukraine). The US alone permanently stations massive numbers of troops around the world. The key implication for scholars studying the relationship between major powers and international institutions is that nuanced, context-specific information – not some aggregate measure of national power – is often necessary to understand when powerful states will support or oppose international institutions.

Lastly, it is worth considering whether the dynamics of the US–ICC relationship generalize to other international courts. On the one hand, there are similarities: the US has an extensive history of worrying about international courts that it cannot control. For example, the International Court of Justice (ICJ), a tribunal that adjudicates disputes between states, allowed Nicaragua to sue the US in the 1980s for mining its harbors. As one of Nicaragua's lawyers put it, they worked through the ICJ instead of confronting the US directly because the ICJ provided a venue where Nicaragua could face the US "on equal terms" and the "outcome [was] not predetermined by the dipartites [sic] of

---

[65] On the importance of distinguishing between power and threat, at least in the context of alliance formation, see Walt 1985.
[66] The UK and France quickly joined the ICC, but Russia never joined the Court despite voting in favor of its creation.

military and economic power between the parties."[67] This was unacceptable to American officials, and the US promptly withdrew from the ICJ's jurisdiction. In another case, the US started as a leading negotiator of the Law of the Sea Convention, a 1982 legal framework for maritime governance. Among other things, joining would have exposed the US to the jurisdiction of the new International Tribunal for the Law of the Sea (ITLOS). Despite gaining significant concessions from other states during the negotiations, the Ronald Reagan administration ultimately declined to join the Convention on the grounds that the concessions were not enough to safeguard American interests. As described in Chapter 3, the Bill Clinton administration made a remarkably similar string of decisions during the ICC negotiations.[68]

On the other hand, there are differences: American animosity toward the ICC is in a class of its own. In contrast to its harsh attacks on the ICC, the US never imposed economic sanctions or threatened to use military force against the ICJ or the ITLOS. The US simply withdrew from ICJ jurisdiction after the *Nicaragua* case and declined to submit itself to ITLOS jurisdiction in the first place. These more subdued American reactions reflect a crucial difference in the design of the international courts. With most courts, including the ICJ and the ITLOS, states do not fall under their jurisdiction without first consenting to it. But that is not the case with the ICC. Individuals from nonmember states are automatically exposed to ICC jurisdiction when they are on the territory of member states. As a result, declining to join the ICC does *not* shield Americans from ICC jurisdiction, an unusual dynamic that underpins much of the US hostility toward the Court.

International Courts in a Political World

The ICC is a legal institution, but it operates in a political world. As ICC Prosecutor Karim Khan acknowledged in a 2024 interview with *CNN*, his investigation of senior Israeli leaders and top Hamas commanders forced the Court to sit atop "the San Andreas fault of

---

[67] Reichler 2001, 38.

[68] On parallels between the negotiations that created the ICC and the Law of the Sea Convention, see Scheffer 2012a, 166. Successive American presidents have flirted with the idea of joining the Law of the Sea Convention, but they have either thought better of it or discovered that Congress was unwilling to go along with their plans.

international politics and strategic interests."[69] My book therefore offers an opportunity to explore how international courts navigate the complex interplay of law and politics.

Despite the considerable efforts to isolate the ICC from political influence, the Court nonetheless has an awkward relationship to power politics. The UN Security Council does not get to pick the ICC's investigations – as the US wanted during negotiations in Rome – but the Security Council can refer situations to the ICC that are outside the Court's standard jurisdiction. For some, the decision to give the Security Council any role calls into question the Court's neutrality and impartiality.[70] This concern came to the fore with the ICC's investigation in Libya – an investigation that resulted from a Security Council referral and coincided with a NATO military intervention – prompting concerns that political power and international justice were too deeply intertwined.[71] Moreover, the ICC's lack of independent enforcement mechanisms means that when states are unwilling to apprehend and transfer suspects to The Hague, the ICC has no way to prosecute and punish the world's worst criminals. ICC Prosecutor Luis Moreno-Ocampo candidly recognized this political reality when he noted that the diplomatic community "is crucial for me, because basically, at the end of the day, the impact of my cases will be defined by them, not by me."[72]

The ICC therefore straddles the legal and the political. This idea, however, is anathema to many ICC supporters, who insist there is a bright line between politics and law. The ICC's founders drew heavily on the school of thought known as "legalism." The essence of legalism, according to Judith Shklar's famous description, is that "politics is regarded not only as something apart from law, but as inferior to law. Law aims at justice, while politics looks only to expediency. The former is neutral and objective, the latter the uncontrolled child of competing interests and ideologies."[73] While this clear division between politics and law is an attractive idea, reality is more

---

[69] Amanpour 2024. [70] Ba 2020, 18.
[71] The rapid speed at which the ICC opened an investigation and issued arrest warrants following the UN Security Council referral was notable to many observers. See, among others, Kersten 2016; Vinjamuri 2016; Bosco 2017; Ba 2020.
[72] Moreno-Ocampo 2010. [73] Shklar 1964, 110.

complex.[74] Regardless of the ICC's desire to be apolitical, it may be pulled into the realm of politics in at least three ways.

First, the Court can have unintended political effects. That is, strategic political actors might respond to the ICC in unexpected ways. Research on how the ICC shapes political violence, sometimes called the "peace versus justice" debate, illustrates this dynamic most clearly.[75] Some worry that the ICC – even if it strictly follows its legal mandate – might interfere with the complex political negotiations that are often required to resolve ongoing conflicts.[76] In particular, the threat of international prosecution at the ICC might generate an obstacle when attempting to coax troublesome leaders out of office with foreign retirements.[77] Rather than head into exile as a "golden parachute" retirement option, oppressive rulers might cling to power, prevent democratic reforms, and fight longer civil wars.[78] The decision-making of Muammar Gaddafi, who opted to fight to the bitter end in Libya instead of going into an uncertain exile during Libya's 2011 civil war, is consistent with this viewpoint.

Second, states decide whether it is in their interest to cooperate with the ICC and, if so, how to do so in a way that advances their interests. All states – the strong and the weak alike – may attempt to use the ICC for their own ends. Major powers can employ their economic and military might to try to steer the ICC in their preferred direction by using UN Security Council referrals, sharing information, withholding funding, enforcing arrest warrants, and a variety of other techniques.[79] Weaker states, for their part, often try to use the international legal

---

[74] On the relationship between politics and law at the ICC, see Roach 2013; Bosco 2014a; Steinberg 2024. For a more general analysis of the connection between politics and law in world affairs, see Hurd 2017.

[75] Of course, political actors react to the ICC in other ways too. On public opinion toward the ICC, see Voeten 2013; Zvobgo 2019; Chapman and Chaudoin 2020; Dancy et al. 2020; Zvobgo and Chaudoin 2025.

[76] The ICC insists that it ignores the political effects of its investigations and arrest warrants for the sake of neutrality. Several ICC officials maintain there is – and should be – a firewall between political issues like resolving civil conflicts and the Court's legal mandate to prosecute the perpetrators of atrocity crimes. See Fatou Bensouda, "International Justice and Diplomacy," *New York Times*, March 19, 2013.

[77] Escriba-Folch and Krcmaric 2017; Krcmaric 2018, 2020.

[78] Escriba-Folch and Wright 2015; Nalepa and Powell 2016; Prorok 2017; Krcmaric 2020.

[79] Bosco 2014a. See also Chapter 4.

environment as a form of "lawfare" to compensate for their material shortcomings.[80] For instance, several African regimes have attempted to use the ICC as a weapon in domestic political struggles, typically by self-referring to the ICC in the hopes of marginalizing their political opponents.[81] In the eyes of some, this makes the ICC "inherently political" because the Court's investigations, arrest warrants, and trials end up drawing distinctions between the "friends" and the "enemies" of the international community.[82]

Third, the ICC might occasionally need to demonstrate some political savvy to survive as an institution. Most notably, the ICC may be hesitant to target major powers with investigations because – to put it bluntly – the ICC needs the major powers more than the major powers need the ICC. This possibility raises significant implications for the US–ICC relationship. In contrast to the American policymakers who allege anti-US bias at the ICC, some scholars anticipate the opposite. That is, they expect the ICC to demonstrate pro-US bias because the ICC has compelling political reasons to avoid getting entangled with the American military.[83] After all, the Court depends on powerful states for funding, intelligence sharing, cooperation at the UN Security Council, and the enforcement of its arrest warrants. Rather than alienate the US, the ICC might try to win over the world's superpower to its cause by avoiding investigations that threaten American interests. The ICC, according to this viewpoint, would inevitably "hamstring itself" by going after the US military.[84]

My book contributes to this debate by drawing a distinction between "being politicized" and "being politically biased." Since the ICC is forced to operate in a political world, I agree with other scholars who have pointed out that the Court has little chance of insulating law from politics entirely. But that does not necessarily mean that the ICC is politically biased. Indeed, my results show there is no merit to allegations that the ICC is biased against the US – arguably the most consequential type of bias for all the reasons outlined previously. My statistical tests instead indicate that the ICC has generally done a good job following its legal mandate: It neither targets nor avoids the

---

[80] On lawfare, see Dunlap 2008.   [81] Ba 2020.
[82] Nouwen and Werner 2010, 941.   [83] Bosco 2014a; Rudolph 2017.
[84] Wedgwood 1998, 23. I empirically assess this possibility in Chapter 5.

world's superpower and instead tends to investigate the world's gravest atrocity crimes.

Road Map

The rest of the book is divided into five chapters. Chapter 2 provides an overview of America's traditional support for international justice institutions and demonstrates the anomalous nature of US opposition to the ICC. Chapter 3 seeks to explain the origins of American opposition to the ICC. After a brief overview of how the ICC works, I turn to the negotiations at the Rome Conference. I describe how America's fear of a rogue ICC prosecutor targeting the US military around the world ultimately ensured that the US opposed the Court's creation. Chapter 4 discusses how American opposition to the ICC has worked in practice in the post-Rome era. I introduce a theory to explain why American hostility toward the Court waxes and wanes over time and across cases, with the US sometimes even opposing one ICC investigation at the exact same moment that it supports another. Chapter 5 outlines my quantitative methodology for assessing the extent of anti-American bias at the ICC and presents results showing that US allegations of ICC bias are overblown. Chapter 6 concludes by considering the future of US–ICC relations. Though this is a speculative exercise, it is possible to weigh the factors that might encourage or discourage a thaw in American hostility toward the Court. Even though there are many reasons to expect the contentious relationship to continue, I offer some reasons for cautious optimism about future US–ICC relations. I also outline practical steps the US can take to assist the Court – and realize its own foreign policy goals in the process – even if the US never joins the ICC.

2 | US Support for International Justice

The simplest potential explanation for America's hostility to the ICC is that the US opposes international justice in general. After all, the international justice movement has its fair share of critics. International tribunals allegedly cost too much money,[1] impose universalist norms on local communities,[2] discourage brutal leaders from relinquishing power,[3] disrupt negotiations to end wars,[4] and undermine the principle of state sovereignty.[5] The possibility that US antagonism toward the ICC may be just one part of a broader campaign against international justice highlights the need for an assessment of America's relationship with other international justice institutions. I provide one in this chapter. To be clear, my goal is not a complete historical accounting of every international tribunal but rather an analysis of American policy toward the key tribunals. Did the US support or oppose their creation? Did the US help them achieve their mandates by providing diplomatic, military, or economic assistance? And why did US policy end up the way that it did?

An examination of the historical record does not support this alternative explanation. The US has been an ardent supporter of international justice institutions both before and after the ICC's creation. In the period immediately following World War II,[6] the US played an indispensable role in creating the Nuremberg and Tokyo tribunals that

---

[1] Cobban 2006.   [2] Hopgood 2013.
[3] Nalepa and Powell 2016; Krcmaric 2018.
[4] Goldsmith and Krasner 2003; Snyder and Vinjamuri 2003; Prorok 2017; Krcmaric 2020.
[5] Rabkin 2007.
[6] The US was interested in using legal means to regulate the horrors of warfare long before World War II. For example, President Abraham Lincoln adopted the Leiber Code during the American Civil War to govern the conduct of the Union army. The Leiber Code represented the first formal codification of the laws of war and later served as an inspiration for The Hague Conventions and the Geneva Conventions. On the Leiber Code, see Witt 2012.

prosecuted political and military elites in Germany and Japan. After the end of the Cold War, the US once again led the way in establishing the "ad hoc" tribunals that addressed genocides in Yugoslavia and Rwanda. Even after the ICC's creation, American support for international justice has remained steadfast. The US has aided several new venues of international justice, devoted significant resources to tracking down wanted war criminals, and elevated international justice issues in its diplomacy. This chapter's key lesson is that there is something about the ICC – and the ICC alone – that piques the ire of American politicians and policymakers.

The Post–World War II Period

World War II was the most devastating conflict in global history.[7] Approximately 50 million people were killed as a direct consequence of the war, while tens of millions more died due to war-related disease and famine.[8] In addition to the magnitude of the death toll, the manner of the killings – Germany's genocide of European Jews, Russia's Katyn massacre, Japan's Bataan Death March, Britain's indiscriminate carpet bombing techniques, and America's use of atomic weapons – shocked the consciences of many around the world. The horrors of World War II sounded the death knell for notions of gentlemanly warfare and instead brought to the fore ideas about warfare as a criminal act. Though the victorious Allies struggled with the decision on how to confront the defeated Axis leadership, the US ultimately pushed forward a pair of international tribunals – Nuremberg and Tokyo – that laid the foundation for modern international criminal justice in general and the ICC in particular.

Nuremberg

On November 21, 1945, Robert Jackson strode to the prosecutor's podium at Nuremberg's Palace of Justice and surveyed the courtroom.

---

[7] A full accounting of the war's destruction is beyond the scope of this book, but for analyses that address the war's devastating effects in Asia and Europe, respectively, see Dower 1986; Snyder 2010.

[8] Precise numbers should be interpreted with a healthy dose of caution since estimating the number of war deaths and casualties is notoriously difficult. See, for example, Andreas and Greenhill 2010.

It must have been an odd moment for Jackson, a US Supreme Court Justice who had taken a leave of absence to serve as America's chief prosecutor at the International Military Tribunal (IMT) at Nuremberg. Instead of the familiar sights of his Supreme Court chambers, surrounded by fellow justices and attorneys from white-shoe law firms, he found himself staring down at the captive leaders of the Third Reich. Though Adolf Hitler had already committed suicide in his Berlin bunker, the defendants in front of Jackson nonetheless represented the worst of the worst. Nearly two dozen infamous Nazis such as Hermann Goering, the *Reichsmarschall* in charge of Germany's war machine, and Ernst Kaltenbrunner, a high-ranking SS officer responsible for overseeing the Holocaust, waited in the prisoner's dock. Sitting in two neat rows, they watched impassively as Jackson opened his case with one of the most celebrated lines in legal history: "That four great nations, flushed with victory and stung with injury, stay the hand of vengeance and voluntarily submit their captive enemies to the judgment of the law is one of the most significant tributes that Power has ever paid to Reason."[9]

In line with Jackson's opening statement, the Nuremberg Tribunal is generally remembered as a triumph of legal principles over political passions and desires for revenge. Nuremberg has become "legalism's greatest moment of glory" and remains "exalted by advocates of war crimes trials."[10] Few would dispute international jurist Geoffrey Robertson's claim that "international law would never be the same again" after Nuremberg.[11] Some even view it as the "trial of the century."[12] Indeed, the Nuremberg Tribunal has cast such a long shadow over the field of international justice that it now seems like an inevitable response to the horrors of World War II and the Holocaust. But that is not the case. The most remarkable aspect of

---

[9] Jackson's statement was – and still is – hailed as a masterstroke. During Nuremberg, the American press feted Jackson, such as when the *Philadelphia Inquirer* labeled his speech "one of the greatest opening statements ever delivered before any court." See Ehrenfreund 2007, 32. Seven decades after Nuremberg, several scholars argued that it remains "one of the most memorable and often-quoted prosecutorial statements in modern history." See Stover, Peskin, and Koenig 2016, 43.
[10] Bass 2000, 203. [11] Robertson 2012, 309.
[12] Joseph Kanon, "The Real Trial of the Century," *New York Times*, June 9, 2002. The O. J. Simpson trial would (regrettably) steal this title from Nuremberg just before the twentieth century ended.

Nuremberg is that the Allies decided to pursue a trial at all. Moreover, if it were not for American insistence, a trial would never have happened.

During the first few years of World War II, the Allies did not have a meaningful policy for addressing German war crimes.[13] Officials in the US, the UK, and the Soviet Union occasionally threatened unspecified consequences when new evidence of Nazi atrocities emerged, but they devoted virtually all of their attention to winning the war. Only after the tide of the war shifted decisively in favor of the Allies did they begin to consider the fate of Germany's political and military elites. At least initially, all three countries preferred a simple solution for dealing with captured Nazi leaders: summary executions.

In the US, Treasury Secretary Henry Morgenthau Jr., President Franklin D. Roosevelt's close friend and trusted advisor, wielded tremendous influence in shaping American plans toward postwar Germany. His strikingly punitive policy, the so-called Morgenthau Plan, had two main components. The first involved the "pastoralization" of Germany, effectively making it impossible for Germany to wage war again by eliminating its industrial capabilities and turning it into an agricultural backwater. The second involved the immediate execution of captured Nazi elites. Specifically, following the identification of Nazi officials by an officer of one of the Allies, the Morgenthau Plan instructed that "the person identified shall be put to death forthwith by firing squads."[14] Morgenthau was far from the only US government official in favor of executing high-ranking German officers and politicians. General Dwight D. Eisenhower, Supreme Allied Commander in Europe, privately told Britain's ambassador to the US that he wanted to "exterminate all of the [German] General Staff" and supported the "liquidation" of the entire Gestapo organization and all Nazi party members holding the position of town mayor or higher.[15] Secretary of State Cordell Hull told his Soviet counterparts that he would like to "bring up all these [Nazis] before a drumhead court-martial, and I would shoot them before sunset."[16] At least initially, American support for executing captured Nazis without trial went all the way to the top: Roosevelt officially signed off on the Morgenthau Plan in September 1944.[17]

---

[13] Smith 1981, 13. [14] Morgenthau Jr. 1944, 163. [15] Taylor 1992, 108.
[16] Morgenthau Jr. 1944, 126. [17] Bass 2000, 151.

The British were staunch supporters of the Morgenthau Plan. Hartley Shawcross, who went on to serve as the UK's chief prosecutor at Nuremberg, dryly summarized the initial British position as, "execution without trial is the preferable course."[18] Others used more colorful language. Foreign Minister Anthony Eden opposed a trial on the grounds that "the guilt of such individuals [Nazi leaders] is so black that they are outside and go beyond the scope of any judicial process."[19] Prime Minister Winston Churchill similarly believed the fate of Nazi officials was a political issue rather than a legal one. He proposed that after high-ranking Nazis were captured, they be brought before an Allied military officer "not for the purpose of determining the guilt or innocence of the accused but merely to establish the fact of identification. Once identified, the said officer will have the outlaw or outlaws shot to death within six hours."[20] Not surprisingly, when Churchill met with Roosevelt in Quebec in September 1944, he enthusiastically endorsed the Morgenthau Plan.

The Soviets were on board with the plan for summary executions as well. They did, however, quibble with one detail: the Soviets wanted to execute a far greater number of Nazis than the Americans or the British. Given Soviet leader Joseph Stalin's notorious penchant for violence and the fact that the Soviets had suffered the most at the hands of the German war machine, this may not have been terribly surprising. Whereas most officials in the US and the UK envisioned summary executions of somewhere between a couple of hundred and a couple of thousand high-ranking Nazis, Stalin preferred orders of magnitude higher. During the Tehran Conference, for example, Stalin shocked Roosevelt and Churchill when he made clear his preference for dealing with postwar Germany: "At least 50,000 and perhaps 100,000 [Germans] must be physically liquated."[21] Roosevelt and Churchill both pushed back against this massive number of executions in their own way. Roosevelt awkwardly joked that the number should not exceed 49,000, whereas Churchill pointed out that ordinary soldiers who had fought for their country should be spared the firing squad.[22] But when it came to the top Nazis, Roosevelt, Churchill, and Stalin all considered summary executions the appropriate course of action.

---

[18] Shawcross 1995, 90–91.   [19] Bass 2000, 185.   [20] Bass 2000, 185–186.
[21] Office of the Historian 1943.   [22] Office of the Historian 1943.

Given that the three Allies agreed that the Nazi leadership ought to be shot as late as September 1944, it is remarkable that they instead created the Nuremberg Tribunal when the war ended the following year. The origins of this rapid reversal involved a maneuver familiar to official Washington: a press leak. Less than two weeks after Roosevelt and Churchill agreed to the Morgenthau Plan at the Quebec Conference, the details of the once-secret plan appeared on the front page of the *New York Times*.[23] The reaction was overwhelmingly negative. Though American public opinion favored executing Nazi war criminals, the pastoralization aspect of the Morgenthau plan was extremely unpopular.[24] Attuned to public opinion, Roosevelt quickly dropped his support for the Morgenthau Plan in its entirety. For a brief moment, the US no longer had a policy for dealing with Nazi war criminals.

The collapse of the Morgenthau Plan created a context in which Henry Stimson, the Secretary of War and Morgenthau's main rival for influence within Roosevelt's cabinet, could put forth an alternative plan. Stimson, a lawyer by training, advocated for what his profession viewed as the natural response to crime: a trial. This trial, however, would have to be unique. More than a decade of Nazi rule, in addition to the general chaos of the war, had thoroughly decimated the German legal system. Given that there was not a functioning German judiciary in 1945 – or, for that matter, any kind of German government – a conventional domestic trial was not a feasible option. The Allies, in Stimson's view, would have to create an international trial.

Stimson and his supporters believed a trial would have two major advantages over summary executions. First, a trial had educational value. If Morgenthau's goal had been to destroy Germany, Stimson's was to rehabilitate it. As War Department attorney Murray Bernays put it, if there was no trial, then Germany "will simply have lost another war. The German people will not know the barbarians they have supported, nor will they have any understanding of the criminal character of their conduct and the world's judgment upon it."[25] In this regard, the Nuremberg Tribunal unambiguously succeeded by introducing to Germany and the world an unassailable record of Nazi

---

[23] "Morgenthau Plan on Germany Splits Cabinet Committee," *New York Times*, September 24, 1944.
[24] Bass 2000, 169.   [25] Smith 1982, 36.

crimes that ranged from damning documents signed by Nazi leaders to video footage of the liberation of the concentration camps.[26] Hugh Trevor-Roper, the British historian famous for authoring *The Last Days of Hitler*, highlighted this enduring legacy of Nuremberg as early as 1946: "Had it not been for [Nuremberg] it would have been possible for a new German movement in ten years' time to maintain that the worst of Nazi crimes were Allied propaganda easily invented in the hour of such total victory. That is now impossible. ... The real nature of Nazism has been confirmed ... by the exacting scrutiny of a court of law."[27]

Second, Stimson believed that a trial was the American thing to do. Only a trial – and a fair one at that – would be consistent with American values. Summary executions, by contrast, were bound to undercut the moral authority of the US. As Stimson wrote to Roosevelt, "The very punishment of these men in a dignified manner consistent with the advance of civilization will have the greater effect on posterity. ... I am disposed to believe that, at least as to the chief Nazi officials, we should participate in an international tribunal constituted to try them."[28] To be sure, a trial was a risk. Morgenthau and his allies worried, with some justification given the lack of precedent for international tribunals, that the Nazi leadership might somehow get off scot-free due to a legal technicality if they were given a fair trial complete with due process protections.[29] But it was a risk that Roosevelt, at Stimson's urging, was willing to take. In early 1945, US policy officially shifted toward putting Nazi leaders on trial.

Roosevelt still faced the formidable task of convincing the other Allies to back his new plan for an international tribunal. Perhaps surprisingly, the Soviets were more amenable to the idea than the

---

[26] The notion that a trial is valuable because it creates a historical record is not without critics. Hannah Arendt reprimanded Nuremberg on these grounds:

> The purpose of a trial is to render justice, and nothing else. Even the noblest of ulterior purposes – "the making of a record of the Hitler regime which would withstand the test of history," as [the prosecution] formulated the supposed higher aims of the Nuremberg Trials – can only detract from the law's main business: to weigh the charges brought against the accused, to render judgment, and to mete out due punishment.

See Arendt 1977, 253.
[27] H. R. Trevor-Roper, "The Lasting Effects of the Nuremberg Trial," *New York Times Magazine*, October 20, 1946.   [28] Robertson 2012, 307.
[29] Bass 2000, 170–172.

British. Stalin's willingness to support a trial, however, had nothing to do with the logic Stimson espoused. Instead, Stalin sought to turn the affair into a political show trial not unlike the infamous "purge trials" his regime carried out in Moscow in the late 1930s – charades where guilt was predetermined, confessions were forced, and defendants were quickly convicted and executed. The tension between America's desire for a reasonably fair trial (even if it did not quite match the due process standards found in US courts) and the Soviet Union's preference for a show trial stubbornly persisted throughout the IMT's lifespan.[30] For example, the American team at Nuremberg was wary when Andrei Vishinsky, the man responsible for engineering Stalin's show trials in Moscow, joined the Soviet delegation. At a booze-fueled dinner for the prosecution teams, American fears were proved justified when Vishinsky declared: "I propose a toast to the defendants. May their paths lead straight from the courthouse to the grave!"[31] Many of the Americans drank to the toast before the translation from Russian to English was complete, and they were mortified when they learned they had inadvertently toasted death sentences for defendants who had not yet been tried.[32]

The British offered stiff resistance to the American plan for an international trial. Even after Roosevelt dispatched an emissary to London to "bring Britain into line,"[33] the British refused to budge from their position that a trial of German war criminals was "neither good nor practicable."[34] The UK's opposition to a trial echoed concerns that Morgenthau had raised within the US government: it was simply too risky. The British worried that Nazi war criminals might escape punishment due to a legal technicality and, even if they were ultimately found guilty, the British fretted about giving Hitler and his henchmen a high-profile platform to engage in Nazi self-justification.[35] Despite this initial stance, the British eventually changed their position due to a pair of developments in the spring of 1945. First, the suicides of several top Nazis – not only Hitler but also Heinrich Himmler and Joseph Goebbels – mitigated the risk of the trial devolving into a Nazi soapbox.[36] Second, Roosevelt finally passed away after a long period

---

[30] It also led to accusations that Nuremberg was a case of "victor's justice," an issue I discuss later.
[31] Taylor 1992, 211.   [32] Taylor 1992, 211.   [33] Bass 2000, 189.
[34] Overy 2001, 11.   [35] Stover, Peskin, and Koenig 2016, 29.
[36] Robertson 2012, 308.

of declining health, elevating Harry Truman to the American presidency. Truman, a former judge with strong personal convictions about the rule of law, appeared even more enamored with the idea of an international trial than his predecessor had been.[37] In early May, Truman publicly announced America's unwavering commitment to building an international tribunal and appointed Supreme Court Justice Robert Jackson as the US representative in this endeavor. One day later, Britain gave up its opposition to a tribunal on the grounds that continued resistance to the American plan would be "inexpedient."[38] At long last, the Allies had reached a tentative agreement to put Nazi leaders on trial.

In June 1945, representatives from the US, the UK, and the USSR, as well as recently liberated France, met in London to sort out the details of the trial. It was a daunting task. They had to create a new international tribunal from scratch and were effectively making up the rules as they went. As Joseph Persico summarized the situation: "There were no precedents, no existing body of law, not even a court. The legal instruments for prosecuting a drunk driver in any county in America were better than those for prosecuting the murderers of millions during a war."[39] After a summer of debate – sometimes polite, other times contentious – the Allies signed the London Charter establishing the International Military Tribunal at Nuremberg on August 8, 1945.

The US mostly got its way when setting up the IMT. One of the key debates concerned where to hold the trial. Nuremberg, a city utterly devastated by Allied bombing raids, was far from an obvious choice. One journalist who covered the trial described his daily commute: "I could smell the stench of death as I walked through the streets of Nuremberg on my way to the Palace of Justice. Beneath the rubble of the shattered city lay the bodies of 20,000 air raid victims."[40] The other Allies preferred London or Berlin, but Jackson and the American team insisted on Nuremberg because it had symbolic value as the former location of Hitler's massive Nazi rallies. Perhaps even more

---

[37] Ehrenfreund 2007, 10.   [38] Bass 2000, 191.   [39] Persico 1994, 11.
[40] Ehrenfreund 2007, xiii. Other than the Palace of Justice, which was miraculously still standing, Nuremberg was largely destroyed. Its streets were littered with the debris of bombed buildings to the point that the city effectively was unnavigable on the eve of the trial. Jackson despaired, but the US military had a ready solution: use German prisoners of war to clear the streets. See Persico 1994, 41.

important, Nuremberg was in the American zone of occupied Germany, giving the US physical control of the site.[41] Jackson's preferences on whom and what to prosecute largely carried the day as well. He cajoled the Allies into settling on three categories of crime: crimes against peace (aggression), war crimes, and crimes against humanity. He also oversaw a process of horse-trading among the Allies, who each had their own views about which Nazis ought to face trial, as they eventually agreed on a list of twenty-four defendants.[42] The deference the other Allies showed to the US in setting up the IMT was largely a product of the geopolitical situation at the war's end: "The Americans had pressed hardest for trying war criminals; they held most of the expected defendants in custody. More to the point, in a Europe enfeebled by war, they were in the best position to pick up the tab for whatever this enterprise cost."[43]

Once the Nuremberg Tribunal was established, the US played an essential role in supporting its operations in war-torn Europe by staffing the court, producing evidence, and apprehending suspects. In terms of the IMT's personnel, the Americans dominated key positions to such an extent that they actually insisted on reserving some roles for representatives of the other Allies simply for the sake of appearances. To be sure, all four of the Allies were equals on paper. Each provided a prosecutorial team headed by a chief prosecutor, a judge, and an alternative judge. In practice, though, it was widely acknowledged at Nuremberg that Jackson "was much the most powerful" of the chief prosecutors.[44] Moreover, after the judges arrived in Nuremberg, Francis Biddle, the American judge who had previously served as the US attorney general under Roosevelt, quickly emerged as a de facto leader and appeared on track to become the tribunal's president (a largely ceremonial role reserved for one of the judges). US officials, including Jackson himself, worried that "Americans already dominated the show" and believed that "a more international flavor" was needed.[45] Biddle was quietly instructed to stand aside so

---

[41] Ehrenfreund 2007, 15.
[42] Taylor 1992, 85–90. The IMT indicted twenty-four Nazis, but only twenty-one were tried at Nuremberg. One defendant committed suicide before the trial began (Robert Ley), one was too ill to stand trial (Gustav Krupp), and one could not be located (Martin Bormann). Genetic testing later confirmed that Bormann had died before the trial began.
[43] Persico 1994, 32.   [44] Taylor 1992, 215.   [45] Persico 1994, 76.

that Britain's judge could become the court's president and thereby mitigate the appearance of an American-dominated tribunal.[46]

The Americans also provided the IMT with an array of evidence used to prosecute the Nazi defendants. The other Allies helped in this regard too, but the American military was responsible for "bringing in the bulk of the documentary evidence."[47] Even before the London Charter was signed, the US began collecting Nazi documents that would prove crucial at the trial. General William "Will Bill" Donovan – the head of the Office of Strategic Services (OSS), forerunner to the Central Intelligence Agency (CIA) – offered his resources to Jackson's prosecution team. Jackson, who was initially doubtful about the prospects of finding high-quality evidence scattered across wartorn Europe, was soon inundated with a "river of documents" from the OSS.[48] For instance, the OSS discovered forty-seven massive crates of documents hidden in an underground cellar that contained the complete files of Alfred Rosenberg, often considered the Nazi Party's chief philosopher for his role in developing the regime's theoretical justifications for anti-Semitism and *Lebensraum*. The capture of Rosenberg's files meant that the Nuremberg prosecutors took possession of "three thousand pounds of the Nazi Party's meticulously recorded past, dating back to 1922."[49] Shortly thereafter, American investigators began receiving tips that led to the discovery of ever greater numbers of Nazi files hidden in barns, cellars, and alpine cabins across Germany.

The combined weight of the documentary evidence that the American military produced was so compelling that it shaped the prosecution's strategy at Nuremberg. Telford Taylor, a member of Jackson's team and the celebrated author of *The Anatomy of the Nuremberg Trials*, recalled the burst of excitement when "we began to realize that the Teutonic penchant for meticulous record keeping would greatly ease our task of proving the criminal charges."[50] Jackson's assessment was more blunt: "I did not think men would ever be so foolish as to put in writing some of the things the Germans did."[51] As a result of the documentary evidence, much of it bearing the signatures of the very Nazis sitting in the dock at Nuremberg, Jackson largely eschewed using witnesses at the trial. Rather than risk

[46] Ehrenfreund 2007, 81.   [47] Taylor 1992, 62.   [48] Persico 1994, 42.
[49] Persico 1994.   [50] Taylor 1992, 57.   [51] Ehrenfreund 2007, 35.

putting someone with an unreliable memory or a personal bias on the witness stand, Jackson let the documents speak for themselves. In short, the evidence that the American military uncovered made it possible to prosecute the Nazis using their own words.

The final pillar of US support involved apprehending suspects. To start, the US and the other Allies created a Central Registry of War Criminals and Security Suspects (CROWCASS) in Paris to circulate information about tens of thousands of wanted Nazi fugitives to military commanders and prisoner of war camp administrations. American military and intelligence agencies also ensured that CROWCASS suspects ended up in the dock.[52] The OSS raided mountain redoubts throughout Bavaria and arrested many die-hard Nazi holdouts, including Ernst Kaltenbrunner, one of the IMT's most high-profile defendants. The Army Counter Intelligence Corps (CIC) joined the OSS in the hunt for Nazi war criminals and stay-behind enemy agents throughout Europe.[53] To be sure, the American commitment to justice was tested and, at times, found wanting. The demands of the nascent Cold War with America's erstwhile ally, the Soviet Union, sometimes trumped the pursuit of war criminals. For instance, in Operation Paperclip, CIC agents scoured Germany and Austria for renowned Nazi scientists and engineers – some of whom arguably were war criminals – and brought them to the US before they could fall into Soviet hands.[54] Overall, though, the American military made detaining war crimes suspects a priority. Indeed, the US apprehended more of the defendants at Nuremberg than any of the other Allies.[55]

---

[52] On the broader effort to apprehend Nazi fugitives, see Walters 2009; Steinacher 2011; Stover, Peskin, and Koenig 2016; Sands 2021.

[53] In a strange historical twist, one CIC officer was a young Henry Kissinger, who spent the immediate postwar period "ferreting out Gestapo and SS officers who were hiding" in Germany. See Stover, Peskin, and Koenig 2016, 39. As discussed in Chapter 3, the future Secretary of State would go on to become a prominent critic of the ICC.

[54] Some of the ex-Nazi scientists brought to the US in Operation Paperclip went on to have distinguished careers, especially in the space race. Wernher von Braun, who developed Germany's V-2 rocket program that wrought destruction on London during the war, became the architect of NASA's Saturn V launch vehicle that propelled astronauts to the moon during the Apollo missions. Kurt Dubus, a colleague of von Braun's in the V-2 program, became the first director of NASA's Kennedy Space Center. Not surprisingly, their Nazi pasts were generally swept under the rug. On American efforts to reckon with this legacy, see Lichtblau 2014.

[55] Persico 1994, 47; Stover, Peskin, and Koenig 2016, 43.

American support for postwar accountability in Europe did not end with the IMT. Instead, the famous IMT was immediately followed by twelve lesser-known American-led Nuremberg Military Tribunals (NMTs). Held at Nuremberg's Palace of Justice between 1946 and 1949, these trials were organized thematically – one for Nazi doctors, one for SS officers, one for German industrialists, and so on – and included another 177 defendants who were not quite notable enough to make it into the IMT's proceedings.[56] The decision to create the NMTs rather than continue with more trials at the IMT was partly the product of fraying relations between the Americans and the Soviets. Indeed, when Jackson returned to the Supreme Court at the IMT's conclusion, he advised Truman against participating in additional international trials. Truman agreed the US would go it alone on future Nazi trials, and the other Allies would be free to hold national tribunals in their respective occupation zones if they wished.[57] Telford Taylor, one of Jackson's deputies at the IMT, became the chief prosecutor at the NMTs. He was assisted by Benjamin Ferencz, then a twenty-seven-year-old lawyer and war crimes investigator, who tried the first case of his career at the NMT's *Einsatzgruppen* trial of SS mobile death squads. Half a century later, Ferencz would draw on this experience and become a prominent – and at times lonely – American advocate for the ICC.

No discussion of Nuremberg would be complete without addressing the "victor's justice" debate. On the one hand, Nuremberg was a case of victor's justice in at least two respects. First, the defeated Germans were put on trial, but the victorious Allies were not. Officials on both sides of the war recognized this reality. Hermann Goering, the highest-ranking Nazi official in the dock at Nuremberg, described the proceedings as the natural consequence of power politics: "The victor will always be the judge, and the vanquished the accused."[58] On the American side, General Curtis LeMay agreed with this assessment when he famously quipped, "I suppose if I had lost the war, I would have been tried as a war criminal. Fortunately, we were on the winning side."[59] As Nuremberg took shape, Jackson feared the Nazi defendants might be able to mount a successful *tu quoque* defense ("you did it

---

[56] Heller 2011.   [57] Heller 2011, 9–24.   [58] Gilbert 1947, 4.
[59] Richard Rhodes, "The General and World War III," *The New Yorker*, June 19, 1995, p. 48.

too") given that the Allies had committed some of the same offenses as the Germans.⁶⁰ However, the Allies worked around this concern by drafting the London Charter in such a way that the IMT's jurisdiction was limited exclusively to European Axis war criminals. Second, the Allies engaged in *ex post facto* law because they charged the Germans with crimes that were not illegal at the time they were committed. Indeed, the concept of crimes against humanity was not created until Nuremberg, and the legal grounds for prosecuting aggressive war in 1945 were shaky at best.⁶¹ Nearly all of the Nazis on trial highlighted the *ex post facto* nature of the charges, but the IMT ruled this defense inapplicable given the "obvious wrongness" of their acts.⁶² Put another way, prosecuting Nazis for crimes against humanity may have been problematic, but the IMT believed it would have been even more problematic to ignore their crimes entirely.⁶³

On the other hand, it is a mistake to dismiss Nuremberg as nothing more than a case of the victors punishing the vanquished.⁶⁴ First, the IMT provided the defendants with several due process protections including the right to provide explanatory testimony, the right to present evidence, the right to conduct one's own defense or appoint counsel on one's behalf (including the counsel of fellow Nazis, if desired), and the right to cross-examine witnesses. While these due process protections may not have been as strong as those found in American courts, they were remarkable given the circumstances in

---

⁶⁰ In a letter to Truman, Jackson acknowledged that the Allies had

> done or are doing some of the very things we are prosecuting the Germans for. The French are violating the Geneva Convention in their treatment of prisoners of war. ...We are prosecuting the Germans for plunder and our allies are practicing it. ...We say aggressive war is a crime and one of our allies asserts sovereignty over the Baltic States based on no title except conquest.

Quoted in Ehrenfreund 2007, 60.

⁶¹ Even some members of the Allied prosecution at Nuremberg, including Telford Taylor, acknowledged the *ex post facto* nature of some of the charges. See Taylor 1992, 635.   ⁶² Van Schaack and Slye 2021, 31.
⁶³ Sheldon Glueck, a Harvard law professor who advised the US government on war crimes issues, captured the prevailing wisdom when he argued that allowing Nazis to escape prosecution on jurisdictional or procedural grounds "would be a triumph of bookish legalism and the death of both common sense and justice." Quoted in Hagan 2003, 24.
⁶⁴ Gary Bass gets it right when he points out Nuremberg's shortcomings but also notes that it "was still far better than anything else that has been done at the end of a major war." See Bass 2000, 205.

which the Nuremberg Tribunal occurred. Second, most of the prosecution teams at Nuremberg – particularly the American side, led by a Supreme Court justice and staffed by respected attorneys and scholars – were legal professionals rather than political hatchet men.[65] Third, the judges – despite being representatives of the Allied nations – acted with a surprising level of neutrality. They frequently allowed the defendants to give long, winding answers over the objections of the prosecutors so that the defendants were afforded every opportunity to explain their actions.[66] Fourth, the IMT did not convict all of the Nazi officials put on trial, as one might expect in a case of victor's justice. Specifically, three defendants were acquitted and another seven received prison sentences rather than the death penalty. That means the Nuremberg Tribunal spared the lives of nearly half of the Nazis on trial – men who otherwise would have been summarily executed if not for the American insistence on a trial.[67]

Tokyo

By the early summer of 1945, the war in Europe was over, but fighting in the Pacific dragged on with no end in sight. Though the "island hopping" strategy brought the US and the other Allies closer to the Japanese home islands, a full-scale Allied invasion of Japan promised to be devastating for both sides. Imperial Japan nonetheless appeared poised for a fight to the bitter end. The calculus changed, however, during one fateful week in August 1945. On August 6, the *Enola Gay*, an American B-29 bomber, took off from Tinian in the Mariana Islands and dropped an atomic bomb on the Japanese city of Hiroshima, marking the first time atomic weapons were used in combat. Three days later, the US dropped a second atomic bomb on Nagasaki. In between these two bombings, the Soviet Union – which had previously focused its formidable manpower on the war in Europe – joined the fight against Japan. The coming days promised

---

[65] One commentator at Nuremberg noted, "The aura of the prevailing New York corporate law firm drifted across the Atlantic and landed in Nuremberg. ... It was as if Sullivan and Cromwell or Milbank, Tweed, Hadley, & McCloy decided to conduct a trial." Quoted in Bass 2000, 24.
[66] Ehrenfreund 2007, 66–68.
[67] In fact, the Soviet judge dissented from Nuremberg's final judgment because he objected to the acquittals.

to bring even more dire news for the Japanese. When President Truman announced America's mastery of atomic weapons technology to the world, he included an ominous warning for Japan's leaders: "If they do not now accept our terms, they may expect a rain of ruin from the air, the like of which has never been seen on this earth."[68]

On August 14, Japan indicated its willingness to surrender via a Swiss intermediary.[69] The following day Emperor Hirohito made a rare public radio address to his subjects announcing Japan's capitulation in the war. Though Japanese officials had long promised to fight to the last man, Hirohito acknowledged that America's "new and most cruel bomb" had changed his thinking and that continuing the war would "result in an ultimate collapse and obliteration of the Japanese nation."[70] Not long after, representatives of the Japanese government unconditionally surrendered to the Allies in a formal signing ceremony aboard the USS *Missouri* in Tokyo Bay. The Japanese surrender raised the same question the Allies had confronted when they defeated Nazi Germany months before: What should they do with the defeated political and military elites of Imperial Japan? The inspiration for their answer came from some 5,000 miles away, where Allied prosecutors were preparing to open the trial at Nuremberg.

The International Military Tribunal for the Far East (IMTFE), or Tokyo Tribunal, shared much in common with its predecessor in Nuremberg. One historian concludes that "the echo of Nuremberg was strong and true,"[71] whereas another describes Tokyo as "almost a Nuremberg copy."[72] The Tokyo Tribunal borrowed liberally from Nuremberg's charter and focused on the same three categories of

---

[68] Sidney Shalett, "First Atomic Bomb Dropped on Japan; Missile Is Equal to 20,000 Tons of TNT; Truman Warns Foe of a 'Rain of Ruin,'" *New York Times*, August 6, 1945. Truman's warning was something of a bluff. The US did not have any more atomic weapons after dropping the two bombs on Hiroshima and Nagasaki, though it was racing to build more in the coming weeks and months.

[69] There is an ongoing debate about why Japan surrendered. A general point of consensus is that the American use of atomic weapons was one contributing factor, but the Soviet decision to join the war against Japan also was crucial. Scholarly disagreements generally concern the relative explanatory weight that should be placed on each factor. For some of the key perspectives on Japan's surrender and America's use of atomic weapons, see Butow 1954; Feis 1966; Sigal 1988; Pape 1993; Asada 1998; Dower 1999.

[70] "Text of Hirohito's Radio Rescript," *New York Times*, August 15, 1945.

[71] Minear 1971, 22.   [72] Ehrenfreund 2007, 113.

crimes: aggression, war crimes, and crimes against humanity. Partly because Tokyo was seen as a duplicate – a Nuremberg for the Pacific – the Western media generally paid scant attention to the trial as it was happening.[73] When they did bother reporting on the Tokyo Tribunal, comparisons to Nuremberg were inevitable. For instance, one foreign correspondent described the Tokyo trial's setting – an auditorium in what had previously been the Japanese War Ministry – as "a third-string road company of the Nuremberg show."[74] Contemporary scholarship, at least outside of Japan, has also granted Tokyo far less attention than its more famous twin at Nuremberg.[75] As Arnold Brackman notes, English-language research on Tokyo is "thin."[76]

One aspect of the Tokyo Tribunal, however, is unambiguous: the dominant American role. Unlike Nuremberg, which arose from months of tedious negotiations between the US, the UK, Russia, and France, the US simply created the Tokyo Tribunal by fiat. General Douglas MacArthur, acting as the Supreme Commander for the Allied Powers in Japan and following orders from the Joint Chiefs of Staff, unilaterally issued a decree establishing the tribunal and setting forth its charter. In MacArthur's words: "I, Douglas MacArthur, as Supreme Commander for the Allied Powers, by virtue of the authority so conferred upon me, in order to implement the Terms of Surrender which requires the meting out of stern justice to war criminals, do order ... there shall be established an International Military Tribunal for the Far East."[77] American allies in the Pacific were not consulted until after MacArthur issued the Tokyo Charter.[78] There was no debate among the Allies over the structure of the tribunal, no arguments over which crimes ought to be prosecuted, and no wrangling over which defendants should stand trial as war criminals. MacArthur's unilateral approach, perhaps surprisingly, produced little friction with the rest of Allies because all parties "relied heavily on the precedent set by the Nuremberg Charter."[79]

---

[73] Brackman 1987, 212.   [74] "Road Show," *Time Magazine*, May 20, 1946.
[75] According to two leading scholars, "[T]he volume and depth of Japanese scholarship on the Tokyo Tribunal dwarfs that produced by Western scholars and, unfortunately, the bulk of the Western scholarship has largely ignored the research of their Japanese colleagues." See Cohen and Totani 2018, 1.
[76] Brackman 1987, 9. An important recent exception, however, is Bass 2023.
[77] Brackman 1987, 59.   [78] Minear 1971, 20.   [79] Minear 1971.

There was, however, an additional reason for the deference shown toward the US at the Tokyo Tribunal: America's geopolitical position in Asia. At the war's conclusion, the traditional European powers were focused on events closer to home, primarily rebuilding after the devastation the war had wrought. To the extent they were interested in pursuing accountability for wartime atrocities, Nuremberg consumed most of their attention. The Soviet Union, as a Eurasian power, was a possible exception. However, the Soviets – who signed a nonaggression pact with Japan in 1941 – only joined the war against Japan in the final days before the Japanese surrender. America's remaining allies in the Pacific were relatively weak states that had neither the means nor the motive to challenge American plans for a trial.[80] Altogether, this put the US in a position to dictate policy in postwar Japan. The manner of the war's termination meant that there was sure to be a preponderance of American troops in the Allied occupation of Japan, giving the US long-term influence in the region. On top of that, there was the perception that the US had made a disproportionate contribution in defeating Japan – initially with its island hopping strategy throughout the Pacific and later with its bombing campaign against Japan's home islands – so it deserved to play the leading role.[81] The US role in crafting the Tokyo Tribunal was so absolute that American officials at one point considered making the trial exclusively about the Japanese attack on Pearl Harbor, though they ultimately decided to take a much broader view of Japan's wartime conduct.[82]

Authority at the Tokyo Tribunal stemmed from MacArthur's position as Supreme Commander for the Allied Powers in Japan. In consultation with official Washington, he wasted little time in putting this authority to use. The US was involved in virtually every aspect of the tribunal, including staffing the court, picking the defendants, collecting evidence, and apprehending fugitive criminals.

American personnel dominated the tribunal's key positions. To be clear, each of the eleven nations that participated in the Tokyo Tribunal – the US and ten other countries that helped defeat Imperial Japan – provided a prosecutor, a judge, and support staff.[83] But the

---

[80] In fact, many of them went on to play a role in the Tokyo Tribunal, primarily by providing judges and associate prosecutors.
[81] Cohen and Totani 2018, 36.   [82] Rudolph 2017, 27.
[83] The ten other countries were Australia, Canada, China, France, India, the Netherlands, New Zealand, the Philippines, the Soviet Union, and the United Kingdom.

details of the Tokyo Charter, issued by MacArthur, afforded American personnel an even greater degree of influence than they had enjoyed at Nuremberg. Recall that Nuremberg had a chief prosecutor from each of the four Allies, who all were granted equal authority.[84] At Tokyo, there was only one chief prosecutor. Not surprisingly, this role went to an American: Joseph B. Keenan, an assistant attorney general who was best known for prosecuting several notorious gangsters during the Great Depression. The other Allies were only allowed to provide an "associate prosecutor" whose position was subordinate to the chief prosecutor. In terms of judges, MacArthur endowed himself with the ultimate authority to make appointments. While each of the Allied nations was allowed to nominate a judge, MacArthur had to approve the nomination.[85] MacArthur also had the right to handpick the tribunal's president from among the judges.[86] Lastly, American personnel played one other unique role in Tokyo: two dozen American lawyers were appointed to the defense counsel, partly in an attempt to head off criticisms of victor's justice.[87]

The IMTFE ultimately charged twenty-eight high-ranking Japanese political and military elites.[88] MacArthur was personally involved in compiling the list of suspects for the trial.[89] Hideki Tojo, Japan's prime minister for most of the war and the man responsible for ordering the attack on Pearl Harbor, was the tribunal's best-known defendant. The most notable aspect of the Tokyo Tribunal's list of defendants, however, concerns who was *not* on the list: Emperor Hirohito. The emperor's absence had little to do with the merits of the case against him. While Hirohito's legacy is complicated, many agree that he reasonably could have been included in the dock at Tokyo. As Lucien Pye summarizes, the emperor was not some passive ruler who was outmaneuvered by a militarist faction but was instead "an active strategic

---

[84] In practice, some believed that the American chief prosecutor, Robert Jackson, wielded the most influence.
[85] For additional details on the Tokyo Tribunal's prosecutors and judges, see Brackman 1987, 54–71.
[86] MacArthur appointed Australia's judge, William Webb, to this position.
[87] Cohen and Totani 2018, 46.
[88] The IMTFE only charged twenty-eight high-profile individuals, but the Allies created many other tribunals throughout Asia that prosecuted lesser-known Japanese war criminals.
[89] Stover, Peskin, and Koenig 2016, 47.

plotter of Japanese wars of aggression – and a certifiable war criminal."[90]

MacArthur and other American officials decided not to prosecute Hirohito for a simple reason: postwar stability. Like the decision to bring Nazi scientists to the US via Operation Paperclip at the same time that the US pushed for trials of other Nazis at Nuremberg, the decision to spare Hirohito from the trial at Tokyo was a geopolitical calculation. As MacArthur relates in his autobiography, "I believed that if the emperor was indicted, and perhaps hanged, as a war criminal, military government would have to be instituted throughout all Japan, and guerrilla warfare would probably break out."[91] In addition to excluding Hirohito from the trial, the US went to great lengths to ensure that the other defendants did not implicate the emperor in their testimonies.[92] The idea was that if the occupying forces retained Hirohito as a figurehead emperor and showed him a sufficient level of respect, he could be a useful, if admittedly somewhat awkward, ally in postwar Japan. In the words of historian Herbert Bix, the US wanted to use the emperor to "bring about a great spiritual transformation of the Japanese people" and "make maximum use of his existing Japanese government organizations."[93] This strategy was controversial with America's allies. Nearly every other country participating in the Tokyo Tribunal vehemently disagreed with the decision to give Hirohito a pass.[94] But like most debates in Tokyo, the American position prevailed.

As the preeminent power in occupied Japan, the US military was almost single-handedly responsible for apprehending wanted war criminals. This was no easy task. After Japan's surrender, its political and military elites knew that arrests were coming given prior Allied statements about postwar Japan and the events unfolding almost contemporaneously in Nuremberg. Some used the interregnum between Japan's surrender and the arrival of US troops to go into hiding,[95] whereas others took the path of preemptive

---

[90] Quoted in Stover, Peskin, and Koenig 2016, 52.
[91] MacArthur 1964, 287–288.
[92] Minear 1971, 113; Stover, Peskin, and Koenig 2016, 53.   [93] Bix 2000, 545.
[94] Minear 1971, 111; Brackman 1987, 51; Rudolph 2017, 29; Cohen and Totani 2018, 42.
[95] One example is Mutsuhiro Watanabe, a now-infamous sadistic guard at a prisoner of war camp, who successfully hid in the hills outside Nagano until a

suicide.[96] Overall, though, the US was generally successful in apprehending the IMTFE's defendants. Of MacArthur's initial list of the forty most wanted Japanese criminals, nearly all were eventually apprehended.[97] More often than not, finding and arresting war criminals was a dramatic affair. For instance, Tojo shot himself in the chest as American troops surrounded his home, but he somehow survived the suicide attempt. In strange turn of events, American military doctors rushed to save the life of their former archenemy, managed to restore his health, and eventually brought him to trial.[98]

The US did what it could to collect and preserve evidence for the tribunal, but the quantity and quality of the documentary evidence is one area where Tokyo fell short of Nuremberg. There are two reasons for the relative paucity of documentary evidence at Tokyo. First, unlike Nazi Germany, Imperial Japan did not go to great lengths to meticulously record its own misdeeds. Second, the Japanese intentionally destroyed much of the documentary evidence that did exist in the days between Hirohito's surrender announcement and the arrival of American troops in Tokyo.[99] As John Dower describes it, "Although the emperor's broadcast put an end to the American air raids ... the skies over Tokyo remained black with smoke for days to come. Bonfires of documents replaced napalm's hell fires as wartime elites followed the lead of their sovereign and devoted themselves to obscuring their wartime deeds."[100] Taken together, these dynamics produced a stark contrast in the nature of the evidence at the two tribunals. At Nuremberg, prosecutors had the luxury of combing through a "river of documents" for particularly incriminating memoranda and letters that allowed them to prosecute the Nazi leadership using their own words.[101] Nothing comparable existed at Tokyo, though at least some documents survived and eventually made their way into the hands of the IMTFE prosecutors.[102]

The Tokyo trial was slow and laborious. Whereas Nuremberg was complete within a year, Tokyo took two and a half years. The tribunal delivered its judgment and sentences in November 1948. The IMTFE started with twenty-eight defendants, though it was down to

general amnesty for war criminals was declared after the end of the Allied occupation of Japan.
[96] Brackman 1987, 51.   [97] Stover, Peskin, and Koenig 2016, 49.
[98] Stover, Peskin, and Koenig 2016, 51–52.   [99] Brackman 1987, 40.
[100] Dower 1999, 39.   [101] Persico 1994, 42.   [102] Brackman 1987, 40.

twenty-five by the end of the lengthy proceedings (two defendants died of natural causes during the trial and one was deemed mentally unfit to stand trial). All twenty-five were found guilty, with seven sentenced to death and the rest receiving prison sentences. Before the sentences were carried out, MacArthur oversaw a review of the tribunal's work, a process that encapsulates the extent to which American military power underpinned the IMTFE. MacArthur promptly confirmed all the verdicts and sentences.[103] In a last-ditch effort to stave off punishment, some of the defendants attempted to file writs of habeas corpus to the US Supreme Court. The Supreme Court considered the argument of the Japanese accused over three days, but it ultimately decided that it had no jurisdiction over the Tokyo Tribunal.[104] After the Supreme Court's decision not to intervene, the guilty were quickly imprisoned or put to death by hanging.

The Tokyo Tribunal raised concerns about victor's justice that mirrored those at Nuremberg. On the one hand, the IMTFE put the vanquished Japanese on trial, but it ignored the behavior of the victorious Allies. Most notably, the tribunal kept America's use of atomic weapons against Hiroshima and Nagasaki out of the trial entirely by declaring evidence related to atomic weapons inadmissible. Partly due to the Tokyo Tribunal's one-sided nature, Judge Radhabinod Pal of India issued a scathing dissenting opinion and argued for the acquittal of the defendants.[105] On the other hand, the Japanese defendants received "a full range of fair-trial protections."[106] This included an international defense team that consisted of a Japanese attorney of the defendant's choosing plus the support of a large group of American lawyers assigned to aid the defense.[107] Some of the defendants were initially reluctant to trust their American defense attorneys given that they were nationals of Japan's former enemy, but their skepticism disappeared once they saw the defense counsel perform in court. As one of the defendants, Koichi Kido, remarked, "I don't know whether it was out of their business-mindedness or love of Japan, but

---

[103] In MacArthur's words: "I can find nothing of technical commission or omission in the incidents of the trial itself of sufficient import to warrant my intervention in the judgments which have been rendered." Quoted in Cohen and Totani 2018, 52.
[104] Cohen and Totani 2018, 52–53.
[105] For an analysis of Pal's dissent, see Cohen and Totani 2018, 431–495.
[106] Cohen and Totani 2018, 53. [107] Minear 1971, 23.

the American lawyers genuinely stood by the accused and did very well."[108] On the whole, the Tokyo Tribunal likely occupies some middle ground in the victor's justice debate: it had enough shortcomings to call into question its status as a just trial, but it was not merely an exercise in political revenge either.

Since its conclusion, the Tokyo trial has become something of a footnote to the Nuremberg trial. Outside of Japan, Tokyo has received considerably less attention than Nuremberg from scholars, policymakers, and the public. But the Tokyo Tribunal nonetheless helped solidify some of the more controversial legal doctrines that were first espoused at Nuremberg. Moreover, it firmly established the US as the world's leader in the emerging field of international justice. Just as with Nuremberg, there would not have been a tribunal at Tokyo without the diplomatic, military, and economic might of the US. Put simply, the US created modern international justice at Nuremberg and Tokyo.

Legacy

The legacies of the post–World War II international tribunals endured long after the courtrooms at Nuremberg and Tokyo were shuttered and returned to the Germans and the Japanese, respectively. The tribunals, especially Nuremberg, produced the core principles of the field of international criminal law and "transformed the way we look at the acts of warring governments and the consequences that we expect to follow victory or defeat."[109] In at least five ways, the Nuremberg legacy shaped the development of the international tribunals that followed it, including the ICC.[110]

First, Nuremberg established the doctrine of individual criminal responsibility for international crimes.[111] Prior to Nuremberg, legal accountability in international politics – to the extent that it occurred at all – took place at the state level (e.g., state-to-state reparations). But

---

[108] Cohen and Totani 2018, 47.   [109] Smith 1981, 4.
[110] For lengthier discussions of Nuremberg's legacy, see Ferencz 1998; Ehrenfreund 2007; Van Schaack and Slye 2021, 25–33.
[111] There were, however, previous attempts to establish a similar precedent. After World War I, for example, the Treaty of Versailles stated that a tribunal should be created to prosecute Germany's Kaiser Wilhelm II. But plans for the tribunal were shelved when the kaiser fled into exile in the Netherlands at the war's end.

the postwar tribunals set the precedent that the specific individuals guilty of ordering or perpetrating horrific crimes personally bore criminal liability. As the Nuremberg judgment famously put it, "Crimes against international law are committed by men, not by abstract entities, and only by punishing individuals who commit such crimes can the provisions of international law be enforced."[112] Every international tribunal since Nuremberg has taken the notion of individual criminal accountability as its starting point.

Second, Nuremberg established the primacy of international law over domestic law. The status quo had historically been that ruling regimes could treat their own populations however they liked without any outside legal interference. With regard to dispensing justice, the principle of sovereignty meant each state wielded total legal authority within its borders but possessed zero authority outside its borders. Prosecuting alleged crimes in another state, even if they were heinous, was viewed as an unwelcome violation of sovereignty. As Jeremy Rabkin summarizes, "If sovereignty means anything, it means very sharp limits to any serious notion of international criminal justice."[113] But both of the postwar tribunals tipped the scales in favor of international justice over state sovereignty when they ruled that some acts were punishable even if they were legal under the domestic law of the country where they occurred.[114] Hence, one of Nuremberg's enduring legacies is that it is now harder for oppressors to evade justice by hiding behind the protective cocoon of state sovereignty.

Third, Nuremberg established the norm that political and military leaders are not immune from prosecution at international tribunals. The idea that a country's leadership can face justice for their crimes in the same manner as foot soldiers may seem unremarkable today, but it was revolutionary at the time. Leading up to the trial, Robert Jackson worried that long-standing respect for head-of-state immunity would complicate the prosecution's case, complaining that "this idea [head-of-state immunity] is a relic of the doctrine of the divine right of kings" and lamenting "the paradox that legal responsibility [is] the least where power is the greatest."[115] The IMT addressed this issue directly when Article 7 of the London Charter asserted that no official position,

[112] International Military Tribunal 1947, vol. 1, 223.   [113] Rabkin 2007, 99.
[114] Nuremberg also set the precedent that "following orders" was not a defense against criminal liability at international tribunals.
[115] Cassese 2008, 245.

including head of state, could free an individual from criminal responsibility. Prosecuting heads of state ultimately became a moot point at Nuremberg (Hitler committed suicide) and Tokyo (Hirohito was spared), but the IMT's stance on immunities paved the way for future international tribunals to prosecute political leaders. The ICC, for instance, has set its sights on Sudan's Omar Bashir, Kenya's Uhuru Kenyatta, Libya's Muammar Gaddafi, the Ivory Coast's Laurent Gbagbo, Russia's Vladimir Putin, Israel's Benjamin Netanyahu, and the Philippines' Rodrigo Duterte.

Fourth, Nuremberg created the new category of crimes against humanity. To be sure, the Allies were more interested in prosecuting Germany's aggressive war than its crimes against humanity, including the horrors of the Holocaust.[116] Jackson made the conscious decision to focus the prosecution's case primarily on the war itself because it was the war that enabled all the other atrocities, a strategy that at times reduced crimes against humanity to "mere afterthoughts" at the IMT.[117] But with the benefit of hindsight, the opposite conclusion is warranted: the crime of aggression has become something of an afterthought to crimes against humanity, which have dominated most international tribunals since Nuremberg.[118] The ICC, for instance, has prosecuted more cases of crimes against humanity than cases of aggression and genocide combined. The focus on crimes against humanity also holds true for the "ad hoc" tribunals of the 1990s, which are discussed in the next section. As Richard Goldstone, the first prosecutor at both the Yugoslav and Rwandan tribunals, put it: "The recognition of crimes against humanity was the most important legacy of Nuremberg."[119]

Fifth, as mentioned earlier, both of the postwar tribunals faced accusations of victor's justice. This legacy of Nuremberg and Tokyo was very much on the minds of the architects of the ICC when they met some five decades later.[120] They went to great lengths to separate international justice from political power so as to avoid even the appearance of victor's justice. For instance, the ICC's founders allowed the ICC prosecutor to select situations to investigate without first getting permission from the members of the UN Security Council or

---

[116] Bass 2000, 147–205. [117] Van Schaack and Slye 2021, 31.
[118] As noted in the book's introduction, Russia's invasion of Ukraine has sparked a renewed focus on the crime of aggression.
[119] Bass 2000, 204. [120] Schabas 2010.

any other political actor. As I explain in Chapter 3, this attempt to make the ICC a purely judicial institution that could avoid the stigma of victor's justice inadvertently helped create the seeds of American opposition to the ICC.

The Post–Cold War Period

After World War II's conclusion, there were high hopes that the Nuremberg precedent might spur the development of additional international tribunals to prosecute atrocity crimes around the world.[121] Geopolitics, however, got in the way. The culprit was the burgeoning American–Soviet rivalry and the onset of the Cold War. As John Hagan summarizes, the post–World War II tribunals occurred during a "window of political opportunity that lasted barely long enough for cooperation in prosecuting the captured Nazi leadership at Nuremberg."[122] By the late 1940s, it was clear that the window of opportunity for pursuing international justice had closed. The Cold War featured a seemingly endless list of atrocities that theoretically could have been investigated and prosecuted, but geopolitical competition dictated a different path. Rather than bring the perpetrators to justice, the two superpowers typically did their best to excuse or cover up atrocities committed by their own allies even as they denounced atrocities committed by the other side. Given this context, serious plans for creating new international tribunals went into hibernation for several decades.

The end of the Cold War and the demise of the Soviet Union created a more favorable context for pursuing international justice.[123] Not even a year after the fall of the Berlin Wall, US President George H. W. Bush and UK Prime Minister Margaret Thatcher backed the idea of establishing "another Nuremberg" to prosecute Saddam Hussein and other Iraqi war criminals for their conduct during the

---

[121] For instance, the newly created United Nations directed a panel of legal experts to explore how the Nuremberg principles might be codified into a permanent international tribunal. The 1948 Genocide Convention also refers to the potential creation of such a court.
[122] Hagan 2003, 28.
[123] For an analysis of the ebb and flow of the international and transitional justice movements, see Teitel 2003.

The Post–Cold War Period 53

Gulf War.[124] This plan never came into fruition, but the sense that international tribunals were once again possible persisted in Western capitals, especially Washington. When two genocides – first in Yugoslavia, then in Rwanda – erupted in the early 1990s, the UN Security Council responded by creating a pair of new international tribunals. The rest of this section documents American policy toward these "ad hoc" tribunals. As I explain below, the American commitment to international justice was not always perfect, but the US did more than any other country to create the tribunals and ensure that they succeeded in prosecuting the architects of atrocities in Yugoslavia and Rwanda.

Yugoslavia

Nearly half a century after the Holocaust and promises of "never again," genocide returned to Europe in the early 1990s. The multinational federation of Yugoslavia, held together by Josip Broz Tito from the end of World War II until his death in 1980, had long managed to keep ethnic nationalism at bay. But after Tito's death, the federation began to unravel due to faltering economic conditions and rising ethnonationalist tensions. Yugoslavia finally imploded in 1991, a process that produced six independent states: Bosnia, Croatia, Macedonia, Montenegro, Serbia, and Slovenia. In some cases, such as relatively homogenous Slovenia, the path to independence was largely peaceful. But in Bosnia – a diverse state featuring large populations of Muslims, Serbs, and Croats – fighting erupted along ethnic lines.[125] Over the course of the war, all three sides engaged in horrific crimes. But Bosnian Serbs, led by notorious war criminals Radovan Karadzic and Ratko Mladic and supported by Serbian leader Slobodan Milosevic, committed the most extensive and systematic atrocities.[126] By the time the fighting finally ended in 1995, over 200,000 Bosnians had been killed and another two million were displaced.

The US initially took a hands-off approach to the escalating violence in Bosnia. America's strategic interests at the dawn of the post–Cold War era lay elsewhere, with an expansionist Iraq and a chaotic Russia

---

[124] Bass 2000, 210.
[125] There is, however, a debate on whether ethnicity was the ultimate cause of the violence. See Mueller 2000.
[126] All three of these individuals would, albeit with significant delays, face trial.

preoccupying US policymakers far more than events in the Balkans. As James Baker, secretary of state in the George H. W. Bush administration, bluntly described the brewing conflict in Bosnia and the rest of the Balkans in 1991: "We don't have a dog in that fight."[127] On top of that, there was a widespread perception that European countries, after decades of deferring to the US during the Cold War, were ready to handle the Bosnian crisis on their own. Indeed, European leaders repeatedly "claimed they had the authority, the strength, and the will to manage [Yugoslavia's] collapse."[128] The US was therefore willing to step aside during the early phases of the conflict.

The calculus changed in the summer of 1992. Roy Gutman of *Newsday* published a chilling series of articles based on eyewitness accounts that described several Serb-run concentration camps in Bosnia where civilian detainees were routinely executed or starved to death. Other reporters, photographers, and television crews raced across Bosnia to locate the camps. In early August, the first images from the camps – filmed with the permission of Serb guards who apparently failed to anticipate their significance for global audiences – circulated around the world. The videos and photos of emaciated prisoners behind barbed wire created a striking visual parallel to the Holocaust that was hard to miss. If, however, someone failed to make the connection, Gutman's reporting did it for them: One of his dispatches carried the evocative headline "Like Auschwitz."[129]

The revelation of the concentration camps put significant pressure on the US and other Western democracies to "do something," even though it was not readily apparent what that something ought to be. Lawrence Eagleburger, who served as secretary of state during the final months of the Bush administration, emerged as a leading spokesperson for war crimes trials. In December 1992, he gave a dramatic speech at a diplomatic conference in Geneva addressing the Yugoslav conflict: "We know that crimes against humanity have occurred, and we know when and where they occurred. We know, moreover, which forces committed those crimes, and under whose command they operated. And we know, finally, who the political leaders are and to whom those military commanders were – and still are – responsible. ... A second

---

[127] Baker and Glasser 2020, 463.   [128] Power 2003, 258.
[129] Roy Gutman, "Like Auschwitz," *Newsday*, July 21, 1992.

Nuremberg awaits [the perpetrators]."[130] Eagleburger went on to "name names" and provided a list of the specific people the US government considered war criminals.[131]

Though Eagleburger's speech made headlines, it was not yet accompanied by a major push for a new tribunal given the American political calendar: Bush had just lost the 1992 presidential election and was set to depart the White House in a few weeks. The incoming Bill Clinton administration would ultimately get to decide whether the US pursued another Nuremberg. As a candidate, Clinton had spoken forcefully about Bosnia, arguing that if "the horrors of the Holocaust taught us anything, it is the high cost of remaining silent and paralyzed in the face of genocide. We must discover who is responsible for these actions and take steps to bring them to justice."[132] But campaign rhetoric does not always translate into presidential action. On the eve of Clinton's presidency, it remained unclear whether he would prioritize international justice in the Balkans. The Senate confirmation hearing of Madeleine Albright for US ambassador to the UN provided a clue. Albright pledged to support a tribunal for Yugoslavia and then "moved quickly at the United Nations to make the creation of the Yugoslav Tribunal her first major achievement."[133] Indeed, Albright – a former Czech refugee whose family fled both Nazism and Communism – took a keen interest in issues of international accountability and eventually earned the nickname "the mother of the tribunals."[134]

While the Clinton administration was ready to create the first new international tribunal for atrocity crimes since Nuremberg and Tokyo, it still needed to convince other countries to support its plan. In the context of the post–Cold War multilateralism that reigned during the 1990s, this meant winning over the other members of the UN Security Council. But that was no easy task. The conversations on the merits of a tribunal for Yugoslavia taking place in the US stood in stark contrast to how the other major powers viewed a tribunal. For example, after Eagleburger gave his speech about the need for a modern-day Nuremberg in Yugoslavia, diplomats from other countries greeted him with "dead silence."[135] The reluctance of other major powers to

---

[130] Elaine Sciolino, "U.S. Names Figures It Wants Charged with War Crimes," *New York Times*, December 17, 1992.
[131] Among others, Eagleburger's list included Milosevic, Karadzic, and Mladic.
[132] Bass 2000, 214.   [133] Scheffer 2012a, 18.   [134] Bass 2000, 262.
[135] Carla Anne Robbins, "Balkan Judgments," *Wall Street Journal*, July 13, 1993.

support a tribunal continued into the Clinton administration. Even as Clinton made the case that a tribunal for Yugoslavia should be "a top United Nations priority," the other permanent members of the Security Council looked for ways to scuttle the tribunal, albeit for different reasons.[136] France and Britain prioritized a diplomatic peace process over a tribunal. Indeed, both initially opposed the creation of a tribunal because they worried that attempts to hold perpetrators accountable for their crimes would complicate efforts to end the war.[137] China and Russia both feared a tribunal for Yugoslavia might set a precedent that would later come back to haunt them given their own treatment of minority groups in places such as Tibet and Chechnya.[138] Moreover, Russia was loath to create a tribunal that was sure to put ethnic Serbs, Russia's traditional allies in the Balkans, on trial.[139]

Despite these reservations, the UN Security Council unanimously adopted Resolution 808 on February 22, 1993, in which it authorized the creation of a new tribunal to prosecute individuals guilty of serious violations of international humanitarian law committed on the territory of the former Yugoslavia since 1991. A second resolution, passed unanimously on May 25, formally established the International Criminal Tribunal for the former Yugoslavia (ICTY). The new tribunal was located at The Hague in the Netherlands, the same location where the ICC would later set up its offices.

The lack of resistance to the American push for the ICTY was primarily due to two factors. First, the 1990s represented the height of the "unipolar moment," making it more difficult than ever to resist the preferences of the US.[140] One Venezuelan diplomat involved in the negotiations that established the tribunal even complained that the ICTY resolution "was rammed down our throats."[141] Second, horrific images, videos, and stories continued to emerge from Bosnia and other parts of the region, creating a context in which it was difficult to

---

[136] Scharf 1997, xv.

[137] The British and French concern that the tribunal could undermine efforts to end the war foreshadowed the "peace versus justice" debate among scholars. See, for example, Goldsmith and Krasner 2003; Snyder and Vinjamuri 2003; Nalepa and Powell 2016; Prorok 2017; Krcmaric 2020.

[138] Bass 2000, 216.

[139] After the tribunal opened, Russian security and intelligence forces helped ethnic Serb war criminals, including Ratko Mladic, avoid capture. See Borger 2016, 283–307.

[140] Krauthammer 1990. [141] Guest 1995, 129.

protest the tribunal's creation. Though other members of the Security Council may have privately opposed the ICTY, blocking it publicly was another matter. As one member of the American negotiating team described the public relations dynamic for reluctant members of the Security Council, "With the situation in the former Yugoslavia spinning out of control, no country was willing to be seen as the spoiler."[142]

The ICTY's founding prompted a pair of opposing reactions. Some criticized the tribunal even before it opened its doors. To be clear, the criticism was directed more toward the major powers that created the ICTY than the ICTY itself. The argument was straightforward: the UN Security Council created the tribunal as a substitute for military intervention.[143] Compared to direct military action – which could have saved countless lives but also would have put troops from the major powers in harm's way – international prosecutions were low-risk. Hence, the decision to create the ICTY may have reflected a crude political calculus more than a principled commitment to international justice.[144] The sense that the tribunal was a "fig leaf" for the lack of military action even held sway within parts of the US government. Due to the Clinton administration's inaction on Bosnia, the US suffered "the largest wave of resignations in State Department history" in the summer of 1993.[145]

Others greeted the ICTY with great fanfare. Many of the court's proponents, both in the US and elsewhere, viewed it as the heir to Nuremberg. Madeleine Albright delivered arguably her best-remembered speech after the UN Security Council established the ICTY, famously proclaiming, "There is an echo in this Chamber today. The Nuremberg Principles have been reaffirmed."[146] UN Secretary General Boutros Boutros-Ghali similarly asserted, "For the first time since the Nuremberg Tribunal, war criminals will know the sanction of

---

[142] Scharf 1997, 62.
[143] According to one legal scholar, "One intention of some people at the beginning of this new period of international law was to use the promise of criminal prosecution as a policy *alternative* to direct intervention – so that an intended consequence (for some, anyway) of this new activity was to reduce the pressure to intervene." See Anderson 2009, 334.
[144] Rudolph 2017, 43.   [145] Power 2003, 315.
[146] Julia Preston, "U.N. Security Council Establishes Yugoslav War Crimes Tribunal," *Washington Post*, February 23, 1991.

international law."[147] Even after the ICTY began operating, its staff continued to draw parallels to Nuremberg, presumably to enhance the legitimacy of the ICTY and burnish its image as part of a great historical undertaking. Louise Arbour, the Canadian jurist who served as the tribunal's second prosecutor, told an interviewer: "Collectively, we're linked to Nuremberg. We mention its name every day."[148]

The constant comparisons to Nuremberg masked a crucial difference between the ICTY and its famous predecessor: the timing of the tribunals. Nuremberg was a case of justice *after* conflict. Yugoslavia, however, was a case of justice *during* conflict. In other words, the ICTY was novel because it represented the first time a war crimes tribunal began to operate in the middle of the armed conflict it was meant to investigate.[149] The ICTY's job was consequently much more difficult. To be sure, Nuremberg (and Tokyo) faced plenty of challenges. But the ICTY quickly learned that it is even harder to collect evidence, investigate suspects, and arrest indicted criminals outside the context of a military occupation in a completely defeated country. The tribunal therefore got off to a slow start. Near the end of 1994, nearly two years after the UN Security Council authorized the creation of the ICTY, the tribunal had little to show for its efforts. As Richard Goldstone, the South African judge who served as the tribunal's first prosecutor described the early years, "We had an empty prison. There was a great deal of frustration."[150]

The turning point for the ICTY occurred not in the courtroom but on the battlefield: the Clinton administration finally decided to use military force in Yugoslavia. The decision was at least partly due to domestic political calculations in the US. In a confidential memo, Anthony Lake, Clinton's national security advisor, made the case that "the administration's weak, muddle-through strategy on Bosnia was becoming a cancer on Clinton's entire foreign policy – spreading and eating away at its credibility."[151] In the late summer of 1995, the US and its NATO allies began a massive bombing campaign against Serb targets that was meant to degrade their military capabilities to the

---

[147] Hazan 2004, 7.
[148] Olivia Ward, "War Crimes Tribunal on a Roll," *Toronto Star*, March 23, 1998.
[149] The pursuit of justice during conflict has become the norm, as exemplified by the permanent nature of the ICC.
[150] Quoted in Hagan 2003, 71.   [151] Woodward 1996, 253.

point that the Serbs might prefer a diplomatic solution to continued war. The bombing campaign quickly paid dividends. The Bosnian Serb leaders, Karadzic and Mladic, and their Serbian benefactor, Milosevic, signaled that they were finally ready to negotiate after more than three years of fighting. On November 1, 1995, the leaders of Bosnia, Serbia, and Croatia joined representatives from the US, Russia, and several European powers at Wright-Patterson Air Force Base outside Dayton, Ohio.[152] After three weeks of intense negotiations, many of them painstakingly mediated by Assistant Secretary of State Richard Holbrooke, the warring parties reached a peace deal and signed the Dayton Accords.

The negotiations in Dayton were extraordinarily complex,[153] but the Accords were relevant to the ICTY for two main reasons. First, the US refused to trade away justice for peace. Before talks began in Dayton, officials from several European countries floated the idea of offering amnesty from ICTY prosecution to Karadzic, Mladic, Milosevic, and others in exchange for their participation in the peace talks, but the US refused to support the plan.[154] Rumors of a similar amnesty-for-peace initiative surfaced again during Dayton, prompting ICTY Prosecutor Richard Goldstone to fear that the tribunal "would be sold down the river at Dayton." In the end, these worries never materialized because, in Goldstone's words, "Holbrooke protected the interests of the tribunal."[155] Second, the Dayton Accords provided for the deployment of a large NATO peacekeeping force, the Implementation Force (IFOR), to Bosnia. IFOR sent nearly 60,000 troops to Bosnia – over one-third of them American – to ensure that the terms of the Dayton Accords materialized on the ground. The arrival of IFOR fundamentally changed the context in which the ICTY operated. Instead of attempting to pursue justice in an active

---

[152] The Bosnian Serb leaders were not permitted to travel to Dayton or participate in the negotiations directly, but Milosevic was allowed to represent their interests at the negotiating table.
[153] For an insider account of the many twists and turns during the Dayton negotiations, see Holbrooke 1999.
[154] Scheffer 2012a, 19.
[155] Scheffer 2012a, 134. In fact, Holbrooke demanded that US government officials be allowed to visit suspected war crimes sites in Bosnia during the Dayton negotiations as "a constant public reminder that even as we sought peace, we were not abandoning the quest for justice." See Holbrooke 1999, 189.

war zone, which had made it all but impossible for the tribunal to gather evidence or for sympathetic nations to arrest suspects, the ICTY now encountered an internationally brokered peace deal backed by the presence of NATO forces. For the first time since the tribunal's creation, it was realistic to imagine bringing major Balkan war criminals to justice.

American support for the ICTY shaped nearly every aspect of the court's operations: the US provided funding, shared evidence, contributed lawyers and investigators, and arrested indicted war criminals. In terms of funding, the ICTY constantly struggled because of the peculiarities of the UN system. Even though the tribunal was a creation of the Security Council, its funding came from the regular budget of the General Assembly, an arrangement that was meant to symbolize the entire world's investment in the tribunal.[156] But it was problematic from the beginning. As Goldstone put it, "A bureaucracy made up of civil servants from 186 countries is more than 186 times worse."[157] Due to recurrent financial crises at the UN, all ICTY staff were forbidden from traveling on multiple occasions. This unsurprisingly hampered the tribunal's ability to accomplish basic tasks. For example, it is nearly impossible for war crimes investigators to gather evidence if they are prohibited from traveling to crime scenes. In his memoirs, Goldstone recalls how he and his staff were required to "spend many days at irritating and time-consuming meetings with United Nations officials" on pay and funding issues when they otherwise could have spent their time and energy investigating crimes in the Balkans.[158] The financial situation became so dire at one point that the UN instructed Goldstone to cancel his address at a diplomatic event commemorating the fiftieth anniversary of the Nuremberg trials unless he could find someone else to cover his travel costs.[159]

Given that the ICTY was perennially underfunded due to the UN's bureaucracy, voluntary contributions from states were sometimes required to allow the tribunal to operate smoothly. The US was the largest overall funder, ultimately covering about a quarter of the ICTY's costs, which totaled more than $2 billion over the course of

---

[156] Scharf 1997, 79. [157] Quoted in Bass 2000, 220.
[158] Goldstone 2000, 85.
[159] Goldstone 2000, 87. Goldstone ultimately was able to speak at the event because the city of Nuremberg graciously covered the travel costs.

the tribunal's lifespan.[160] On some occasions, the US even volunteered additional money to the tribunal without first receiving a specific request. For instance, Congress used the Emergency Supplemental Appropriations Act to identify an extra $18 million for the ICTY beyond the funding the Clinton administration had already requested for the tribunal.[161] Though some other states were willing to pitch in financially, many were not. For instance, when the tribunal first opened its doors, the value of just the computers donated by the US government equaled the total voluntary contributions from all other countries combined.[162] Even critics of the ICTY, eager to cast the tribunal as a tool of Western imperialism, acknowledged the unique role the US played in funding the tribunal's operations. According to journalist Michael Parenti, "The International Criminal Tribunal for the former Yugoslavia was set up by the United Nations Security Council in 1993 at the bidding of Madeline Albright and the US government. It depends on NATO countries for its financial support, with the United States as the major provider. ... It hardly qualifies as any kind of independent judicial body."[163] In other words, the court's supporters and detractors could debate whether American financial support compromised the ICTY's independence, but the underlying fact that American funding was essential to the tribunal's operations was indisputable.

The US also played a key role in staffing the fledgling tribunal. Like at Nuremberg, the US was concerned about the optics of an American-dominated tribunal and hoped to create a more international flavor. Secretary of State Warren Christopher therefore decided the ICTY's first prosecutor should not be an American and refrained from campaigning for candidates from other countries to avoid having the tribunal appear "as an American show."[164] In hindsight, this may have been a mistake. The fifteen members of the UN Security Council, acting in the spirit of post–Cold War multilateralism, made a de facto agreement to pick the prosecutor unanimously.[165] But it took them well over a year to reach a consensus as many countries aggressively lobbied for their preferred candidates and blocked the nominees of their rivals. The protracted fiasco was only resolved after an intervention from Nelson Mandela, paving the way for South

---

[160] Ford 2011, 971–973. [161] Scheffer 2012a, 287. [162] Hazan 2004, 53.
[163] Parenti 2000, 128. [164] Scharf 1997, 77. [165] Scheffer 2012a, 31.

Africa's Goldstone to get the tribunal's top job.[166] Once Goldstone was installed, it became possible to staff the rest of the tribunal. The US quickly decided to share twenty-two government employees – such as FBI investigators and attorneys from the departments of State, Defense, and Justice – with the ICTY.[167] The secondees, whose salaries and expenses were paid for by the US government rather than the underfunded tribunal, were an essential "jump-start" for Goldstone and the ICTY.[168] In fact, given that Goldstone's initial staff was only forty people, the secondment of twenty-two American lawyers and investigators represented the majority the prosecutor's office.[169]

Several other countries were less than thrilled about the prominence of the American staff at the ICTY, leading to grumbling about the influence of the tribunal's "American mafia."[170] This attitude, especially common in European capitals, did not sit well with many ICTY personnel. The ICTY's first president, Antonio Cassese (an Italian himself) noted, "The French, Italian, and German governments questioned me, 'Why are you accepting all these Americans?' I told them, 'Do the same thing!' They did nothing of the sort."[171] Similarly, ICTY spokesman Christian Chartier recalls European governments routinely complaining about the heavy presence of Americans, with one even claiming that the CIA had somehow infiltrated the tribunal. But it was not lost on Chartier that "these same governments had sent us no personnel while we cried famine and did nothing even when we asked them for help."[172] To be sure, there were some within the ICTY who were concerned about the preponderance of Americans staffing the tribunal. Graham Blewitt, an Australian who served as the deputy prosecutor, worried at one point that "this is going to become an American judicial office if we're not careful."[173] In the end, however,

---

[166] Hagan 2003, 60–61.
[167] In addition to these attorneys and investigators, the US also provided one of the ICTY's judges, Gabrielle McDonald. In 1997, she was elected president of the tribunal.
[168] Goldstone 2000, 82.
[169] Some of these secondees from the American government to the ICTY went on to have long and distinguished careers in the international justice field. For instance, one of them – Brenda Hollis – later became the prosecutor of the Special Court for Sierra Leone, another US-supported international tribunal.
[170] Bass 2000, 222. [171] Hazan 2004, 53. [172] Hazan 2004.
[173] Hagan 2003, 9.

the prominent role for American staff was inevitable because the US was willing to contribute far more to the ICTY than any other country.

Another channel of American support for the ICTY involved sharing evidence. As soon as the tribunal opened its doors, the US pledged to provide it with information necessary for the prosecution of war criminals. A small team of American officials began to organize information about atrocity crimes in the Balkans for delivery to the tribunal, but it quickly ran into a problem: the most helpful information was almost always classified.[174] American intelligence agencies, not surprisingly, were reluctant to share extremely sensitive material with an international institution whose staff had not gone through the standard security clearance vetting process.[175] To determine what information it could safely provide to the ICTY without revealing American sources and methods for intelligence collection, the US created the Interagency Working Group on War Crimes Evidence in May 1993, directed by deputy National Security Advisor Sandy Berger. Despite this effort from American officials, the flow of information to the tribunal remained woefully slow from the perspective of the ICTY. A frustrated Goldstone visited Washington in 1995 to complain about "the unacceptably long time it was taking for [his] office to receive responses to requests for intelligence information."[176] He was granted meetings with senior American officials – including National Security Advisor Anthony Lake and CIA Director John Deutch – and the visit came to an amicable end when the CIA expanded the unit tasked with processing requests from the ICTY and created a secure communications link between Washington and The Hague. As Goldstone put it, "I got everything I was seeking [from the US]."[177]

After the US and the ICTY implemented new procedures for sharing information, the flow of evidence went from a trickle to a flood. This often involved capitalizing on the American intelligence community's comparative advantage in technology, particularly aerial reconnaissance photos, which allowed the tribunal to identify and analyze mass graves throughout Bosnia. The scale of the information that the US

---

[174] On the early struggles of the Washington bureaucracy to share information efficiently with the ICTY, see Scheffer 2012a, 35–44.
[175] For a broader analysis of how "disclosure dilemmas" influence when and how states share secretive information with international institutions, see Carnegie and Carson 2020.
[176] Goldstone 2000, 91. [177] Hagan 2003, 135.

provided to the ICTY is difficult to overstate. According to one US official involved in the process: "A great deal of information was made available to the tribunal, especially aerial imagery. ... Sometimes we gave them so much that it would pile up at the US embassy in The Hague, where it was archived and the tribunal had access to it."[178] Among other things, images from American reconnaissance aircraft helped the ICTY reconstruct exactly what happened during the infamous massacre at Srebrenica, when some 8,000 Bosnian Muslim men and boys were killed in the deadliest slaughter on European soil since World War II.[179] In addition to sharing classified intelligence material, the US assisted the tribunal with its investigations by pressuring Balkan leaders to allow ICTY personnel access to crimes scenes,[180] deploying FBI forensic teams to the Balkans to collect evidence that could be shared with the ICTY,[181] and allowing US military officers to serve as witnesses for the ICTY prosecution.[182] The US stood out among the major powers for the extent to which it helped the tribunal gather evidence. As one journalist described it, "With the exception of the United States, none of the great Western states [shared] intelligence with the tribunal beyond dribs and drabs."[183]

The final pillar of American support concerned the apprehension of ICTY fugitives. Like intelligence sharing, the arrest of ICTY fugitives started slowly but eventually transformed into a success story. The arrival of NATO peacekeepers after the Dayton Accords, as mentioned earlier, created a far better context for arresting suspects than while the fighting still raged. But bizarre rules of engagement initially handicapped NATO forces. Put simply, NATO soldiers were not supposed to take the initiative in tracking down ICTY suspects, though they were

---

[178] Hagan 2003.

[179] Scheffer 2012a, 41–42. This American-generated evidence proved crucial to the ICTY's prosecution of crimes at Srebrenica. As one tribunal judge recalled,

> I found most astounding in the Srebrenica case the satellite aerial image photography furnished by the US military intelligence which pinpointed to the minute movements on the ground of men and transports in remote Eastern Bosnian locations. These photographs not only assisted the prosecution in locating the mass grave sites over hundreds of miles of terrain, they were also introduced to validate its witnesses' accounts of where thousands of civilians were detained and eventually killed.

See Wald 2001, 101.

[180] Hagan 2003, 115–116. [181] Scheffer 2012a, 289–290.
[182] Hagan 2003, 165–168. [183] Hazan 2004, 91.

permitted to arrest indicted war criminals if they happened to bump into them in the course of their other peacekeeping duties.[184] This policy was largely the result of loss aversion in Washington and the European capitals: the Western powers were willing to deploy their troops to Bosnia via the NATO peacekeeping force, but they were unwilling to put them in risky arrest scenarios. The legacy of the 1993 intervention in Somalia, where eighteen Americans died in the Black Hawk Down incident while attempting to capture Somali warlord Mohammed Farah Aideed, still loomed large in NATO decision-making on Bosnia.[185] The Western powers worried that Serb forces – who remained well-armed – might kill or capture their troops in retaliation for arrests.[186] This timid initial approach to arrests was a source of frustration for the ICTY.[187] As Goldstone lamented, "If arrests are left to luck or stupidity, they aren't going to happen."[188]

Goldstone's prediction proved accurate. When he left his position as ICTY prosecutor in 1996 to return to South Africa, only a handful of low-ranking suspects were in the tribunal's custody. His successor, Louise Arbour, realized that the ICTY needed to implement an entirely different arrest strategy. Rather than badger reluctant NATO states to undertake arrest operations that they perceived as excessively risky, she sought a way to convince them that arrests could be done with minimal risk to their troops. Her solution was to start issuing "sealed" (i.e., secret) arrest warrants instead of publicly announcing new indictments as the tribunal had done previously. The idea underpinning Arbour's strategy was simple: it is harder to arrest someone – especially

---

[184] Scheffer 2012a, 140.   [185] Bass 2000, 224.
[186] That said, some in the US government pushed the Clinton administration and the Pentagon to make arrests a priority. Holbrooke, for example, pressed Clinton and Gore to devote the resources necessary to capture Karadzic and Mladic, insisting the apprehension of the Bosnian Serb leaders was "the most critical issue that was not resolved at Dayton." See Holbrooke 1999, 327. Another US official argued that having Karadzic and Mladic at large in the Balkans "was akin to leaving Goering and Goebbels in Germany after World War II." See Bass 2000, 259.
[187] The NATO arrest policy was especially striking because the whereabouts of many ICTY fugitives were known, with some suspects living openly under their own names. At times, enterprising journalists managed to track them down. In other cases, the manhunts took a comical turn, such as when a group of journalists were mistaken for CIA agents and inadvertently sparked a political imbroglio in the Balkans.
[188] Scheffer 2012a, 124.

if that someone is a heavily armed war criminal with loyal forces at his command – when they know they are being pursued. The sealed indictments offered peacekeeping forces the element of surprise and, along with it, a reduction in the likelihood of sustaining casualties during arrest operations.

Arbour just needed a willing partner to demonstrate that her sealed indictment strategy could work. She found one in Jacques Klein, the American general in charge of the UN authority in Eastern Slavonia (Croatia). Arbour informed Klein that Slavko Dokmanovic, a Serb responsible for massacring hundreds of hospitalized Croatian soldiers, was secretly indicted and was known to visit the territory under Klein's command. Klein promptly organized a joint American–Polish arrest mission that apprehended Dokmanovic without incident and transferred him to the tribunal.[189] This seemingly mundane arrest – the first by international peacekeeping forces – produced a powerful demonstration effect. Other countries realized that if the Americans and the Poles could nab war crimes suspects in the Balkans without suffering causalities or inciting retaliatory attacks, they likely could do so too. As one ICTY official described it, "Once they pulled that off, this developed some sort of peer pressure for the [peacekeepers] in Bosnia ... and it just snowballed."[190] In the coming years, the ICTY continued to use the sealed indictment strategy to great effect with the cooperation of the US and other NATO countries. Some even consider the pursuit of Balkan war criminals "the world's most successful manhunt."[191]

The zenith of American support for apprehending war criminals in the Balkans involved the region's most powerful person: Serbian leader Slobodan Milosevic. Milosevic had managed to avoid an ICTY indictment as violence engulfed Yugoslavia in the early 1990s, but the tribunal indicted him in 1999 after he ordered a brutal assault on Kosovo, then an autonomous province in Serbia. Getting Milosevic to the ICTY, however, was a challenge. Even after he was voted out of office in 2000, the prospects for a trial were bleak since the successor regime in Serbia was unwilling to extradite him to the ICTY. In the US,

---

[189] Borger 2016, 25–44. Klein and Clint Williamson, an American attorney working at the ICTY (who would later become the US Ambassador-at-Large for War Crimes Issues), took the lead in directing the operation, which was carried out by Polish special forces.
[190] Hagan 2003, 105.   [191] Borger 2016.

the newly installed George W. Bush administration decided to use America's economic might to ensure that Milosevic ended up behind bars. Secretary of State Colin Powell not only threatened to withhold from Serbia hundreds of millions of dollars in American aid but also repeatedly delayed an international donors' conference where over a billion dollars of reconstruction aid was at stake. The new Serbian Prime Minister Zoran Djindjic and others in official Belgrade quickly realized that it was in Serbia's interest to capitulate since American economic pressure had turned Milosevic into "Serbia's most valuable export commodity."[192] In 2001, Serbian authorities arrested Milosevic and transferred him to the ICTY, where he later died of a heart attack in the midst of his trial.

For a tribunal that got off to such an inauspicious start, from not being able to pay for its employees' travel to the frustrations of letting its jail cells sit empty, the ICTY reached a remarkable conclusion. The tribunal indicted a total of 161 individuals and had zero fugitives remaining fugitives by 2011. In other words, every single indicted war criminal – including figures that once seemed untouchable such as Milosevic, Karadzic, and Mladic – was eventually apprehended or died. Having fulfilled its mandate to a degree that even the court's most enthusiastic supporters considered unlikely, the ICTY formally closed its doors in 2017.[193]

Rwanda

Just months after the UN Security Council created the Yugoslav tribunal, another genocide broke out in Rwanda. On April 6, 1994, the airplane carrying Rwandan president Juvenal Habyarimana and Burundian president Cyprien Ntaryamira was shot down in mysterious circumstances.[194] The death of Habyarimana, who had ruled Rwanda for more than two decades, was the spark that turned long-standing tensions between Rwanda's Hutu and Tutsi ethnic groups into a full-

---

[192] Quoted in Hagan 2003, 210.
[193] A residual mechanism was set up to oversee the tribunal's few outstanding cases.
[194] There is still no consensus on who was responsible for the assassination of the two leaders. One theory holds that the RPF shot down the plane. Another theory maintains that Hutu hardliners within Habyarimana's own government orchestrated the killing to justify seizing power and exterminating the Tutsi.

blown genocide. There was a history of recurrent violence between the two groups dating back to Rwanda's colonial period, when Belgian colonizers manipulated ethnic identities and favored the minority Tutsi over the majority Hutu. After Rwanda became independent in 1962, many Tutsis fled the country as they feared retribution at the hands of the newly empowered Hutu. Most recently, Habyarimana's Hutu-led Rwandan government and the Rwandan Patriotic Front (RPF), a Tutsi rebel army based primarily in neighboring Uganda, had fought a three-year civil war that ended with the signing of the Arusha Accords in 1993. But the brief period of calm following the Arusha Accords was shattered when Habyarimana's plane exploded in the skies over Kigali, Rwanda's capital city. Within hours, Hutu extremists seized control of the government and orchestrated the mass murder of Rwanda's Tutsi and moderate Hutu populations.[195]

The international community made no serious attempt to stop the slaughter as it unfolded.[196] In the evocative words of Samantha Power, the US and other major powers were "bystanders to genocide" in Rwanda.[197] A pair of factors help explain America's hesitancy to intervene. First, the brutal killing of eighteen American soldiers on the streets of Mogadishu, Somalia on what was supposed to be a low-risk peacekeeping and humanitarian relief operation was still a fresh memory. The lesson of Somalia for many American policymakers was that intervention in Africa was an inherently risky venture that had little upside but plenty of downsides. Indeed, the debacle in Somalia "had an enormously negative impact for years thereafter on Washington's attitude about military engagements in Africa ... and it shaped the context for failing to intervene to end Rwanda's genocide."[198] Second, many US government officials knew almost nothing about Rwanda's politics given that the country had previously been of little concern to American foreign policy. Wesley Clark, the American general who would later become famous for leading the NATO bombing campaign against Serbia in 1999 and running for president in 2004, remembers officers debating, "Is it Hutu and Tutsi or Tutu and Hutsi?"[199] The US, however, cannot be singled out for its unwillingness to intervene militarily: no other major power was willing to do

---

[195] On the causes of the genocide, see Straus 2006.
[196] On the international response (or lack thereof) to Rwanda's genocide, see Des Forges 1999; Kuperman 2001; Barnett 2002; Power 2003.
[197] Power 2001. [198] Scheffer 2012a, 47. [199] Power 2003, 330.

so either.[200] Moreover, the UN did nothing to stop the genocide. After Hutu militias killed ten Belgian peacekeepers on the day after Habyarimana's assassination, the UN not only declined to send reinforcements but also decided to withdraw nearly all the peacekeepers who were already in Rwanda. These moves effectively abandoned Rwanda's Tutsi population to the Hutu killing squads prowling the country.

With no international intervention forthcoming, the RPF and its primarily Tutsi fighters invaded Rwanda from Uganda. Led by Paul Kagame – Rwanda's future president – the RPF proved to be a much more effective fighting force than what the Hutu extremists could muster. The RPF took Kigali on June 4 and captured the last Hutu stronghold in mid-July. The genocide was over. In the preceding 100 days, Hutu extremists had killed an estimated 800,000 Tutsis and moderate Hutus, making the Rwandan genocide "the fastest, most efficient killing spree of the twentieth century."[201]

There is a debate on exactly what the international community could and should have done to stop the genocide, but the consensus is that even small actions taken early in the genocide would have made a big difference. Romeo Dallaire, the Canadian officer in charge of the UN peacekeeping mission established in Rwanda after the Arusha Accords, pleaded with his superiors at UN headquarters for a total of only 5,000 well-armed troops, which he believed would be enough to stop the killing.[202] An analysis from the Carnegie Corporation supported Dallaire's claims and concluded that the timely deployment of 5,000 international peacekeepers authorized to use force "could have stemmed the violence in and around the capital, prevented its spread to the countryside, and created conditions conducive to the cessation of [violence]."[203] Even Bill Clinton, who never seriously completed using military force in Rwanda, later expressed remorse and asserted that he could have saved some 300,000 Rwandan lives if he had deployed troops to the country.[204]

---

[200] In the final days of the genocide, France sent soldiers to Rwanda in Operation Turquoise. Instead of protecting Tutsi victims, the French forces deployed to areas where Hutus were fleeing the advancing RPF. As a result, France was criticized for protecting the genocidaires and giving them an opportunity to escape beyond Rwanda's borders.
[201] Power 2003, 334.   [202] Power 2003, 350.   [203] Feil 1998.
[204] Dana Hughes, "Bill Clinton Regrets Rwanda Now (Not So Much in 1994)," ABC News, February 28, 2014.

After the genocide ended, the US emerged as "the driving force" pushing for the creation of an international tribunal for Rwanda.[205] As a bureaucratic first step, the UN created a commission of experts to analyze which crimes may have been committed in Rwanda and make a recommendation to the Security Council on the best course of action. The Clinton administration made it clear that it preferred another tribunal. In mid-July, right as the genocide was ending, the White House issued an official statement demanding "that those Rwandans responsible for genocidal killings and other crimes against humanity be brought to justice" and indicating that it "hoped that the United Nations would act swiftly ... to create a war crimes tribunal."[206]

Two dynamics underpinned American support for a tribunal. First, there was a moral imperative. The US and other members of the UN Security Council felt the need "to redeem themselves" by doing something in the post-genocide period after doing nothing during the genocide.[207] In this sense, the Rwandan Tribunal was born out of the same substitution logic between military intervention and international prosecutions that appeared in debates on Yugoslavia. The international community would once again try to prosecute the crimes that it had failed to prevent. Second, there was a regional security logic. As the RPF swept across Rwanda, Hutu genocidaires hid among millions of Hutu civilians fleeing the country for neighboring Zaire (now known as the Democratic Republic of the Congo). The UN-supported refugee camps in Zaire inadvertently provided the genocidaires with a safe haven to regroup, assert physical control over the camps, and possibly launch attacks back into Rwanda.[208] The US therefore feared that Paul Kagame, Rwanda's new de facto leader, would send his RPF fighters into Zaire to eliminate the Hutu threat, sparking a regional war.[209] John Shattuck, the US Assistant Secretary of State for Democracy, Human Rights, and Labor, described the situation as follows: "I was convinced that unless we moved quickly to set up an international tribunal and

---

[205] Cruvellier 2006, 29.   [206] Scheffer 2012a, 71.   [207] Peskin 2008, 159.
[208] On refugee flows and humanitarian aid as possible sources of conflict, see Lischer 2005; Krcmaric 2014.
[209] Two years later, this fear became a reality as Rwanda invaded Zaire. Rwandan forces attacked the refugee camps and then joined with several other countries to overthrow Zaire's leader, Mobutu Sese Seko. The chaos after Mobutu's ouster helped fuel a devastating regional conflict, sometimes considered "Africa's world war." See Prunier 2008.

arrest the leaders of the genocide, a new cycle of vengeance would destabilize all of central Africa. Rwanda was not just a tragedy we had failed to prevent; it was another crisis in the making."[210]

The US faced far less pushback to its plans for a tribunal in Rwanda than it did previously for the tribunal in Yugoslavia. Recall that only a year earlier, the other four permanent members of the UN Security Council were initially opposed to the Yugoslav Tribunal, though they eventually supported the American position. When it came to Rwanda, only China expressed reservations about creating a tribunal to address the genocide.[211] For France, Britain, and Russia, the debate was on *how*, not *if*, a tribunal should be set up. The sticking point concerned the relationship between any new tribunal for Rwanda and the existing tribunal for Yugoslavia. At one extreme, some wanted to expand the jurisdiction of the Yugoslav Tribunal to include Rwanda and thereby avoid the delays associated with creating a new tribunal from scratch. At the other extreme, some preferred a separate tribunal for Rwanda that had no linkages to the tribunal for Yugoslavia. The Security Council eventually settled on a compromise that all five permanent members found acceptable: there would be separate tribunals, but they would share a prosecutor and an appeals chamber, a decision that made the ICTY's Richard Goldstone the first prosecutor at the new Rwandan Tribunal as well. On November 8, 1994, the UN Security Council adopted Resolution 955 and formally established the International Criminal Tribunal for Rwanda (ICTR).

The ICTR, as hinted above, shared a great deal with the slightly older tribunal for Yugoslavia. Given that they were created around the same time, shared a prosecutor, and had similar rules and procedures, one journalist reasonably concluded that the ICTR was "a replica of the ICTY for Rwanda."[212] Indeed, it is not uncommon to see the Rwandan Tribunal described as the neglected sibling of the Yugoslav Tribunal. Goldstone himself acknowledged that there was a widespread perception that the ICTR was little more than "some sort of poor relation" of the ICTY, though he personally disagreed with this characterization.[213] In a dynamic that mirrors the relative neglect of the tribunal at Tokyo compared to its slightly older twin at Nuremberg, the tribunal for Rwanda has generally received less

---

[210] Shattuck 2003, 68. [211] Scheffer 2012a, 71. [212] Cruvellier 2006, 6.
[213] Goldstone 2000, 113.

attention from scholars, the media, and the public than the tribunal for Yugoslavia.[214]

One area where the ICTR did receive plenty of attention was in Rwanda itself, where the new Tutsi-led government had an awkward relationship with the tribunal. Though Rwanda initially threw its support behind plans for an international tribunal, it soured on the ICTR after discovering it would have little control over the court's institutional design.[215] Rwanda's biggest objection to the ICTR was the tribunal's unwillingness to impose capital punishment. For many in Rwanda, judicial punishments short of the death penalty paled in comparison to the genocide. Moreover, the ICTR's decision to prohibit the death penalty created a strange incongruity in punishments: the leading architects of the genocide would only receive prison sentences at the ICTR, whereas low-level perpetrators tried in Rwanda's domestic courts could be put to death. Rwanda also was dismayed that the Security Council decided to locate the new tribunal in Arusha, Tanzania. The international community believed holding trials in Rwanda – where demands for rough justice were ubiquitous – would compromise the tribunal's impartiality, but the Rwandan government did not see it that way. Finally, Rwanda and the Security Council differed on the ICTR's temporal jurisdiction. Rwanda wanted the tribunal's jurisdiction to end on July 17, 1994, the day the genocide ended. But the Security Council gave the ICTR a mandate to investigate crimes committed in Rwanda during any part of 1994, which meant that the ICTR could theoretically investigate RPF reprisals against Hutus in the aftermath of the genocide. Rwanda's disenchantment with the ICTR's rules grew to the point that Rwanda, which just happened to hold a rotating seat (i.e., a seat without veto power) on the UN Security Council, was the only country to vote against creating the tribunal.[216] Despite this "no" vote, the Rwandan government generally cooperated with the tribunal and the two sides enjoyed a "cordial relationship" most of the time.[217]

---

[214] To be clear, there is a voluminous academic and popular literature on the Rwandan genocide, but the tribunal itself – with a few notable exceptions – has received less attention.

[215] See, for example, Goldstone 2000, 110–111; Peskin 2008, 156–167; Scheffer 2012a, 80–84.

[216] China abstained on Resolution 955. Every other country voted in favor.

[217] Goldstone 2000, 112. There were, however, a few notable clashes on whether high-profile defendants would be prosecuted at the ICTR or in Rwanda.

Once the ICTR was established, the US played an essential role in supporting all aspects of its operations. To start, American financial resources were crucial to the ICTR given that the tribunal cost nearly two billion dollars over the course of its lifespan.[218] As with the ICTY, the US was the ICTR's largest overall funder and ultimately paid for approximately one quarter of the tribunal's expenses.[219] The US also went to great lengths to help raise extrabudgetary international funds for the ICTR that could be used to cover shortfalls in UN funding. Goldstone, for example, recalls how he was "enthusiastically supported" by the State Department's John Shattuck when he held a donors' conference in Kigali for the ICTR. Despite a "lukewarm reception" from the UN itself, Shattuck and the Dutch minister of developmental aid organized a successful conference that raised millions and went "well beyond [the ICTR's] expectations."[220] Overall, American generosity toward the tribunals in both Rwanda and Yugoslavia meant that the US effectively became "the convenient one-stop shopping ally of the war crimes tribunals."[221]

The US also played a pivotal role in staffing the ICTR with qualified lawyers, judges, and investigators. This was especially important given that the tribunal's personnel, especially in the early years, were frequently accused of corruption and incompetence.[222] In one particularly embarrassing episode, the tribunal unknowingly employed one of its own suspects – a former genocidaire living under a false identity – as an investigator.[223] Against this backdrop, both the quantity and the quality of the American staff at the ICTR stood out. Though Americans may not have dominated the ICTR quite as thoroughly as the ICTY, the US provided more personnel to the tribunal than any other country.[224] Americans also tended to rise through the ranks quickly. The ICTR's second prosecutor, Louise Arbour, was willing to ruffle feathers among tribunal staff by promoting young but talented American prosecutors over more experienced but less competent attorneys from elsewhere.[225] In fact, the US arguably sent its best and brightest minds in the international justice realm to the ICTR. Three Americans who worked on the ICTR's prosecution team – Pierre-Richard Prosper, Stephen Rapp, and Beth Van Schaack – later

[218] Ford 2011, 960.   [219] Ford 2011, 974.   [220] Goldstone 2000, 114.
[221] Scheffer 2012a, 29.
[222] Scheffer 2012a, 114; Stover, Peskin, and Koenig 2016, 201.
[223] Peskin 2008, 195.   [224] Shattuck 2003, 71.   [225] Cruvellier 2006, 25.

became the US Ambassador-at-Large for Global Criminal Justice,[226] the top position in the US government devoted to international justice issues. American influence on accountability efforts in Rwanda was significant enough that the UN High Commission for Human Rights complained that "the operation was being run by Americans."[227]

The US also aided the tribunal by providing high-quality evidence that proved essential in ICTR prosecutions. Like in Yugoslavia, the sort of information that the US shared with the tribunal in Rwanda often took advantage of America's comparative advantage in sophisticated technology. Though the full scope of the genocide was not yet clear, the US had unambiguous evidence starting in the genocide's earliest days that Hutu extremists were initiating large-scale massacres thanks to the Pentagon's Defense Intelligence Agency (DIA). Within twenty-four hours of Habyarimana's plane being shot down, the DIA began acquiring satellite photos and communication intercepts from Kigali and its environs. While the DIA initially acquired this information to prepare for the evacuation of US embassy staff from Rwanda, it quickly realized that Rwandan officials were in the process of ordering mass killings of Tutsis. In response, DIA officials requested that American satellites take additional photos of Kigali and other suspected massacre sites throughout the country.[228] After the ICTR opened its doors, the US shared satellite imagery to aid the prosecution of some of the tribunal's most prominent defendants.[229] Moreover, the

---

[226] This position was originally called "Ambassador-at-Large for War Crimes Issues" when the Clinton administration created it, but the name changed to "Ambassador-at-Large for Global Criminal Justice" during the Obama administration.

[227] Scheffer 2012a, 71.

[228] Kuperman 2001, 32–37. However, the DIA's information did not quickly make its way to Clinton's desk because other intelligence agencies were more sanguine about events in Rwanda during the first few weeks of the genocide.

[229] As with other tribunals, such as MacArthur's decision to pardon Hirohito at Tokyo, the American commitment to full and impartial justice at the ICTR sometimes conflicted with its geopolitical goals. In the post-genocide environment, the US and other Western governments gave generous political and economic support to the new Tutsi-led government. The US had little interest in seeing Kagame and the RPF, who were already being cultivated as a key regional ally, prosecuted in Arusha. At the same time that the US provided evidence of Hutu crimes during the genocide, it generally withheld evidence from the ICTR concerning possible atrocity crimes connected to the RPF in the post-genocide period. See Peskin 2008, 210–212; Carnegie and Carson 2020, 232–234.

The Post–Cold War Period 75

CIA provided communications intercepts to the ICTR showing the extent to which the Hutu-controlled radio station Radio Television Libre des Mille Collines (RTLM) broadcast virulent messages branding Tutsis as enemies and encouraging Hutus to participate in the killings.[230] This evidence helped with the ICTR's *Media* case, which established an important precedent by prosecuting individual members of the media for broadcasts meant to incite genocide.

Lastly, the US helped with the apprehension and transfer of genocide suspects to the ICTR. To be clear, American assistance with the arrests of ICTR fugitives played out in a different fashion than it did for prior tribunals because the context was distinct. Unlike Germany, Japan, and Bosnia (in the post-Dayton Accords period), there was not a massive American military presence in Rwanda to make arrests. To the contrary, the US pulled its personnel out of the country during the genocide. Moreover, the manner in which the genocide ended created a special challenge for apprehending genocide suspects. In the chaos surrounding the RPF's takeover of Rwanda, the genocidaires intermingled with millions of Hutu refugees who fled into neighboring Zaire. Over the coming months, those with financial resources or political connections – often the Hutu elites most responsible for instigating the genocide – quietly left the squalor of Zaire's refugee camps with the aid of fake passports and disguises.[231] Many headed to Kenya, where President Daniel arap Moi, a longtime ally of Habyarimana's Hutu-dominated government, offered them a warm welcome and promised protection from the tribunal. Others sought safety in Europe, especially Belgium and France, where they could hide among large Hutu exile communities. By the time the ICTR was ready to issue arrest warrants, the "former regime's elites who had been ousted ... were now scattered to the four corners of Africa and Europe."[232]

Despite this challenge, the US still found ways to help the ICTR get its suspects in the dock. This primarily involved sharing information with the ICTR's "tracking team," an investigative unit established within the tribunal to locate fugitives hiding around the world. David

---

[230] Carnegie and Carson 2020, 233. On the role of "hate radio" in Rwanda's genocide, see Straus 2007.
[231] On the flight of Rwanda's former Hutu elites to other parts of Africa and Europe, see Stover, Peskin, and Koenig 2016, 201–202.
[232] Cruvellier 2006, 33.

Scheffer, the US Ambassador-at-Large for War Crimes Issues, met frequently with the American intelligence community and nongovernmental experts on Rwanda to discuss locating and apprehending genocide suspects who had gone off the grid. Armed with new information on their possible whereabouts, Scheffer "traveled to Kigali and Arusha often ... to arrange U.S. assistance for tracking down the large number of indicted fugitives."[233] While the ICTR tracking team had no authority to make arrests, it could coordinate with police forces in the countries where suspects were located to ensure that the right individual was apprehended and transferred to the tribunal. The information the US supplied – ranging from classified signals intelligence such as satellite imagery and communications intercepts to human intelligence – played a decisive role in arrests made around the world. Indeed, after briefings with US officials, the tracking team and its national police force partners were able to "sweep up indictees in Kenya and West Africa by the dozens, including some of the significant accused."[234] Beyond sharing information with the ICTR on the whereabouts of fugitives, the US took additional steps to ensure that suspects actually ended up facing prosecution at the tribunal. Among other things, the US pressured countries sympathetic to Hutu interests, such as Kenya and Zaire, to cooperate with the tribunal and make arrests,[235] offered rewards of up to $5 million for information leading to the arrests of ICTR fugitives,[236] and extradited one fugitive who managed to slip into the US back to the tribunal.[237]

The ICTR, like the ICTY, came to a remarkable conclusion after an admittedly slow start. The ICTR indicted ninety-five individuals for crimes committed during the genocide and has no remaining fugitives today.[238] Having completed its mandate to bring the leading perpetrators of the Rwandan genocide to justice, the ICTR was formally shuttered in 2015, though a residual mechanism was created to oversee

---

[233] Scheffer 2012a, 112.
[234] Anonymous official quoted in Carnegie and Carson 2020, 234–235.
[235] Stover, Peskin, and Koenig 2016, 209–218.   [236] Cruvellier 2006, 54.
[237] Scheffer 2012a, 119–123. On the politics of extradition in American foreign policy, see Krcmaric 2022.
[238] The ICTR crossed the last two remaining fugitives off its list in 2024, when the court's residual mechanism announced it had accumulated enough evidence to conclude that its final two fugitives were dead and buried in unmarked graves. Julian Borger, "Rwanda Genocide War Crimes Tribunal Wraps Up Mission after 29 Years," *The Guardian*, May 15, 2024.

its few remaining cases. This level of success would not have been possible without American support. As Richard Goldstone put it long after his retirement from the two ad hoc tribunals,

> From my experience as the first chief prosecutor of both, I can assure you that neither of them would have been set up and neither of them would have got off the ground without the support from the United States. ...Personnel, financial assistance, computer technicians, you name it – the United States provided crucial assistance.... One cannot overemphasize the importance of the role played by the United States.[239]

After the ICC

This chapter set out to show that American antagonism toward the ICC is anomalous. Thus far, it has demonstrated that the US was the leading proponent of each of the international criminal tribunals – Nuremberg, Tokyo, Yugoslavia, and Rwanda – that preceded the ICC. But since these examples all predate the ICC, it is conceivable that American antagonism toward the ICC may simply reflect an over-time shift in US preferences for pursuing international justice rather than something about the ICC itself.

It is feasible to explore this possibility empirically because the international community has continued to build new tribunals even after the ICC was created at the Rome Conference in 1998.[240] Though the ICC's global reach and permanent nature make it "the pinnacle" of the tribunal-building process,[241] there has also been a complementary movement to create other tribunals tailored to the specifics of certain humanitarian crises.[242] Many of these tribunals are considered "hybrid" or "quasi-international" since they mix elements of international and domestic law in addition to having international and domestic prosecutors, judges, and administrators. Prominent examples

---

[239] Goldstone 2007, 765.
[240] The international justice landscape therefore is an example of "international regime complexity" featuring several partially overlapping institutions. See Alter and Meunier 2009.
[241] Kersten 2016, 2.
[242] Advocates of hybrid tribunals point out that they help mitigate some of the alleged shortcomings of international tribunals, such as imposing justice that fails to account for local context and holding trials far away from victimized communities.

include the Special Panels for Serious Crimes in East Timor (created in 2000), the Special Court for Sierra Leone (2002), the Extraordinary Chambers in the Courts of Cambodia (2003), the Special Tribunal for Lebanon (2009), the Extraordinary African Chambers (2013), the Special Criminal Court in the Central African Republic (2015), and the Kosovo Specialist Chambers (2016).

The US has not opposed the creation of any of these tribunals. To the contrary, the US has gone to extraordinary lengths to support their operations, providing personnel, funding, and evidence, among other sources of support.[243] Moreover, American lawyers and judges have assumed key leadership positions at many of the tribunals.[244] One simple way to quantify the extent American support for international tribunals in the modern era is to examine the amount of money spent relative to other countries because "money talks" in international politics. According to this metric, the extent of American support is deep: the US spent more than $1 billion across all tribunals combined during the 1993–2015 period, making it the world's largest financial contributor to international criminal tribunals.[245]

For a closer look at the dynamics of American support for international justice in the post–ICC period, it is worth zeroing in on the Special Court for Sierra Leone (SCSL). The SCSL is a good case to examine because it helps highlight the uniqueness of American opposition to the ICC. At the exact same time that the US orchestrated a virulent campaign to destroy the ICC in the early 2000s, the US also

---

[243] In addition to these traditional channels of support, American assistance has taken a variety of other guises. To give just one example, Congress passed the Cambodian Genocide Justice Act in 1994 to encourage the creation of an international tribunal to prosecute atrocities committed during the oppressive reign of Pol Pot and his Khmer Rouge supporters. This act also provided funding for a center based at Yale University, the Cambodia Genocide Program, that produced a systematic catalogue of atrocity crimes during the Khmer Rouge era. When the Extraordinary Chambers in the Courts of Cambodia (ECCC) were established nearly a decade later, a trove of evidence was waiting for prosecutors.

[244] For an accounting of the many Americans who assumed leadership positions at international tribunals, see Buchwald and Van Schaack 2021, 96.

[245] Ford 2011, 956. The depth of American financial support for tribunals other than the ICC is even more impressive when one considers that this statistic includes the considerable amount of funding that other states provided to the ICC (to which the US gave nothing).

championed the cause of the SCSL. Moreover, many American politicians and policymakers known for their hostility to the ICC – for example, officials in the George W. Bush administration – were unabashed supporters of the SCSL. Thus, the case of the SCSL unambiguously shows that American antagonism toward the ICC is not simply due to an over-time shift in US international justice policies. In the post–ICC period, Democrats and Republicans alike tend to support international justice initiatives – as long as they are not connected to the ICC.

The SCSL was founded in response to crimes committed during a civil war in the 1990s that pitted the embattled Sierra Leonean government against a rebel group called the Revolutionary United Front (RUF). The RUF gained global notoriety for the brutal tactics that its undisciplined fighters used against not only government forces but also Sierra Leone's civilian population. For instance, when the RUF attacked and then occupied the capital city of Freetown, it committed nearly every type of human rights violation imaginable. As one journalist described the carnage, "Civilians were gunned down in the streets, thrown from the upper floors of buildings, used as human shields, and burnt alive in cars and houses. They had their limbs hacked off with machetes, eyes gouged out with knives, hands smashed with hammers, and bodies burned in boiling water."[246] The movement for a tribunal in Sierra Leone rapidly gained momentum in 2000 when the government managed to capture the RUF's leader, Foday Sankoh. Fearing that their war-ravaged country lacked adequate security for Sankoh's imprisonment and legal capacity for his prosecution, officials from Sierra Leone contacted the UN about partnering to create a court that would prosecute RUF atrocities. The inquiry eventually led to the establishment of the SCSL in 2002. Its mandate was to prosecute the specific individuals most responsible for war crimes and other serious violations of international humanitarian law committed on Sierra Leone's territory after November 30, 1996.

Other than Sierra Leone itself, no country did more to facilitate the creation of the SCSL than the US. Following Sierra Leone's request for UN assistance in creating a tribunal, the path to establishing the SCSL was far from straightforward. Sierra Leonean President Ahmed Tejan Kabbah initially communicated that he preferred using a UN Security

---

[246] Gberie 2005, 130.

Council resolution to create a hybrid court. This plan, however, quickly ran into a problem: After helping to foot the bill for the Yugoslav and Rwandan tribunals, most members of the Security Council had little interest in paying for a tribunal in Sierra Leone. The result was gridlock: A purely national prosecution was not feasible given Sierra Leone's postwar challenges, but the typical pathway to international involvement was blocked. The US Ambassador-at-Large for War Crimes Issues, David Scheffer, found a way out of this impasse that ironically relied on the recently concluded ICC negotiations. As Scheffer recounts in his memoirs, "I was lost in thought walking along Second Avenue when the idea struck me: If the International Criminal Court was to be created by *treaty* among governments, why not also establish the Special Court for Sierra Leone as an international criminal court with a treaty between the United Nations and the government of Sierra Leone?"[247] This unusual proposal offered a legal mechanism for the UN to create a new hybrid tribunal without committing reluctant members of the Security Council to become involved with it. After many revisions involving officials from the US, the UN, and Sierra Leone, Scheffer's idea became the formal basis of the SCSL's creation.

Once the SCSL was established, the US ensured that its operations got off the ground quickly. The initial challenge facing the court was money. Since the SCSL was created by a treaty rather than a Security Council resolution, it could not count on any funding from the UN, putting it in an even more precarious financial position than the tribunals for Yugoslavia and Rwanda. The SCSL instead had to rely on voluntary contributions from sympathetic governments. The US helped this fill void by becoming the SCSL's largest funder at a time when many other governments were unwilling to contribute. In fact, only three countries – the US, the UK, and the Netherlands – provided nearly all of the SCSL's budget during its first several years.[248] The US also took a keen interest in staffing the SCSL. Given the court's hybrid nature, Sierra Leone not surprisingly had the most personnel working at the SCSL. But the US was close behind, and Americans were overrepresented among the tribunal's senior roles.[249] The Bush administration also "backed aggressively" the candidacy of David Crane, a

---

[247] Scheffer 2012a, 329.   [248] Stover, Peskin, and Koenig 2016, 267.
[249] Perriello and Wierda 2006, 21.

Department of Defense lawyer, for the tribunal's top job: prosecutor.[250] Despite some misgivings at the UN about Americans potentially exerting too much influence at the SCSL, UN Secretary General Kofi Annan appointed Crane to the post. Over the tribunal's lifetime, three of the four prosecutors were Americans.[251]

The SCSL's biggest target, oddly enough, was not a Sierra Leonean. That distinction went to Charles Taylor, the warlord turned president of neighboring Liberia. Taylor was elected in 1997 after nearly a decade of brutal civil war in Liberia. All sides in the conflict exhibited virtually no regard for civilians caught in the path of war, but the behavior of Taylor's forces, the National Patriotic Front of Liberia (NPFL), was particularly heinous as they killed, raped, and pillaged their way across the country.[252] These crimes, however, fell outside the SCSL's jurisdiction because they occurred on Liberian territory. The SCSL targeted Taylor for his connection to the RUF and its nominal leader, Foday Sankoh. In the eyes of many, including SCSL prosecutors, the RUF was "functionally a faction of [Taylor's] NPFL"[253] and was employed as "Charles Taylor's foreign legion."[254] As Abdul Tejan-Cole explains, "Charles Taylor acted as mentor, patron, banker, and weapons supplier for this motley collection of Sierra Leonean dissidents, bandits, and mercenaries."[255] The relationship between Taylor and Sankoh was largely one of mutual benefit: Sankoh funneled valuable "blood diamonds" to Taylor in exchange for the weapons Taylor supplied to the RUF.[256] Though Taylor grew extraordinarily wealthy, his regime was on the verge of collapse by 2003. Liberians openly revolted against his rule, neighboring Guinea and the Ivory Coast sponsored anti-Taylor rebel groups, the UN Security Council imposed economic sanctions for his role in the blood diamond trade, and the SCSL issued a warrant for his arrest. In August 2003, Taylor fled Liberia for exile in Nigeria, where President Olusegun Obasanjo

---

[250] Perriello and Wierda 2006.
[251] The other two American prosecutors at the SCSL were Stephen Rapp and Brenda Hollis.
[252] For a description of atrocities committed by Taylor's forces, see Waugh 2011, 132–137.
[253] Tejan-Cole 2009, 209.   [254] International Crisis Group 2002, i.
[255] Tejan-Cole 2009, 208.
[256] The arms-for-diamonds trade between Taylor and Sankoh was worth between $25 million and $125 million annually. See Tejan-Cole 2009, 209.

offered safe haven and promised that he would not hand over Taylor to the SCSL.[257]

The prospects for justice appeared bleak at this point. Taylor himself was convinced he would never see a jail cell at the SCSL and put a great deal of faith in Obasanjo's promise of protection, asserting that "my brother will never betray me."[258] But that is exactly what happened three years later. Shortly after Taylor's ouster, the SCSL and several NGOs such as Amnesty International, Human Rights Watch, the Soros Foundation, and No Peace without Justice began working to shame Nigeria for providing an indicted war criminal with a luxurious exile.[259] The US soon threw its weight behind the movement to put pressure on the Nigerian leadership for sheltering Taylor from the SCSL.[260] Democrats and Republicans joined forces to issue a Congressional resolution calling on Nigeria to transfer Taylor to the SCSL. Congress also made headlines when it authorized a $2 million bounty for Taylor's capture, which President Bush quickly signed into law.[261] In the face of mounting international pressure, much of it from the US, Obasanjo made a concession in 2005 when he agreed that Nigeria would send Taylor back to Liberia *if* the newly elected Liberian government requested his extradition.

This put Taylor's fate in the hands of Ellen Johnson Sirleaf, Liberia's new president. Sirleaf initially made it clear that putting Taylor on trial was not a priority for her administration – in fact, she saw bringing Taylor to justice as little more than a distraction from her larger goals of rebuilding Liberia's economy and consolidating its fragile peace.[262] The US, now firmly committed to the idea that Taylor deserved to face justice at the SCSL, sought to change her mind. Secretary of State Condoleezza Rice quietly communicated to Sirleaf that the US government thought it was time for Taylor to stand trial.[263] When that did not get the desired response from Sirleaf, the US threatened to withhold

---

[257] "Nigeria Would Shield Taylor from Trial," *CNN News*, July 10, 2003.
[258] Waugh 2011, 284.   [259] Alter 2014, 271.
[260] This was a remarkable policy reversal given that the US originally supported the plan to ease Taylor into exile as a mechanism to resolve the ongoing conflict in Liberia. On the political logic underpinning this sort of reversal for exiled leaders, see Krcmaric 2020.
[261] "In $87.5 Billion Bill, $2 Million Bounty for Exiled Liberian," *New York Times*, November 10, 2003.
[262] "Taylor 'Not Priority' for Liberia," *BBC News*, January 27, 2006.
[263] Tejan-Cole 2009, 217.

economic aid to Liberia if she did not request Taylor's extradition.[264] In an interview, Sirleaf noted, "We also are facing ... pressure – I must use that word – from the UN, from the US, from the European Union, who are all our major partners in development, on the need to do something about the Charles Taylor issue."[265] This pressure proved decisive: Sirleaf formally requested that Nigeria extradite Taylor on March 17, 2006.

Not long after, Taylor disappeared from his villa in Nigeria. Some believe Taylor went on the run, whereas others think Nigeria tried to help Taylor escape into Cameroon to avoid the embarrassment of backtracking on its promise of safe haven.[266] Either way, the timing for Obasanjo was terrible: he was scheduled to visit the White House only a few days later. The Bush administration wasted no time before threatening unspecified "consequences" for Nigeria if Taylor was not arrested and transferred to the court.[267] White House officials also let Obasanjo know that his meeting with Bush would be cancelled if Taylor was not immediately apprehended.[268] At this point, Nigeria caved to American pressure to bring Taylor to justice. Speaking at the White House the next day, Obasanjo announced to the world that his government had apprehended Taylor and put him on a plane to Liberia. Once in Liberia, Taylor was transferred to a UN helicopter and then taken to the SCSL. In 2012, the SCSL found Taylor guilty and sentenced him to 50 years in prison, guaranteeing he will spend the rest of his life behind bars.

In addition to its support for tribunals in the post–ICC period, it is also worth noting two other ways in which the US has elevated the role of international justice issues in American foreign policy. First, the US was the world's first country – and, at the time of writing, remains the only country – with an ambassador-level position dedicated to international justice issues. Established by the Clinton administration and continued by each successive president, the ambassador-at-large position ensures that there is a high-ranking official supported by the

---

[264] Lydia Polgreen, "Nigeria Says Ex-President of Liberia Has Disappeared," *New York Times*, March 29, 2006.
[265] Johnson-Sirleaf 2006.
[266] "Nigeria Faces Anger over Taylor," *BBC News*, March 29, 2006.
[267] Felix Onuah, "Wanted Liberian Warlord Disappears in Nigeria," *Reuters*, March 28, 2006.
[268] Tejan-Cole 2009, 218.

Office of Global Criminal Justice within the State Department to advocate specifically for international justice issues in US foreign policy as well as liaise with international tribunals. Second, the US created the War Crimes Rewards Program, which offers up to $5 million to people who provide information that aids with the arrest, transfer, or conviction of perpetrators of genocide, crimes against humanity, and war crimes.[269] The program started with the ICTY, then expanded to the ICTR and the SCSL, and now includes any international or hybrid tribunal. The rewards program, in the words of Ambassador Stephen Rapp, has proven "very successful in generating information that has led to the arrest of some of the world's worst criminals."[270]

Conclusion

The purpose of this chapter was to examine America's historical relationship with international justice institutions other than the ICC. This is a crucial starting point for an analysis of American hostility toward the ICC because it allows me to address the simplest alternative explanation: the US might oppose international justice in general. But this chapter proved that is not the case. The US has been an unabashed supporter of international tribunals both before and after the establishment of the ICC. As William Schabas rightly summarizes, "Since international criminal justice first became truly operational, in 1945, it has had no greater friend or promoter than the United States."[271]

If the US opposes the ICC against this backdrop of support for virtually every other international justice initiative, it raises a natural follow-up question. What exactly is it about the ICC that makes nearly every corner of official Washington – Republicans and Democrats, the White House and Congress, the State Department and the Pentagon – so concerned? Chapter 3 provides an answer.

---

[269] Some may doubt whether these rewards really induce cooperation with international tribunals, but consider the following example: One ICTY informant provided information that helped the tribunal locate the whereabouts of one of the Srebrenica killers. An ICTY employee who walked the informant to the US embassy to claim a $250,000 reward recalled, "He was shaking. It was 81 years' salary for him." See Borger 2016, 175.
[270] Rapp 2012.   [271] Schabas 2004, 702.

3 US Opposition to the ICC Origins

In the summer of 1998, diplomats from around the world gathered in Rome. Their mission was to create something that had long been discussed as an intriguing but unlikely possibly: a permanent International Criminal Court.[1] Rome was a fitting location for this bold experiment in international law. As participants in the Rome Conference vividly described it,

What delegate, gazing out over Il Palatino and the ruins of the Forum, or seeing Castel Sant'Angelo, where Pope Clement was besieged for months while soldiers looted the city and tormented and killed its inhabitants, could not feel the weight of history upon him or her, or understand the historic purpose for which all were gathered? Indeed, what better place in which to argue, on behalf of humanity, that the excesses of war should be restrained by the Rule of Law?[2]

The Rome Conference was held in the United Nations Food and Agricultural Organization building, a structure whose beautiful views compensated for its lack of air conditioning during a Roman heatwave. In addition to the national delegations, hundreds of nongovernmental organizations (NGOs) descended on Rome to observe and, in some cases, participate in the conference.[3] These NGOs, who coalesced under the umbrella of the Coalition for the International Criminal Court, were prepared to criticize and cajole diplomats whenever their commitments to international justice appeared to waver. At one memorable point during the conference, Amnesty International organized a mass demonstration – activists lay down like corpses in the streets surrounding the Colosseum snarling Rome's formidable traffic – to remind the diplomats of what was at stake in the ICC negotiations.

---

[1] As early as 1946, the United Nations created a panel to investigate how the Nuremberg principles might be codified into a permanent court.
[2] Sadat and Carden 2000, 385.
[3] On the role of NGOs at the Rome Conference, see Schiff 2008; Roth 2025.

After five grueling weeks of haggling over the details of the proposed tribunal, the overwhelming majority of the national delegations voted in favor of the Rome Statute, the treaty that formally established the ICC. Many participants at the Rome Conference saw the ICC's creation as a turning point in history, the moment when concerns about justice and accountability finally trumped crude calculations of power and political expediency. After the vote passed, normally staid diplomats went wild and "abandoned themselves to cheers and chants, tears and embraces, and rhythmic stomping and applause."[4]

The US, however, did not join the celebrations. As I detail in this chapter, the US was one of the few countries to vote against establishing the ICC. But this outcome was not a foregone conclusion. The American delegation arrived in Rome hoping to support the ICC but was dismayed when it lost control of the negotiations. The Court's structure evolved in a way that, from the US perspective, unfairly put American troops around the world at risk of facing politically biased investigations and prosecutions. The US may have wanted *an* International Criminal Court, but it did not want *the* International Criminal Court that emerged from the Rome Conference.

The rest of this chapter proceeds in two main sections. First, I provide relevant background information about how the ICC works. Second, I explain why many in official Washington were – and still remain – convinced that a new foreign policy threat was born in Rome.

How the ICC Works

This is a book about America's relationship with the ICC, not the intricacies of the ICC's jurisprudence. But before it is possible to understand American opposition to the ICC, it is first necessary to know something about how the Court actually works. The section therefore describes the ICC's organization as well as the key legal concepts and provisions found in the Rome Statute across four distinct areas: jurisdiction, investigations, arrests, and trials.

Organization

All state parties to the ICC – that is, the states that sign and ratify the Rome Statute – get a seat in the Assembly of State Parties (ASP). The

---

[4] Bosco 2014a, 50–51.

ASP meets at least once per year and helps guide the overall direction of the Court. It does this primarily by electing the ICC's prosecutor and judges. Every member of the ASP, regardless of the country's wealth or power, gets a single vote when electing the ICC's personnel. The ASP also sets the ICC's budget, which primarily comes from state party contributions. The ICC has an annual budget of nearly 200 million Euro and a staff of 900 individuals – ranging from judges to war crimes investigators to bureaucratic staff – hailing from approximately 100 different countries.

Despite its general oversight role, the ASP has little to do with the Court's day-to-day operations. That role falls to the ICC's staff, who are divided into four organs.[5] The most consequential of these is the Office of the Prosecutor (OTP). As David Bosco summarizes, the ICC's "most important discretionary authority – whether to open investigations and seek arrest warrants – centers on the prosecutor rather than judges."[6] The ICC's chief prosecutor (often just "prosecutor") heads the OTP and is elected in the ASP with a majority vote. In line with the wishes of the delegates at the Rome Conference, the prosecutor is isolated as much as possible from political interference and intrigue. In particular, the prosecutor serves a single nonrenewable nine-year term to avoid having reelection motives potentially cloud his or her judgment. The prosecutor's job is to decide which investigations to open, request arrest warrants for specific individuals, and finally prosecute those individuals if and when they are put on trial at The Hague.

As the most prominent member of the ICC, the prosecutor's background and experiences are frequent topics of public discussion. Thus far, the Court has had three prosecutors. The first, Luis Moreno-Ocampo, was an Argentine initially known for his role in prosecuting former members of Argentina's military junta responsible for the "Dirty War" of the late 1970s and early 1980s. Moreno-Ocampo's impressive legal battle against the junta caught the eye of the US State Department, who put forward his name as a candidate to lead the Yugoslav tribunal in 1993, but he ultimately was not selected. Moreno-Ocampo instead entered private practice in Argentina and later took a teaching post a Harvard Law School, which he held before

---

[5] For an analysis of "management culture" among the ICC's staff, see Clements 2024.
[6] Bosco 2014a, 18.

joining the ICC. The second prosecutor, Fatou Bensouda, was a Gambian who previously served as her country's justice minister and attorney general before becoming Moreno-Ocampo's deputy at the ICC. For some, Bensouda's government service during the regime of Gambian dictator Yahya Jammeh was a source of controversy.[7] But many others, including the African Union, applauded the decision to appoint an African to the ICC's top post given the Court's frequent focus on Africa.[8] The third (and current) prosecutor, Karim Khan, is a British lawyer who previously worked as a prosecutor at the Yugoslav and Rwandan tribunals, a defense counsel at the ICC, and the leader of a UN probe investigating the Islamic State's war crimes in Iraq.

Beyond the prosecutor, the ICC has eighteen judges.[9] Like the prosecutor, the judges are elected by the ASP and serve nonrenewable nine-year terms. According to ICC rules, no two judges can be nationals of the same state. Moreover, the ASP is supposed to select a diverse slate of judges that represents the world's major legal traditions, ensures an equitable distribution of men and women, and establishes a fair representation of geographic regions.[10] The judges are split into three different chambers. The pretrial chamber supervises the prosecutor's investigations and, when deemed appropriate, grants the arrest warrants that the prosecutor requests. The trial chamber presides over trials of the accused, makes determinations of innocence or guilt, and imposes sentences for convicted criminals. The appeals chamber gets involved if either party – prosecution or defense – decides to appeal a previous decision made by one of the other chambers, including judgments and sentencing decisions.

---

[7] Cruvellier and Darboe 2019.

[8] According to one profile of Bensouda, "Supporters of the court now hope that the presence of an African prosecutor could tone down some of the fierce criticism it has received from Africa, where many have labeled it a neocolonial tool in the hands of the West." See Marlise Simons, "Gambian Will Lead Prosecution in Hague," *New York Times*, December 12, 2011.

[9] These eighteen judges form a second organ of the ICC, the Chambers. The judges also elect three individuals from among their own ranks to form a third organ, the Presidency. The fourth and final organ of the ICC is the Registry, which provides administrative support.

[10] Some have questioned the ICC's criteria for selecting judges. According to Courtney Hillebrecht, "This procedure has achieved the stated goals of gender equality and regional diversity on the bench, but it has failed to ensure that the judges nominated to the bench were actually qualified to run an international criminal tribunal." See Hillebrecht 2021, 125.

Jurisdiction

Though the "international" in its name may suggest worldwide jurisdiction, the ICC's jurisdiction has limits. It cannot investigate or prosecute anyone, anywhere, anytime. To start, there is a sharp temporal cutoff to ICC jurisdiction: the Court cannot under any circumstances investigate or prosecute crimes committed before 2002. This temporal restriction is the result of language in the Rome Statute stipulating that ICC jurisdiction would begin once sixty states ratified the treaty, which happened to occur on July 1, 2002.

Beyond that, ICC jurisdiction is largely the product of whether or not a country joined the ICC as a state party. The Court automatically has jurisdiction over crimes committed on the territory of an ICC state party.[11] This territorial jurisdiction even applies to the nationals of countries that never signed up for the ICC as long as they are on a state party's territory. As discussed later, this has long been a sticking point in the US–ICC relationship. The ICC also has automatic jurisdiction if the accused is a national of a state party. This nationality jurisdiction applies even if the individual is on the territory of a non-state party. Hence, if an individual's government signed up for the ICC, that person is subject to the ICC's jurisdiction regardless of where they are geographically. In addition to the Court's automatic jurisdiction, the UN Security Council can refer situations to the ICC. This gives the ICC potentially global reach – but only if the five permanent members of the Security Council all agree to involve the ICC.

Given that a country's status as a state party plays a crucial role in establishing ICC jurisdiction, it is worth considering the Court's members in more detail.[12] At present, there are 125 ICC state parties, countries that both signed and ratified the Rome Statute (shaded dark

---

[11] ICC also has jurisdiction over crimes committed on the territory of states that have otherwise accepted the Court's jurisdiction. This typically happens through an Article 12(3) declaration, a special agreement that allows non-state parties to grant the ICC jurisdiction over crimes committed on their territory in an ad hoc fashion.

[12] There is an ongoing debate on the politics of joining the ICC. Some argue that only states with little to fear from the ICC will join the Court. Others insist that ratification gives states with a history of atrocities and weak institutions – the very countries most likely to find themselves on the wrong end of an ICC investigation – a way to signal their commitment to avoiding future abuses. See Simmons and Danner 2010; Chapman and Chaudoin 2013.

Figure 3.1 ICC membership

grey in Figure 3.1).[13] ICC state parties span all world regions, though the Court's membership is concentrated most heavily in the Americas, Europe, and Africa. There are another twenty-nine countries that signed but never ratified the Rome Statute and therefore are not state parties (shaded light grey). This group includes some countries that may soon ratify and thereby join the ICC as well as other countries – such as the US and Russia – that have declared they have no intention to ratify. The rest of the world's countries (shaded white) have neither signed nor ratified the Rome Statute.[14]

Overall, 125 ICC members – about two-thirds of the states recognized by the UN – is an impressive number that exceeds what even the Court's most optimistic supporters initially thought possible.[15] But it is also worth emphasizing which countries have *not* joined the ICC. The

---

[13] These ICC membership statistics are accurate as of January 1, 2025.

[14] In this group, I include the two countries – Burundi and the Philippines – that formally withdrew from the Court after initially joining the ICC as state parties. Two other countries – Afghanistan and Hungary – recently indicated they have plans to withdraw from the Court, but they have not officially done so yet. For an analysis of the politics of withdrawing from the ICC, see Hillebrecht 2021.

[15] At the conclusion of the Rome Conference, many diplomats thought it would take decades to get sixty states to sign and ratify the Rome Statute, thereby bringing the ICC into existence. According to the ICC's first president, Philippe Kirsch, "When we finished the conference in Rome, the pessimists were saying twenty years and the optimists were saying ten years." See James Bone, "War Crimes Court Pits United States against the World," *The Times*, April 11, 2002. Instead, the ICC got the required sixty ratifications in less than four years and passed one hundred state parties shortly thereafter.

world's current superpower, the US, its emerging superpower, China, and its fading superpower, Russia, all remain outside the ICC. Moreover, a host of regional powers such as India, Pakistan, Turkey, Egypt, Israel, Saudi Arabia, and Indonesia declined to join the Court. As a result, the majority of the world's population and most of the world's armed forces are not in ICC member states.[16]

The ICC has jurisdiction over only a small set of crimes that the Rome Statute calls "the most serious crimes of international concern," which are genocide, war crimes, and crimes against humanity. These three crimes, collectively known as atrocity crimes, are often difficult to identify in the real world. Many criminal acts – for example, razing a village and killing its inhabitants – might conceivably be a war crime, a crime against humanity, or a genocide. The characterization of a crime often hinges on the context in which it took place and the intent of the perpetrator.

I discuss the legal definitions of these atrocity crimes – and some of the controversies surrounding their application to real-world cases – at length in Chapter 5. But it is worth briefly describing them here. Genocide is an attempt to destroy a national, ethnic, racial, or religious group. The ICC has only leveled a charge of genocide against one individual: Sudanese leader Omar Bashir for his role in trying to destroy ethnic minority groups in the Darfur region of Sudan. Historically, the archetypical case of genocide is Nazi Germany's attempt to exterminate European Jews before and during World War II. War crimes refer to serious and large-scale violations of the laws of war, such as the Geneva Conventions. The ICC has issued many arrest warrants for war crimes, including one for the infamous Ugandan rebel leader Joseph Kony, whose fighters are believed to have killed over 100,000 people and abducted thousands of child soldiers. Crimes against humanity refer to widespread and systematic attacks against any civilian population. Given its broad definition, ICC has also issued several arrest warrants for crimes against humanity. For instance, the ICC indicted Libyan leader Muammar Gaddafi for crimes against humanity after he ordered his security forces to kill civilians protesting against the regime in the early stages of the 2011 Libyan revolution.

Under a very limited set of circumstances, the ICC also has jurisdiction over a fourth crime: aggression. While the crime of aggression – in

---

[16] Bosco 2014a, 5–7.

effect, starting an unprovoked war – was set aside at the Rome Conference in 1998 to focus on atrocity crimes, governments amended the ICC's founding treaty at a 2010 review conference. While meeting in Kampala, Uganda, the delegates defined aggression and specified when the ICC would have jurisdiction over it.[17] The ICC's jurisdiction over the crime of aggression is far narrower than its jurisdiction over the three atrocity crimes: The ICC cannot investigate or prosecute the nationals of non-state parties for aggression. This means that Americans, regardless of where they are geographically, will not be charged with the crime of aggression.[18] Moreover, ICC jurisdiction over state parties for aggression is limited to those who ratified the Kampala amendments (i.e., even ICC members can "opt out" for the crime of aggression).[19] Since the ICC's jurisdiction over aggression is so circumscribed – to date, the ICC has never charged anyone with the crime of aggression – my book focuses primarily on the three atrocity crimes.

The crimes committed as part of Russia's war against Ukraine offer a useful summary of how the ICC's jurisdiction works. ICC prosecutor Karim Khan announced the Court was opening an investigation into the situation in Ukraine on March 2, 2022, just days after the Russian invasion began. In some ways, this was an easy decision for Khan, as stories of Russian atrocities – such as indiscriminate attacks in densely populated urban areas – grabbed the world's attention. Indeed, there is mounting evidence that Russia's political and military leaders are responsible for aggression, war crimes, crimes against humanity, and genocide.[20] But the ICC can only investigate some of the alleged Russian crimes. The Court has jurisdiction over war crimes, crimes against humanity, and genocide committed by Russian forces on the territory of Ukraine because Ukraine accepted the ICC's

---

[17] On the process of criminalizing aggression in international law, see Dannenbaum 2018; Weisbord 2019.

[18] For the US perspective on the crime of aggression, see Koh and Buchwald 2015.

[19] The ICC's temporal jurisdiction over aggression is also limited to the period after July 17, 2018.

[20] The evidence for aggression, war crimes, and crimes against humanity is overwhelming. But it is debatable whether Russia has committed genocide in Ukraine. See, for example, Philippe Sands, "What the Inventor of the World 'Genocide' Might Have Said about Putin's War," *New York Times*, April 28, 2022; and Eugene Finkel, "What's Happening in Ukraine is Genocide. Period." *Washington Post*, April 5, 2022.

jurisdiction.[21] Yet, even though there is little doubt that Russia initiated an illegal war of aggression against Ukraine, the ICC is unable to charge Russian president Vladimir Putin and his top advisors with the crime of aggression because Russia is not an ICC state party. Given that the ICC path to accountability for Russia's aggressive war is blocked on jurisdictional grounds, some have labeled it "a crime in search of a court" and explored the possibility of creating a new special tribunal to investigate Russia's decision to go to war that could work in tandem with the ICC investigation into atrocity crimes committed during the war.[22]

Investigations

The ICC prosecutor can choose to open an investigation into any situation where the Court has jurisdiction. The use of the term "situation" is intentional. While the ICC ultimately prosecutes specific individuals, it first opens investigations of overall situations, typically large-scale violence within one country's borders. Investigations begin by examining situations as a whole, meaning that the prosecutor should follow the evidence wherever it leads and avoid giving a free pass to individuals on any of the "sides." Hence, ICC investigations are named after the country where the situation is located. To date, the ICC has opened seventeen investigations: Uganda, Democratic Republic of the Congo, Sudan, Central African Republic, Kenya, Libya, Ivory Coast, Mali, Central African Republic II, Georgia, Burundi, Myanmar, Afghanistan, Palestine, the Philippines, Venezuela, and Ukraine.

There are three different ways to trigger an investigation. First, a state party may refer alleged atrocity crimes to the ICC. In a state party referral, the state might refer violence on its own territory or elsewhere to the ICC.[23] The majority of ICC investigations have arisen from state party referrals. Second, the UN Security Council can refer alleged

---

[21] Ukraine was not an ICC state party when the Court initially opened the investigation, but the ICC had jurisdiction over crimes committed on Ukraine's territory because Ukraine made an Article 12(3) declaration. Ukraine later joined the ICC as a state party.

[22] Hathaway 2022.

[23] At first glance, it is puzzling that governments sometimes refer violence on their own territory to the ICC since doing so exposes them to possible prosecution. But many governments have strategically self-referred to the ICC in the hopes of marginalizing their political opponents. See, for example, Ba 2020; Hashimoto 2020; Johns and Parente 2024.

crimes to the ICC. This is relatively rare since it requires unanimous consent among the permanent five members, but it happened in two cases: Sudan and Libya. For these first two triggers it is important to note that the ICC prosecutor is not obligated to open an investigation following a referral – that is, the prosecutor ultimately decides to initiate an investigation, not a state party or the UN Security Council. Third, the prosecutor can choose to open an investigation entirely on his or her own volition (the prosecutor's so-called *proprio motu* authority).[24] As discussed later in this chapter, the prosecutor's independent authority to launch investigations was one of the most controversial and hotly debated issues at the Rome Conference.

The ICC's rules give the prosecutor a tremendous amount of discretion when opening investigations, but two general principles are supposed to guide the prosecutor's selection of situations to investigate. The first is the gravity principle, which holds that of all the potential crimes the ICC might investigate, it should prioritize investigating the world's gravest abuses. The ICC should generally pass on investigating situations that fail to meet the gravity threshold.[25] The second is the complementarity principle, which asserts that the ICC is a "court of last resort." It is meant to complement, not replace, national courts. In practical terms, the complementarity principle means that the ICC should defer to national courts that make genuine efforts to investigate and prosecute atrocity crimes that occur within their jurisdictions. The ICC should only step in when necessary.[26]

In terms of technical steps, it is important to note that the ICC conducts preliminary examinations before opening investigations.[27] A preliminary examination effectively is an information gathering exercise: the ICC inquires whether there is plausible evidence and proper jurisdiction to open an investigation and makes initial assessments about gravity and complementarity.[28] To be clear, many

---

[24] When the prosecutor initiates a *proprio motu* investigation, the judges in the ICC's pretrial chamber must first approve the prosecutor's request to open the investigation.
[25] For a discussion of the gravity principle, see deGuzman 2020.
[26] For a discussion of the complementarity principle, see El Zeidy 2002; Nouwen 2014. On its political salience, see Zvobgo and Chaudoin 2025.
[27] On preliminary examinations, see Bosco 2017.
[28] During this phase, the prosecutor also makes an "interests of justice" determination. That is, the ICC might not proceed with an otherwise permitted investigation if the prosecutor determines that opening the investigation would

preliminary examinations never become investigations. For example, the ICC opened a preliminary examination into possible war crimes and crimes against humanity committed in Colombia as part of a decades-long conflict involving the Colombian government, guerrilla groups such as the Revolutionary Armed Forces of Colombia (FARC), and numerous paramilitary forces. However, the ICC decided to terminate the preliminary examination without opening an investigation because the Colombian government appeared willing and able to make genuine efforts to prosecute atrocity crimes in its national courts. Hence, an ICC investigation was not warranted under the principle of complementarity.

If the prosecutor decides there is a reasonable basis to proceed after conducting the preliminary examination, then he or she formally opens an investigation.[29] Once an investigation is opened, the ICC starts to collect evidence, interview witnesses, and take any other necessary steps to gather all information connected to the alleged crimes. The goal is to assess exactly which crimes were committed and who is most responsible so that the prosecutor is well-positioned to request arrest warrants.

Arrests

The ICC shifts its focus from general situations to specific individuals at the arrest warrant stage.[30] If an investigation yields credible evidence suggesting that a person is responsible for atrocity crimes, then the prosecutor requests that the judges in the pretrial chamber issue an arrest warrant.[31] The practice of making the prosecutor go through the judges to get arrest warrants is intended to serve as a check on the prosecutor pursuing questionable or frivolous cases. Indeed, the judges

---

not serve the interests of justice. There is no consensus on which factors determine whether a given investigation is in the interests of justice. However, two common interpretations are that the prosecutor can decide not to pursue investigations that (a) risk undermining a peace process and (b) have little chance of success.

[29] The UN Security Council – if the five permanent members all agree – has the right to delay ICC investigations for one year.

[30] On the challenges of identifying individual responsibility when most atrocity crimes are collective in nature, see Jain 2013.

[31] Instead of an arrest warrant, the ICC can issue a summons if the judges are confident that the accused will voluntarily appear before the Court.

can decline the prosecutor's request for an arrest warrant if the prosecutor fails to convince them that there are reasonable grounds to believe the individual is responsible for the alleged crimes. In practice, however, the judges usually grant the prosecutor's requests for arrest warrants.

The ICC's central weakness – enforcement – becomes clear after it issues arrest warrants. Simply put, the ICC has no way to arrest its own suspects. Unlike national courts, which are backed by each country's law enforcement agencies, the ICC does not have an independent police force. It must instead rely on sympathetic states to apprehend and transfer suspects to The Hague.

This creates several challenges for the ICC. To start, state officials – including political leaders themselves – are often implicated in atrocity crimes. But it is extraordinarily difficult for the ICC to hold political leaders accountable. Recalcitrant government officials targeted with arrest warrants are not going to hand themselves over to the ICC. Nor are many third-party states willing to intervene militarily against a sitting head of state. As a result, political leaders are almost untouchable as long as they hold onto power because they exert control over their state's military and police forces.[32] Even liberal states that care deeply about the protection of human rights are typically unwilling to risk the lives of their own soldiers in interventions designed to oust oppressive rulers and bring them to justice.[33] Consequently, abusive leaders – even those facing universal condemnation – can usually remain safe behind their own national borders.

The prospects for enforcement improve when suspects, either voluntarily or involuntarily, leave their own national borders and travel abroad. Even then, however, state cooperation with the ICC has been mixed.[34] States that never signed up for the ICC, not surprisingly, have generally been reluctant to help the Court track down its suspects. But even the states that joined the ICC – and therefore have a legal obligation to arrest wanted individuals on their territory – have at times shown little interest in aiding the ICC. Due to the ICC's lack of enforcement mechanisms, there is a clear gap between the Court's lofty

---

[32] Krcmaric 2020.   [33] Bass 2000.
[34] For more on state cooperation with the ICC and other international tribunals, see Meernik 2008; Berlin 2016; Hillebrecht and Straus 2017.

mission of ending impunity and the resources the Court has at its disposal to make that goal a reality.[35]

The case of Sudanese leader Omar Bashir highlights the problematic nature of the ICC's enforcement gap.[36] In 2009, the ICC issued an arrest warrant for Bashir for his role in masterminding atrocity crimes committed in the Darfur region of Sudan. Bashir nonetheless continued to travel widely throughout much of Africa and the Middle East. He started cautiously, only traveling to friendly states that had not joined the ICC. But Bashir quickly become bolder as he realized he could travel abroad with impunity. Bashir's itinerary created some awkward moments: He received the "red carpet treatment" when he traveled to Qatar for an Arab League summit, a meeting that UN Secretary General (and ardent ICC supporter) Ban Ki-moon also attended.[37] The gathered Arab leaders not only made it clear that they would never apprehend Bashir but also used the opportunity to criticize the ICC.[38] Things only got worse from there, as Bashir openly traveled in the coming years to ICC state parties – the very countries that promised to arrest ICC suspects – such as Chad, Kenya, Djibouti, and Malawi without facing any repercussions.[39] To be fair, however, Bashir did have some close calls. He traveled to South Africa in 2015 for an African Union summit after South Africa's ruling party, the African National Congress, promised it would flout the ICC arrest

---

[35] As a result, gloomy predictions about the ICC are pervasive. For example, shortly after the Court's creation, Jack Goldsmith predicted the ICC's lack of enforcement powers could render it irrelevant:

> The ICC is unlikely to punish the Husseins and future Milosevics of the world because it is unlikely to get its grip on them. The ICC has no inherent enforcement powers. It depends completely on member states to arrest and transfer defendants. So the efficacy [of the ICC] depends on the uncertain resolve of nations to use military or economic force to extricate an oppressive leader from his country.

See Goldsmith 2003, 92.

[36] Henningsen and Gissel 2020.
[37] Michael Slackman and Robert F. Worth, "Often Split, Arab Leaders Unite for Sudan's Chief," *New York Times*, March 30, 2009.
[38] Andrew England, "League Rejects Warrant for Bashir," *Financial Times*, March 30, 2009. Some of the Arab leaders who criticized the ICC during the 2009 meeting in Qatar – most notably Libya's Muammar Gaddafi – would soon have their own brushes with the ICC after targeting civilians during the Arab Spring.
[39] Bosco 2014a, 158.

warrant. But during his visit, South Africa's High Court made the dramatic announcement that South Africa, an ICC state party, had a legal obligation to arrest Bashir and send him to The Hague. In the midst of this confusion, Bashir fled the summit on his presidential jet and returned to the safety of Sudan.[40]

As this example shows, enforcing ICC arrest warrants depends on the actions of states whose commitments to the ICC are often fickle.[41] Getting suspects to The Hague has been a challenge since the Court's founding and will remain a major obstacle whenever the ICC attempts to punish the perpetrators of war crimes, crimes against humanity, and genocide. Nonetheless, the ICC has had more success in getting its hands on alleged criminals than many of the Court's critics anticipated. To date, the ICC has issued arrest warrants for 53 individuals for allegedly committing atrocity crimes.[42] Nearly one-third (16) of these individuals have been apprehended and transferred to The Hague. While in ICC custody, defendants are held in a special section of Scheveningen prison in the Netherlands.[43] Of the other thirty-seven individuals who were never surrendered to The Hague, twenty-eight remain at-large fugitives, seven have died, and two had their charges withdrawn.[44]

---

[40] Norimitsu Onishi, "Omar al-Bashir, Leaving South Africa, Eludes Arrest Again," *New York Times*, June 15, 2015. Four years after his hasty escape from South Africa, a domestic revolution in Sudan ousted Bashir. He currently is under arrest in Sudan.

[41] Given the unreliability of states, many NGOs have tried to make the ICC more effective by shaming states that harbor war criminals, collecting evidence, and connecting victims and witnesses with the ICC. See Eilstrup-Sangiovanni and Sharman 2022, 64–68.

[42] The ICC has issued arrest warrants for several more individuals for "offenses against the administration of justice," such as witness tampering. I do not include them here since they do not directly involve the commission of atrocity crimes. Additionally, the ICC has issued several summonses for individuals to appear voluntarily before the Court. I do not include them here since this is a voluntary process that does not require state cooperation to apprehend fugitives on the run.

[43] The ICC detention center at Scheveningen prison has been an occasional source of controversy. Some deem the facilities, which include a tennis court and space for conjugal visits, too good for the alleged perpetrators of genocide, war crimes, and crimes against humanity. One report even notes that prisoners and guards jokingly refer to it as "The Hague Hilton." See Anna Holligan, "Scheveningen Prison," *BBC News*, May 16, 2012.

[44] These ICC apprehension statistics are accurate as of January 1, 2025.

Trials

If a wanted individual is apprehended and transferred to the ICC, the case can go to trial (there are no in absentia trials at the ICC).[45] On one side, the prosecutor presents evidence in an attempt to establish the defendant's guilt. On the other side, defendants may choose to represent themselves or seek outside legal counsel. Like other international criminal tribunals, including the Yugoslav and Rwandan tribunals, there is no jury at the ICC. The judges of the trial chamber not only preside over the trial but also make determinations of guilt or innocence. If the judges convict the defendant, they are responsible for imposing a sentence, which can include prison time, fines, and reparations. Both the defendant and the prosecutor have the right to appeal the judges' decisions.

The ICC has struggled mightily in its attempts to convict the suspected perpetrators of genocide, war crimes, and crimes against humanity. As Tom Ginsburg quips, the ICC "surely must hold the record among international tribunals for the highest ratio of scholarly literature to output."[46] At the time of writing, the ICC has sustained only six convictions for atrocity crimes. All six of them – Dominic Ongwen, Thomas Lubanga, Bosco Ntaganda, Germain Katanga, Ahmad al-Mahdi, and Al Hassan Ag Abdoul Aziz – were members of rebel groups in Africa. The ICC has never sustained the conviction of a government official anywhere in the world. Moreover, some of the ICC's most high-profile cases – those involving "big fish" defendants such as heads of states – have ended in an embarrassing fashion. For example, ICC judges shocked much of the world when they acquitted former Ivory Coast president Laurent Gbagbo on the grounds that the ICC's prosecution team failed to prove its case that Gbagbo was responsible for atrocity crimes committed after the country's disputed 2010 election.

The ICC's dearth of convictions is a far cry from what many of the Court's supporters initially envisioned. Even the ICC's most passionate backers have questioned its ability to bring trials to successful completions. For instance, Aryeh Neier, a founder of Human Rights Watch

---

[45] There is a technical intermediate step after an individual's surrender to the ICC and the start of a trial in which the pretrial chamber confirms or dismisses the prosecutor's charges.

[46] Ginsburg 2009, 501.

and longtime champion of the ICC, admitted that "the ICC's performance has left much to be desired."[47] In a similar vein, some of the countries that have traditionally bolstered the ICC's work have started to doubt the Court's ability to fulfill its lofty goal of ending impunity for the world's worst criminals. At the 2018 meeting of the ASP, the United Kingdom pulled no punches in expressing its disappointment: "We cannot bury our heads in the sand and pretend everything is fine when it isn't. The statistics are sobering."[48] Even former ICC insiders have critiqued the Court. Most notably, the first four presidents of the ASP jointly published a remarkable essay in 2019 lamenting "a growing gap between the unique vision captured in the Rome Statute, the Court's founding document, and some of the daily work of the Court."[49]

At the same time, the ICC has always managed to weather past crises.[50] That may be the case yet again. Just as handwringing about the ICC's performance reached a fever pitch, the "Ukraine moment" triggered a cascade of support for the Court. Indeed, Putin's war may galvanize enthusiasm for the ICC in a way that seemed impossible before Russian forces invaded Ukraine on February 24, 2022. The ICC's decision to open an investigation into possible atrocity crimes committed on the territory of Ukraine shortly thereafter received enthusiastic support from many national governments. Moreover, several states are backing up their words with their actions by giving sizeable extrabudgetary contributions to the ICC and seconding lawyers, investigators, and forensic experts to the Court to aid its investigation. This rapid mobilization in support of the ICC is without precedent, marking "a quiet revolution in terms of the backing the Court has received."[51] Even countries that do not generally support the ICC – including the US – have taken steps to help the ICC's Ukraine investigation, an issue I address in Chapter 4.

---

[47] Neier 2019.   [48] Foreign and Commonwealth Office 2018.
[49] Al Hussein et al. 2019.
[50] For example, there were rumors of a mass withdrawal of African states from the ICC in 2016, prompting a slew of op-eds that asked whether "the end" of the ICC was at hand. See Kate Cronin-Furman and Stephanie Schwartz, "Is This the End of the International Criminal Court?" *Washington Post*, October 2016; and Karen Allen, "Is This the End for the International Criminal Court?" *BBC News*, October 24, 2016. But the ICC survived the crisis as the mass withdrawal never materialized (only Burundi left).
[51] Vasiliev 2022, 896.

Why the US Fears the ICC

Following the creation of the Yugoslav and Rwandan tribunals, a movement to establish a permanent international court gained momentum. As important as the two UN-backed ad hoc tribunals had been, continuing to build new tribunals from scratch for each new case of atrocities was a daunting task. Many suspected that "tribunal fatigue" would creep into the UN Security Council.[52] The political will to wade through the tedious diplomacy of crafting new tribunals would eventually dry up. Moreover, even if the political will existed, establishing ever more tribunals was inefficient. As Ruth Wedgwood put it, creating a new ad hoc tribunal each time the need arose amounted "to starting over with a blank piece of paper, with inevitable delays to build or adapt a courthouse, to hire personnel, and to begin operations."[53] For many advocates of international justice, the solution was obvious: a permanent international court that stood ready to launch investigations whenever atrocity crimes occurred.

Given that the ICC was the logical extension of previous American-supported tribunals – the Nuremberg and Tokyo tribunals after World War II and the tribunals for Yugoslavia and Rwanda in the early 1990s – it was natural to expect American backing for a permanent international tribunal. That expectation was borne out in early discussions about setting up the ICC. In 1994, the UN Generally Assembly delegated the task of writing a draft ICC proposal to the International Law Commission (ILC), an expert group of legal scholars.[54] Despite quibbling over some of the details, the US generally supported the ILC proposal. President Bill Clinton publicly voiced support for establishing the ICC on at least six occasions before the Rome Conference,[55] arguing that "all nations around the world who value freedom and tolerance [should] establish a permanent international criminal court to prosecute, with the support of the United Nations Security Council, serious violations of humanitarian law."[56] In line with Clinton's wishes, American diplomats actively participated in a series of preparatory meetings in the mid-1990s that helped lay the groundwork for the Rome Conference.

---

[52] Scheffer 2012a, 168–174.   [53] Wedgwood 1999, 40.
[54] On the International Law Commission, see Morton 2000.
[55] Scheffer 1999, 13.   [56] Quoted in Schabas 2004, 713.

Hopes were high heading into Rome. The conference occurred during a unique moment in global politics, after the end of the Cold War and before the terrorist attacks of 9/11, where the security concerns of many major powers were considerably lower than they had been in the past and would become in the future. This created a window of opportunity for states not only to consider but even to prioritize non-core security initiatives such as the ICC. Moreover, the stars aligned with regard to the timing of the Rome Conference. There just happened to be political leaders who prized multilateralism and international institutions in office in the US and many of the key European states.[57] In this context, the US delegation – which was led by Ambassador-at-Large for War Crimes Issues David Scheffer and included dozens of other US government attorneys, some of them veterans of the tribunals for Yugoslavia and Rwanda – arrived in Rome. Their instructions were to negotiate the creation of an ICC was broadly consistent with the preferences of US politicians and policymakers back in Washington.

However, the US quickly lost control of the negotiations in Rome. With the benefit of hindsight, this may seem unsurprising given the complicated and chaotic nature of the Rome Conference. As the conference chairman Philippe Kirsch acknowledged,

> This is easily the most complex international negotiation I have ever been involved in ... We have representatives here from 162 countries confronting, many of them for the first time, a draft document of over 200 pages, consisting of 120 articles, and containing 1,300 brackets. That is to say, 1,300 issues which the six preparatory conferences couldn't resolve, leaving multiple options to be tackled one by one by everybody gathered here.[58]

Though Kirsch is correct that there were an almost unlimited number of issues discussed and debated at the Rome Conference, US opposition to the ICC is relatively straightforward. It is the result of the American delegation losing two key battles during negotiations in Rome: The first concerns the ICC's jurisdiction over American servicemembers overseas, whereas the second involves the independence of the ICC's prosecutor. Taken together, these two institutional features of the ICC – at least from the US perspective – put American troops around the world at risk of facing politically biased investigations and prosecutions.

---

[57] Bosco 2014a, 43–44.   [58] Weschler 2000, 85.

America's Exposed Military

The first losing battle for the US delegation at the Rome Conference involved the conditions under which the ICC would have jurisdiction over American troops while they were deployed abroad. To understand why this issue was paramount to the US, it is necessary to step back and explore the history of America's global military presence.[59]

The US stands out as the only nation in the world with a string of military bases circling the globe. This overseas military presence is generally associated with World War II and the broader shift from isolationism to internationalism in US foreign policy, but the American experience with foreign military bases goes back to the country's earliest days. For instance, the construction of a series of military fortifications went hand-in-hand with the westward expansion of the US. These frontier bases, many of which still exist in some form, are now part of the US proper, but they were established on territory that was *not* considered part of the US at the time.[60] An example is Fort Leavenworth in Kansas – currently the home of the Army Command and General Staff College – which was originally built in the 1820s to protect the easternmost starting point of the Santa Fe Trail. The bases that sprouted up across North America in the late eighteenth and early nineteenth centuries served a pair of related functions for the US. First, they helped the young country project military power against more established colonial powers – the British, French, and Spanish – who still maintained vast territorial possessions on the continent. Second, the bases were meant to help protect white settlers who increasingly came into contact (and conflict) with indigenous populations. This process culminated with the Indian Removal Act of 1830, which evicted all Native Americans living east of the Mississippi River and mandated that they relocate to the west – at gunpoint if necessary. As one historian summarizes, the US military presence at these western bases became the "advance agent" of American expansion across the North American continent,[61] turning the idea of a manifest destiny into a reality.

America's foray into building military bases outside North America began in the late 1800s. Most notably, the US intervened in Cuba's war

---

[59] On the history of America's overseas military bases, see Blaker 1990; Sandars 2000; Baker 2004; Calder 2007; Vine 2015.
[60] Vine 2015, 19.   [61] Baker 2004, 4.

of independence against Spain, declaring war on the Spanish following the mysterious sinking of the USS *Maine* in Havana Harbor. After the US emerged victorious in the Spanish–American War in 1898, it took direct control Spain's colonies including the Philippines, Puerto Rico, and Guam, the future sites of some of America's largest overseas bases. It also pressured the new Cuban government into signing an indefinite lease that gave the US complete jurisdiction over forty-five square miles along the shores of Guantanamo Bay. Shortly thereafter, the Guantanamo Bay Naval Base became the first permanent American military base located outside of the present-day United States. In addition to the spoils of the Spanish-American war, the imperial ambitions of the US continued in other parts of the world. After the US annexation of American Samoa, Wake Island, and Hawaii, several military bases – including Pearl Harbor, the future headquarters of the US Pacific Fleet – soon followed. Moreover, the US purchased the Virgin Islands and claimed dozens of small, sometimes uninhabited, islands throughout the Pacific and the Caribbean to use as naval coaling stations (which were crucial for new steamship technology).[62] By the early 1900s, the US possessed an extensive collection of bases abroad that, with the exception of the British Empire, could compete with those of the traditional European colonial powers.

World War II transformed America's overseas military presence into the global behemoth that it is today. Even before the Japanese attack on Pearl Harbor and Roosevelt's subsequent declaration of war, the context of World War II offered opportunities for the US to expand its military footprint around the world. On September 2, 1940, the US and the UK struck the destroyers-for-bases deal: the US transferred fifty aging warships to the Royal Navy in exchange for ninety-nine-year leases on military bases located in British territorial possessions sprinkled throughout the Western Hemisphere.[63] This agreement is notable because it was not only the start of the renowned Roosevelt–

---

[62] In addition to their value as naval bases, the US also sought some of these islands to mine guano (i.e., bird droppings), a valuable agricultural commodity at the time. See Immerwahr 2019, 46–58.

[63] In an interesting historical twist, future Nuremberg prosecutor Robert Jackson (who was then Roosevelt's attorney general) wrote the controversial legal opinion that allowed the president to conclude the destroyers-for-bases deal as an executive agreement that did not require Congressional approval. On Jackson's role in the destroyers-for-bases affair, see Casto 2012.

Churchill wartime partnership but was also the origin of America's contemporary global military presence. Specifically, the US acquired basing rights in Newfoundland (Canada) and several Caribbean islands, including Antigua, the Bahamas, Bermuda, Jamaica, Saint Lucia, and Trinidad. But this was only the beginning for the US. After it entered the World War II as a belligerent, it acquired more and more bases as it waged a multi-continent war ranging from the heart of continental Europe to the deserts of North Africa to the islands of the Pacific. At the end of World War II, the US emerged in command of a global military presence unlike any other country. Indeed, in just five years, the US built the biggest collection of overseas military bases in world history.[64]

The end of the war raised a fundamental question for American foreign policy: What should the US do with all the foreign bases it had acquired during the conflict? Newly installed President Harry Truman left no ambiguity on the American position when he met with Churchill and Stalin at the Potsdam Conference in 1945 to plan the postwar peace. Truman informed the other members of the Big Three that "we are going to maintain the military bases necessary for the complete protection of our interests and world peace." Moreover, Truman signaled that the US likely was not done establishing bases abroad: "Bases which our military experts deem to be essential for our protection we will acquire."[65] A similar mood prevailed in Congress, where many members were reluctant to hand back bases to conquered nations after the lives of so many American servicemembers had been sacrificed in their pursuit. F. Edward Hebert, a member of the House of Representatives from Louisiana, captured the conventional wisdom about America's overseas bases in the immediate postwar period: "We fought for them, we've got them, we should keep them."[66] Within the military establishment, a comparable logic prevailed as well, especially regarding new American bases in the Pacific. Indeed, there was "a bureaucratic consensus about turning the Pacific Basin into an 'American lake.'"[67] Thus, the US ultimately kept many of its wartime bases either through military occupation (e.g., Germany and Japan) or via bilateral contracting with host nations (e.g., the US

---

[64] Vine 2015, 27.   [65] Quoted in Calder 2007, 15.
[66] Quoted in Vine 2015, 29.   [67] Friedman 2000, 1.

signed a ninety-nine-year lease for bases in the Philippines after the war).[68]

The decision to maintain a massive network of military bases around the world in peacetime marked a key shift in thinking about America's role in the world. In a sense, it was the fulfillment of Henry Luce's grandiose vision for an "American century" in which US power and principles transformed world politics.[69] On a more practical level, it was closely linked to the growing consensus in Washington that "the superior coercive power of the United States [was] required to underwrite a decent world order."[70] While America's foreign military presence has faced plenty of criticisms, it offered the US one clear advantage: the ability to project military power rapidly in every region of the world.

From Washington's perspective, the case for maintaining overseas bases only became stronger with the emergence of the Cold War.[71] America's bases were a lynchpin in its efforts to contain the Soviet Union.[72] In some cases, this involved massive deployments at bases – such as Ramstein Air Base in Germany, Camp Humphreys in South Korea, and Subic Bay Naval Base in the Philippines – that more closely resembled fully fledged American cities inserted into foreign countries than stereotypical military bases. These mega-bases were meant to signal a long-term commitment to the host country that would both reassure America's allies and deter its adversaries. In other cases, the US used much smaller deployments to act as "tripwires," such as the garrison of 7,000 American troops in West Berlin. As famously celebrated in Thomas Schelling's *Arms and Influence*, the purpose of this relatively small military outpost was not to stop a Red Army

---

[68] Cooley 2008, 30–31.   [69] Luce 1941.   [70] Wertheim 2020, 7.
[71] Debates about how to protect American troops overseas from foreign legal systems began around this time (and thus predate the ICC by several decades). The primary solution for the US was to sign status of forces agreements with countries hosting American troops. The terms of these agreements can vary, but they often grant US courts jurisdiction over crimes that American servicemembers commit in the course of their official military duties. See Efrat 2023.
[72] Given the ideological component of the Cold War, the global network of bases also offered a potent symbol of American strength. As James Blaker, a former advisor to the Joint Chiefs of Staff, described the early Cold War years, "Next to the U.S. nuclear monopoly, there was no more universally recognized symbol of the nation's superpower status than its overseas basing system." See Blaker 1990, 37.

invasion – that would have been impossible given their inferior numbers – but rather to commit the US to a devastating response should the Soviets attack West Berlin first.[73] Cold War competition also demanded the creation of additional bases in strategically important regions. Nowhere was this clearer than in the Middle East. In response to two major foreign policy setbacks in 1979, the ouster of the US-backed Shah during the Iranian Revolution and the Soviet invasion of Afghanistan, President Jimmy Carter warned the Soviet Union that the US was prepared to use military force to prevent it from gaining control of the Persian Gulf. This policy, later dubbed the Carter Doctrine, included a burst of new base construction efforts to help protect the flow of oil.[74] America's Cold War basing infrastructure also enabled it to fight a pair of major wars – first in Korea and later in Vietnam – on the other side of the globe.

The end of the Cold War punctured the consensus, albeit briefly, about America's need for a massive network of overseas bases. The fall of the Berlin Wall in 1989 and the formal collapse of the Soviet Union in 1991 led some to believe that the US would slowly wind down, if not quickly dismantle, its global system of military bases. After all, if a key justification for maintaining the bases was to contain Soviet aggression, then the demise of the Soviet Union presumably meant the US no longer needed its overseas bases in the way that it once did. Consequently, there was a "come home, America" movement among both scholars and the public.[75] But this movement ultimately failed. While the US did substantially reduce the total number of troops stationed abroad after the Cold War's end, it was generally loath to give up the bases themselves, especially those in strategically important locales. As one Pentagon official described America's overseas military presence in the early post–Cold War period, "We shrank in place. But we didn't really reposition."[76] Instead of dramatically reducing its foreign military footprint, the US appeared more interested in finding new strategic purposes for bases whose original missions had become outdated. After the 9/11 attacks, for example, the US repurposed

---

[73] Schelling 1966, 22.
[74] Calder 2007, 28–29. Some of the bases constructed in response to the Carter Doctrine later played important roles in America's post–Cold War military conflicts in the Middle East.
[75] See, for example, Gholz, Press, and Sapolsky 1997.
[76] Quoted in Vine 2015, 52.

military bases previously meant to contain the Soviet Union for its global war on terrorism. A string of overseas bases has played a major role in waging wars in Afghanistan and Iraq, transporting suspected terrorists as part of the CIA's extraordinary rendition program, and carrying out drone strikes and special forces raids around the world.

The prevalence of American overseas bases has sparked a debate on whether the modern US constitutes an empire. For some, the answer is clear: the US is an empire due to its unparalleled dominance of global military and economic affairs.[77] Even though American politicians might shun the empire label, America's vast military presence beyond its own borders makes the US an empire in denial. As one proponent of this view, Niall Ferguson, quips, "The dilemmas faced by America today have more in common with those faced by the later Caesars than with those faced by the Founding Fathers."[78] Others push back against claims that the US is an empire, at least in the formal sense. Formal empire, according to this view, is a system of rule, not a distribution of power. Though the US in the post-Cold War era is the world's "hegemon" or "unipole," this does not necessarily make the US an empire because it does not rule via an imperial core–periphery model.[79] Still others take a middle-ground position: The US is an empire, but it is fundamentally different than the empires that the traditional European colonial powers once built. Instead of controlling large swaths of land around the world, the US projects its power and influence abroad through its network of overseas military bases, nothing more than "tiny specks" on a world map.[80] As Mark Gillem summarizes, "Today's [American] empire does not so much require vast territories, dependent colonies, or puppet governments. Rather, it needs places for its soldiers to sleep at night and pavement to park its warplanes."[81]

Regardless of where one stands on the empire debate, the key point is that the American global military presence is unique. No other country has a network of overseas bases that can rival the US. In fact, the rest of the world *combined* cannot compare to the US. According to David Vine's data on foreign military bases, discussed in

---

[77] Johnson 2000, 2004; Ferguson 2005.   [78] Ferguson 2005, viii.
[79] Ikenberry 2004; Nexon and Wright 2007; Spruyt 2008.
[80] Immerwahr 2019, 18.   [81] Gillem 2007, 17.

detail in Chapter 5, the US has approximately 800 bases abroad, whereas the number of foreign bases belonging to every other country totals just 30.[82] Most of these other bases belong to Britain, France, and Russia, whose overseas bases are primarily in countries where they have strong historical legacies (former colonies for Britain and France, and the "near abroad" former Soviet republics for Russia). China, presumably America's greatest geopolitical competitor in the coming years, currently has only one overseas base, which opened in Djibouti in 2017.[83] There is speculation that China may be in the process of seeking additional foreign bases in other parts of Africa, as well as Sri Lanka, the Maldives, Tajikistan, and Cambodia.[84] But even if these rumored bases come into fruition, the gap between the US and China will remain massive for the foreseeable future. Indeed, Vine's numbers suggest that over 96 percent of all the overseas military bases in the world belong to the US.

Returning to the context of the ICC, this enormous discrepancy in overseas military presence informed the American negotiating position at the Rome Conference. Depending on how the delegates defined the rules for the ICC's jurisdiction, US troops were at risk of being significantly more exposed to ICC investigations and prosecutions than troops from other countries. As a result, the American delegation in Rome and politicians back in Washington became "fixated on the prospect of that lone American marine … getting nabbed on some capricious charge and inexorably dragged into the maw of the machine" at the ICC.[85] This fear turned negotiations over the ICC's jurisdiction into the "battle royale" in Rome.[86]

Given that well over 100 countries participated in the ICC negotiations, initial proposals for the Court's jurisdiction varied considerably. At one extreme, a group of countries led by Germany wanted to grant the ICC truly universal jurisdiction: the right to investigate and prosecute crimes irrespective of where they occurred or the nationality of the perpetrator and the victim.[87] At the other extreme, the US and a handful of other countries favored setting up the Court with much

---

[82] Vine 2015, 5. These numbers represent all known overseas military bases as of 2015.
[83] Oddly enough, Camp Lemonnier, the largest American military base in Africa, is located only a few miles away from China's base in Djibouti.
[84] Doshi 2021, 295.   [85] Weschler 2000, 95.   [86] Bosco 2014a, 55.
[87] On the politics and law of universal jurisdiction, see Macedo 2004.

narrower jurisdiction, though they did not always agree on the details. Most national delegations fell somewhere in the middle. Ultimately, the participants at the Rome Conference reached a compromise position – one that gave the ICC wide but not unlimited jurisdiction – that most states could live with even if it was not their preferred outcome.[88] Specifically, the ICC can claim jurisdiction over atrocity crimes on the basis of nationality (if the perpetrator is a national of a member state) or territory (if the crime took place on the territory of a member state).[89]

The US strenuously objected to granting the ICC territorial jurisdiction for a pair of reasons. First, it disproportionately exposed the US military to ICC authority. Given its unique global military presence, American soldiers would fall under the ICC's jurisdiction whenever they were stationed on the territory of a country that joined the Court. This was not some farfetched concern: Many countries hosting US troops were enthusiastic ICC supporters and appeared poised to join the Court quickly (125 countries ultimately did so). Countries without a foreign military presence would not have to worry about similar exposure arising from the ICC's territorial jurisdiction. From the American perspective, this was unfair. Its military was deployed around the world not just for the sake of US national security but also to help keep peace in strategically important regions with a history of violence – something that benefited the rest of the world too. But America's reward for this apparently thankless task was relatively higher exposure to the prosecutors and judges of the ICC. As David Scheffer defended the US position in Rome:

> The American armed forces have a unique peacekeeping role, posted to hot spots all around the world. Representing the world's sole remaining superpower, American soldiers on such missions stand to be uniquely subject to frivolous, nuisance accusations by parties of all sorts [at the ICC]. And we

---

[88] This compromise produced a loophole called the "traveling dictator exception." Specifically, a dictator could commit even the most horrendous atrocities and have nothing to fear from the ICC as long as the dictator never joined the ICC and the abuses were committed within his own borders. This hypothetical dictator could travel abroad – including to ICC member states – with legal impunity due to the loophole in the ICC's jurisdiction. As Jack Goldsmith pithily described it, "Even if human rights abusers from non-signatory nations vacation in The Hague, they cannot be arrested and tried by the ICC." See Goldsmith 2003, 91.

[89] As described earlier, the ICC also has jurisdiction if the UN Security Council refers a situation to the Court.

simply cannot be expected to expose our people to those sorts of risks. We are dead serious about this.⁹⁰

Second, US officials argued that the ICC's territorial jurisdiction violated the long-standing principle that states are not subject to the rules of international treaties that they did not sign and ratify. As Abram and Antonia Chayes famously put it, "The most basic principle of international law is that states cannot be legally bound except by their own consent."⁹¹ But the ICC's territorial jurisdiction meant that Americans – soldiers and civilians alike – would be exposed to potential ICC investigation and prosecution while on the territory of member states *even if the US never joined the Court*. This did not sit well with the US. As the American delegation repeatedly argued, it violated both historical precedent and the Vienna Convention on the Law of Treaties, which require ratification for states to be bound by the terms of treaties.⁹² Back in Washington, several senators were in an uproar as well, such as when Jesse Helms decried the ICC's territorial jurisdiction as "baloney."⁹³ But other delegations in Rome pushed back against this assertation, arguing that the ICC was different because it exercised jurisdiction over individuals rather than states. The ICC's territorial jurisdiction therefore did not represent some sort of revolutionary change because Americans on foreign soil have always been subject to the local law of the land. The only difference with the Rome Treaty, the argument went, was that states were delegating the right to prosecute atrocity crimes to an international court. The US, not surprisingly, rejected this logic.⁹⁴ From the American viewpoint, the ICC's territorial jurisdiction represented a "dangerous drift ... toward universal jurisdiction" even if it formally stopped short of it.⁹⁵

The US wanted the ICC's jurisdiction to be based on nationality alone, an arrangement that would limit ICC jurisdiction exclusively to individuals whose countries signed up for the Court.⁹⁶ From the US

---

⁹⁰ Weschler 2000, 91–92.   ⁹¹ Chayes and Chayes 1993, 179.
⁹² Weschler 2000, 101.   ⁹³ Senate Committee on Foreign Relations 1998.
⁹⁴ For a defense of the American position, see Morris 2000. For a criticism, see Scharf 2001.
⁹⁵ Scheffer 1999, 20.
⁹⁶ This position was sometimes called "state consent." While several different definitions of state consent were debated in Rome, ratifying the ICC's Rome Statute would have been considered equivalent to granting consent under some proposals.

perspective, this would solve the aforementioned problems associated with the ICC's territorial jurisdiction because Americans would never fall under the Court's jurisdiction if the US decided not to join it. Decades after the Rome Conference's conclusion, the relationship between the ICC and nonmember states remains an enduring point of contention for the US. American officials claim that the ICC should never be allowed to investigate or prosecute individuals from nonmember states,[97] whereas the ICC (and its 125 member states) asserts that it can as long as the crimes take place on the territory of a member state.

Almost every other country represented at Rome pointed out an obvious flaw in the American position on the ICC's jurisdiction. If the ICC could not attain jurisdiction over individuals from nonmember states, then it had little chance of holding the world's worst criminals accountable. In fact, other delegations argued that the ICC would have a hard time even getting cases if the American plan came into fruition. Oppressive leaders and rogue regimes – those most likely to commit the sort of crimes the ICC was meant to punish – could escape the ICC's jurisdiction simply by not signing up for the Court. In the words of the head of the South Korean delegation in Rome, "In order to protect against this less-than-one-percent chance of an American peacekeeper's becoming exposed, the US would cut off Court access to well over ninety percent of the cases it would otherwise need to be pursuing. Because what tyrant in his right mind would sign such a treaty?" The South Korean diplomat continued with a hypothetical that was on the minds of many in the late 1990s involving Saddam Hussein's Iraq. "What applies to America also applies to Hussein; and simply by not signing, he could buy himself a pass."[98] Given this, the rest of the world saw the American position as frustratingly self-serving: the US was willing to critically weaken the ICC in order to eliminate the tiny chance of an American servicemember facing an ICC investigation or prosecution.

Opposition to American plans primarily came from a loose coalition of states calling itself the "like-minded group." This informal group had a diverse, global membership that eventually grew to some sixty

---

[97] The Biden administration briefly retreated from this position when the ICC opened an investigation in Ukraine that implicated individuals from Russia (another nonmember state). I discuss this policy shift in detail in Chapter 4.

[98] Weschler 2000, 101.

states, with delegations from Argentina, Australia, Canada, Germany, and the Netherlands emerging as its most vocal leaders.[99] As relatively weak or middling powers, the like-minded group brought a different perspective to the negotiations than the US. In fact, members of the like-minded group believed they were better positioned to build a "fair and legitimate" ICC precisely because they were not engaged in foreign wars or encumbered by global security commitments.[100] While the members of the like-minded group did not agree on everything, they concurred on a basic set of principles that should guide the ICC: the new tribunal should have extremely broad jurisdiction, maintain independence from political actors, and stand ready to investigate the strong and the weak alike, thereby removing any taint of victor's justice or double standards.

This vision for the ICC clashed with American plans for the Court. To be fair, some members of the US delegation expressed a modicum of sympathy for the perspective of the like-minded group, acknowledging that the American position was "almost counterintuitive."[101] On the one hand, the US was a longtime supporter of international justice that repeatedly stated its desire to create a permanent international court to take the place of ad hoc tribunals in future humanitarian crises. Once in Rome, the US was heavily invested in building the ICC. American contributions to the text of the Rome Statute were substantial enough that nearly everyone could agree the US "played an extremely important and in many ways constructive role throughout the negotiations."[102] On the other hand, the US was determined to shield its troops scattered around the world from ICC authority – even if that meant guaranteeing impunity for individuals from all other countries that opted not to join the Court.[103] Exposing its own troops was

---

[99] On the role of the like-minded group at the Rome Conference, see Benedetti and Washburn 1999.
[100] Bosco 2014a, 39.   [101] Scheffer 2012a, 167.   [102] Schiff 2008, 71.
[103] Mitchell and Powell's distinction between "originators" and "joiners" helps make sense of America's seemingly bizarre stance in Rome. Originators actively participate in an international court's creation and get to shape its institutional design. Joiners, by contrast, decide to support a court only after its creation and therefore must accept the institutional rules that have already been established. With the ICC, the US was an originator – and it therefore expected to get a say over the Court's design. But it was an originator that failed to achieve its main objectives during the Rome negotiations, prompting it to become an opponent of the Court's creation. See Mitchell and Powell 2011.

simply too high a price to pay. Due to America's unwillingness to compromise on matters of jurisdiction, members of the American delegation were aware that they inadvertently looked like "the guardian of impunity rather than its slayer."[104] Not surprisingly, many countries were "confused by and annoyed with" the American strategy in Rome.[105]

The disagreement between the US and other countries, particularly the like-minded group, was largely about dueling conceptions of equality in international affairs.[106] The primary concern for most countries was the *equality of nations* before international law. The basic idea was that the ICC should apply the exact same set of standards to all countries regardless of their military might, economic wealth, or political influence. Granting special privileges to the US to accommodate its concerns about its exposed global military was anathema to many states because it was inconsistent with notions of equality before the law. As a result, ICC supporters "implored the United States to recognize that an explicitly two-tiered system of justice, applying one law for the United States and a different law for all other countries, would undermine the ICC's most precious resource – its legitimacy."[107]

The US rejected this logic. While the equality of nations may have seemed uncontroversial in theory, American officials pointed out that in practice it translated into *inequality of risk*. No other country's military would be exposed to the ICC in the same way as America's. Given this, the US wanted the rest of the world to agree to the American position on ICC jurisdiction or create some sort of carve-out for American forces deployed abroad. In effect, the US was rather transparently in favor of a double standard: America's unique security responsibilities deserved unique accommodations. As Scheffer argued in Rome: "You can't approach this on the model of the equality of all states. You have to think in terms of the inequality of some states." He continued that in order for the US to keep providing its global peacekeeping and global policing roles, "American interests are going to have to be protected and American soldiers shielded."[108] This view enjoyed widespread popularity back in Washington, where it was

---

[104] Scheffer 2012a, 168. [105] Scheffer 2012a, 167.
[106] The fight over conceptualizing equality at the ICC is consistent with Erik Voeten's argument that international institutions are sites of ideological conflict about the basic principles of world order. See Voeten 2021.
[107] Orentlicher 2004, 428. [108] Weschler 2000, 102–103.

articulated most forcefully by Pentagon officials who argued both privately and publicly that "massive deployments justified exceptional protection for American forces" from the ICC.[109]

In the end, American pleas about the ICC's jurisdiction fell on deaf ears in Rome. The US delegation failed to cobble together a coalition of states that could compete with the superior numbers of the like-mind group. Many opponents of the US position dismissed American calls for special protections from the ICC as "mere hypocrisy."[110] Even those who were somewhat sympathetic to America's unique security burden thought the US position was not worth supporting because it contradicted the logic underlying the entire ICC project: to eliminate, or at least mitigate, impunity by making it more difficult for the perpetrators of atrocity crimes to evade accountability on the basis of sovereignty and nationality.[111]

Losing the fight over the ICC's territorial jurisdiction meant that the ICC could, in theory, investigate and prosecute American soldiers while they were deployed abroad. But would it actually happen? The second big fight in Rome, which concerned the independence of the ICC's prosecutor, convinced American officials that the ICC would, in fact, target their troops scattered around the world.

The ICC's "Rogue" Prosecutor

The second key battle for the Americans in Rome revolved around who, exactly, would get the right to launch the ICC's investigations. This fight over initiating investigations was closely linked to the fight over territorial jurisdiction. If the ICC was going to assert jurisdiction over American soldiers when they were on the territory of ICC members, then the US wanted to make certain that it had a way to block investigations of its troops. Once again, however, the US ended up on the losing side of the debate.

The American position on investigations was clear: the US wanted the UN Security Council to control the ICC's investigations. Under this plan, the ICC would only be able to open new investigations when the Security Council referred a specific situation of atrocity crimes to the Court. The ICC would have no independent authority to pick its own

---

[109] Scheffer 2012a, 228.   [110] Schiff 2008, 171.   [111] Leigh 2001, 127.

investigations.[112] The American vision for the ICC was essentially a permanent version of the two ad hoc tribunals. While there were, of course, some differences – most notably, the ICC would have much wider geographic reach than just Yugoslavia or Rwanda – the key point was that the Security Council would select the countries on which the ICC focused its attention. As Bill Richardson, the US Ambassador to the UN, characterized the American position during a speech at the outset of the Rome Conference: "A permanent Court cannot stand alone. It must be part of the international order, and supported by the international community. The United Nations Security Council remains a vital part of that world order … the United States believes that the Council must play an important role in the work of the permanent Court, including the Court's trigger mechanism [for investigations]."[113]

From the American perspective, Security Council control of the ICC's investigations was attractive because it offered a way to shield US troops exposed to ICC jurisdiction while they were deployed to the territory of ICC member states. As one of the five permanent members of the Security Council, the US enjoys veto power over any action the Security Council considers. In practice, this meant that the ICC would never be able to initiate an investigation unless the US signed off on it.

Nearly all the other states in Rome viewed the US position as another instance of American double standards. India's top negotiator captured this perspective, arguing that granting the Security Council sole control of ICC investigations would put the Council's permanent five members "above the law" since they would have de facto immunity from the ICC.[114] The contingent of NGOs observing the negotiations in Rome also cried foul on plans to give the Security Council authority over ICC investigations. The head of the Coalition for the

---

[112] The American position on the role of the UN Security Council was very similar to the International Law Commission's 1994 draft proposal for the ICC. If the final version of the Rome Statute had more closely resembled the commission's original draft, the US likely would have joined the Court. American opposition to the ICC solidified when most delegations in Rome insisted on downgrading the role of the Security Council and empowering the ICC prosecutor to open investigations independently. See Schabas 2004. For an analysis of why some states changed their positions on the ICC's independent prosecutor between the 1994 ILC draft and the 1998 Rome Conference, see Goodliffe and Hawkins 2009.

[113] Richardson 1998.   [114] No Peace without Justice International 1998.

International Criminal Court, William Pace, proclaimed that it would reduce the ICC to "a sham ... one which would dispense international criminal justice only to small and weak countries, never to violators in powerful nations."[115] More broadly, small states, NGOs, and other advocates of international justice hated the idea of making the ICC subordinate to the Security Council for the exact same reason the US loved the idea: It would grant special privileges to the powerful. By the end of the Rome Conference, it was clear to the US delegation that their insistence on making the Security Council the only pathway to ICC investigations was "toxic" to most of the world and had no chance of surviving a vote.[116]

Contrary to American preferences, the delegates in Rome ultimately created three different ways to trigger an ICC investigation. The first reflects what the US had hoped would be the only pathway: the UN Security Council can refer alleged crimes to the ICC for investigation. The second gives ICC member states the right to refer alleged crimes to the ICC for investigation. The third gives the ICC prosecutor the right to open an investigation entirely on his or her own volition, often called the prosecutor's *proprio motu* authority. In each case, the ultimate decision on whether to open an investigation is the prosecutor's (i.e., the prosecutor is not obligated to open an investigation after a referral). Of the various triggers for ICC investigations, the US supported the first, expressed moderate concern about the second, and openly feared the third.

This third trigger – granting the ICC prosecutor the independent authority to select which situations to investigate – marked a radical departure from other international tribunals that the US had supported previously. Indeed, none of the prosecutors at the tribunals that preceded the ICC enjoyed a comparable level of discretion. In each of those cases, a handful of powerful states (the victorious World War II Allies for Nuremberg and Tokyo, and the UN Security Council for Yugoslavia and Rwanda) picked the conflicts and the countries on which tribunal prosecutors would focus their investigative attention.[117] Moreover, the powerful states that established these tribunals

---

[115] Quoted in Bosco 2014a, 41. [116] Scheffer 2012a, 181.
[117] To be clear, tribunal prosecutors were responsible for deciding which specific individuals to indict within the broader situations that powerful states wanted investigated. Even then, however, powerful states sometimes meddled in the operations of the tribunals, such as when General MacArthur helped draw up a list of suspects in Tokyo.

carefully tailored the rules to ensure that prosecutors would focus on the crimes of others. At Nuremberg and Tokyo, this involved drafting the founding charters of the tribunals in such a way that Allied wartime conduct fell outside of their remit. At the tribunals for Yugoslavia and Rwanda, it meant narrowly tailoring the geographic and temporal jurisdiction of the tribunals to the crimes the Security Council wanted investigated. But at the ICC, there are no comparable restrictions. The ICC itself – specifically, the prosecutor – makes decisions about which countries and episodes of violence will face the scrutiny of an investigation. This unprecedented discretion delegated to the prosecutor was very much on the minds of ICC personnel as the Court set up its operations. In the words of Luis Moreno-Ocampo, "The most distinctive feature of the Court, as compared to the other international tribunals, is the power given to the Court to independently select situations to investigate."[118]

There is a cruel irony in the politics surrounding the discretion given to the ICC prosecutor. Most delegations in Rome, especially those of the like-minded group, championed an independent prosecutor to create a firewall between the ICC and the political biases associated with the UN Security Council.[119] However, as the American delegation pointed out, an independent prosecutor creates a context where a different type of political bias is possible. The very independence that enables the prosecutor to ignore the wishes of powerful states also provides the prosecutor with the opportunity to inject his or her own political biases into the ICC's activities. From the perspective of American officials, giving the ICC prosecutor the right to initiate prosecutions carried a far greater risk of politicization than allowing the Security Council to control the Court.[120] A Security Council decision at least reflected the collective agreement of five countries, whereas an ICC endowed with an independent prosecutor could be subject to the whims of a single individual.

---

[118] Moreno-Ocampo 2009, 13.
[119] Once the ICC was established, the Court's personnel concurred with this perspective. According to Luis Moreno-Ocampo, the ability of the ICC prosecutor to open investigations without having to rely on Security Council action "ensures that the requirements of justice can prevail over any political decision." Moreno-Ocampo 2009, 14.
[120] Schabas 2004, 713.

To American critics of the Court, the power concentrated in the hands of the ICC prosecutor created "an open invitation to abuse."[121] There would be little to stop an overzealous prosecutor from going rogue and unfairly targeting American soldiers dispersed around the world. For the Clinton administration, the overriding fear was "a runaway court – one that would respond sympathetically to politically-motivated charges against US nationals."[122] More specifically, US officials argued that anti-American bias could pervade the ICC's investigations and prosecutions in two ways.

First, the ICC prosecutor might himself or herself have anti-American biases. The precise reason why the prosecutor would bring an anti-American perspective into the job was rarely specified in American complaints, but the general assumption was that the prosecutor would inevitably harbor some sort of resentment toward US power and dominance in global affairs.[123] Given the ICC prosecutor's wide latitude to pick his or her investigations, any anti-American bias could potentially translate into a foreign policy threat for the US. A Clinton administration spokesperson, for example, warned that the ICC prosecutor would become "the most powerful man in the world" due to his unparalleled global investigative powers.[124] Others drew a parallel between the ICC prosecutor and Kenneth Starr, the hard-charging independent counsel whose "Starr Report" led to Clinton's impeachment in the House of Representatives shortly after the Rome Conference.[125] Starr was initially tasked with investigating Clinton's

[121] Rivkin Jr. and Casey 1999. [122] Orentlicher 2004, 421.
[123] Contrary to the US government position, some scholars argue that ICC bias toward the US likely goes in the opposite direction. That is, the ICC might exhibit pro-American bias. The logic underlying this perspective is that the ICC has incentives to garner American support by avoiding investigations that threaten the US military or US interests more broadly. See, for example, Wedgwood 1998; Bosco 2014a; Rudolph 2017.
[124] Leigh 2001, 128. Though this claim was an exaggeration, the US was correct that the role of the ICC prosecutor represented a new source of influence in world politics. In fact, the ICC's first prosecutor described his position as that of "a new autonomous actor on the international scene." Moreno-Ocampo 2009, 14. Additionally, leading scholars noticed the trend toward court personnel – such as judges and prosecutors – becoming "quasi-autonomous foreign policy actors" in the late 1990s. See Slaughter 1997, 188.
[125] Policymakers and pundits made comparisons between the ICC prosecutor and independent counsels so frequently that legal scholars spilt much ink highlighting the similarities and differences of these positions. See, for example, Danner 2003.

pre-presidential real estate investments, but the investigation quickly ballooned – inappropriately, in the eyes of some – into a wide-ranging investigation of the president's life that included the release of sordid details of Clinton's sexual relationship with Monica Lewinsky. Capturing the zeitgeist of the late 1990s, US officials worried that the ICC prosecutor would similarly overstep his authority and become "an untethered international Kenneth Starr, floating free" and casting judgment on American military actions around the world.[126]

Second, even if the ICC prosecutor was not personally biased, anti-American states could pressure the prosecutor into opening investigations that damaged US interests. In making this argument, American opponents of the ICC drew on the experience of the Yugoslav Tribunal. Some in the US believed ICTY prosecutors were overly eager to find Croats and Bosnians to indict so that the tribunal would appear more evenhanded in its prosecution of Serbs, the primary perpetrators of atrocity crimes. According to one Pentagon attorney included in the American delegation in Rome,

I can almost guarantee you that a similar thing will happen one day up ahead [at the ICC]. Say, it's something like Desert Storm, and the prosecutor has been able to round up and indict dozens of Iraqis. You just watch: the Iraqi government will be lodging all sorts of trumped-up, phony complaints about Americans. And the prosecutor will come under terrific pressure to indict a few of them as well, just to demonstrate fairness.[127]

Even if this politicized manipulation of the ICC never resulted in US soldiers facing prosecution at The Hague, American officials insisted that other states would have no trouble turning the ICC into a forum for airing grievances about US foreign policy.[128]

As a result of these potential biases, the US was convinced the ICC prosecutor would unfairly target American servicemembers around the world. Representative Tom DeLay warned the ICC was bound to become "a rogue court" that would "indict, try, and convict American troops for broadly defined and openly interpreted crimes."[129] Senator Jesse Helms lambasted the ICC as an "international kangaroo court"[130]

---

[126] Weschler 2000, 95. For additional discussion of the "international Ken Starr problem," see Senate Committee on Foreign Relations 1998.
[127] Weschler 2000, 95.   [128] Nash 2000, 159.   [129] DeLay 2005.
[130] Steven Mufson, "Helms Calls for Abolishing AID, Increasing Support for Taiwan," *Washington Post*, January 12, 2001.

and insisted it "will turn into a petty claims court that will spend its time taking up complaints about the United States."[131] In Congressional testimony, expert witnesses supported these claims, arguing that the ICC's true purpose was to create "a platform for show trials" of Americans.[132] Even the elder statesman of US foreign policy, former Secretary of State Henry Kissinger, joined the long list of ICC critics by warning that the Court could "turn into an instrument of political warfare" and set its sights on American troops and officials.[133] Given these fears, opposition to the ICC's independent prosecutor became a bottom line for the US during negotiations in Rome. As Clinton administration officials publicly promised in the midst of the negotiations, "We won't support the treaty if it has this self-initiating independent prosecutor. That's for sure."[134]

It is worth emphasizing exactly what US officials meant when they argued that the ICC prosecutor would inject political biases and unfairly target American soldiers. The overriding fear was that the ICC would investigate and prosecute US troops *even if they did not commit any atrocity crimes*. Consider the following statements from cabinet-level foreign policy figures from both political parties. Bill Richardson, a Democrat who served as the US Ambassador to the UN in the Clinton administration, insisted that the ICC was flawed because "soldiers deployed far from home need to do their jobs without exposure to politicized proceedings."[135] The implication was clear: Even troops that merely did their jobs and refrained from committing atrocity crimes might still face the scrutiny of an ICC prosecutor harboring an anti-American agenda. John Bolton, a Republican who served in the Reagan, Bush, and Trump administrations, similarly argued that Americans could be "swept up in a conflict and used as scapegoats simply because they were Americans."[136] Likewise, the prevailing bipartisan consensus in Congress was that "the ICC could be used to harass and detain American soldiers on foreign soil for purely political reasons."[137] The same concern dominated thinking among military leaders: the ICC would "unfairly" target US

---

[131] Barbara Crossette, "Helms Vows to Make War on U.N. Court," *New York Times*, March 27, 1998.
[132] Rabkin 2000. [133] Kissinger 2001, 94.
[134] Alessandra Stanley, "U.S. Argues against Strongly Independent War Crimes Prosecutor," *New York Times*, June 18, 1998.
[135] Ibid. [136] Bolton 2007, 86. [137] Ireland and Bava 2016, 1.

servicemembers for "legitimate actions" simply because those actions were unpopular.[138]

As negotiations progressed in Rome, other countries were acutely aware of America's concerns with the ICC, even if they disagreed with them. In an attempt to get the US to buy into the ICC without sacrificing the Court's independent prosecutor, other delegations agreed to several safeguards designed to prevent the prosecutor from initiating unwarranted investigations. The most important of these was the complementarity principle. As described earlier, the complementarity principle holds that the ICC should intervene only when national courts are unable or unwilling to conduct genuine investigations (and prosecutions, if appropriate). In practice, complementarity meant that the US could stop any ICC investigation of American forces simply by carrying out a credible investigation of its own. Given the generally high quality of US military courts – and the fact that the US military justice system already dictated the investigation and prosecution of servicemembers responsible for the sort of abuses the ICC was meant to punish – many believed complementarity offered the US meaningful protection from frivolous ICC scrutiny.[139] Indeed, legal scholars described the likelihood of an American soldier ever facing justice at The Hague as a "theoretically possible [but] highly improbable" outcome[140] or even "a virtual impossibility"[141] due to the complementarity principle.

Many of the other delegations in Rome hoped that enshrining the complementarity principle and other safeguards into the Rome Statute would be enough to get the US on board for the ICC. A Canadian lawyer, for instance, argued that American fears of the Court were "a moot point ... thanks to the complementarity provisions."[142] The European Union took a similar stance and issued a statement proclaiming: "The Rome Statute provides all necessary safeguards against the misuse of the Court for politically motivated purposes."[143] Others used more colorful language, such as when a member of the Swedish delegation injected a moment of levity into the negotiations by telling

---

[138] Holt and Dallas 2006, 5.
[139] In addition, the US military has one of the world's premier law of armed conflict (LOAC) training programs, which should reduce the likelihood of atrocity crimes occurring in the first place. For evidence suggesting that America's LOAC training is effective, see Bell 2022.
[140] Sadat 2004, 587. [141] Sewall, Kaysen, and Scharf 2000, 11.
[142] Weschler 2000, 101. [143] Quoted in Orentlicher 2004, 431.

his American counterparts, "We are not afraid of a Dr. Strangelove prosecutor" in reference to Stanley Kubrick's beloved political satire film.[144] The implication, of course, was that the US should not fear a rogue prosecutor either.

These arguments failed to sway the US. The American position was simple: The complementarity principle was useful, but it was not enough since it failed to offer 100 percent protection to American troops exposed to the ICC's jurisdiction around the world. In the eyes of US officials, the complementarity principle, like the ICC itself, might be hijacked for nefarious purposes. Particularly alarming to the Americans was the fact that a panel of three ICC judges – not national authorities – gets to make the final determination on what counts as a "genuine" domestic investigation. Given that US officials were already convinced that ICC personnel would harbor anti-American leanings, they had little faith that the ICC judges would rule fairly on complementarity.[145] Pentagon lawyers consequently "threw their grenades at the concept [complementarity] and insisted on seal-tight ways to immunize all soldiers from the reach of the International Criminal Court."[146]

In the end, the independence of the ICC prosecutor was a stumbling block that repeatedly got in the way of attempts to bring the US into the ICC's fold. On the one hand, most of the world, especially the like-minded group, was committed to maintaining the independence of the ICC prosecutor. They refused to gut the Rome Treaty to accommodate American concerns, even if that meant facing the wrath of the US. In fact, many of them directed their frustration right back at the Americans. Richard Dicker, who attended the Rome Conference on behalf of Human Rights Watch and worked closely with the like-minded group, captured the prevailing mood when he argued, "U.S. concerns about [the independent prosecutor] are so completely misplaced, they verge on hysterical or irrational."[147] On the other hand, the US was committed to Security Council control of the ICC's

---

[144] Scheffer 2012a, 200.
[145] Evidence from other international courts, however, suggests that international judges generally do not let geopolitical biases interfere with their rulings. See Voeten 2008.
[146] Scheffer 2012a, 181.
[147] Thomas W. Lippman, "America Avoids the Stand," *Washington Post*, July 26, 1998.

investigations. As Jesse Helms, the influential Chairman of the Senate Foreign Relations Committee, promised before, during, and after the Rome Conference, the ICC was "dead on arrival" if the US did not receive veto power over the Court's decisions.[148] The impasse was ultimately resolved with a vote, and the US once again was on the losing side.

Endgame in Rome

The US could have supported the ICC, or at least refrained from attacking it, if the American delegation had lost only one of the two key battles in Rome. Imagine, for example, an ICC with territorial jurisdiction but not an independent prosecutor. While the ICC technically would have jurisdiction over American troops while they were on the territory of ICC members, the likelihood of an American ever facing ICC scrutiny would effectively fall to zero if the UN Security Council controlled the initiation of the Court's investigations. The US would always be able to shield its nationals by using its veto power on the Security Council. Now imagine the inverse: an ICC with an independent prosecutor but no territorial jurisdiction over American forces overseas. The US could have lived with this scenario as well. The lack of territorial jurisdiction would mean that the ICC – even if its independent prosecutor harbored anti-American biases – only had the right to investigate the crimes of others. US officials could have ensured that Americans would always remain safe from the ICC's scrutiny by simply not joining the Court.

The US, however, lost both of the negotiating battles. By losing them both, the US failed to eliminate the possibility that its nightmare hypothetical scenario could someday become a reality: Another country's police, acting on an ICC arrest warrant, might apprehend and transfer an American servicemember to The Hague for a trial.

To be sure, the risk of the ICC unfairly targeting the American military was not the only reservation US officials expressed about the ICC. Beyond concerns about protecting American troops on foreign soil, there was a "muddle of arguments from the United States" against the ICC.[149] For instance, some American officials criticized the ICC for infringing on US sovereignty and for failing to guarantee defendants

[148] Senate Committee on Foreign Relations 1998. [149] Schabas 2004, 719.

certain due process protections that Americans would typically receive under the Bill of Rights (such as the right to a trial by jury).[150] These other concerns, however, were secondary to the ICC's perceived threat to America's global military.[151] For example, Scheffer described the exposure of US troops as "our most fundamental concern"[152] and noted that in his interactions with other US government officials "every deliberation turned on the fear of prosecution of American soldiers and officials."[153] Likewise, the Senate – the body that would need to ratify the Rome Statute before the US could ever join the ICC – zeroed in on the same issue. Several key members of the Senate Foreign Relations Committee were "utterly and almost uniquely transfixed by [the ICC's] exposure implications for American troops."[154] Hence, there were other US objections to the ICC, but none of them can explain American hostility to the ICC nearly as effectively as the Court's ramifications for American troops abroad.

After five weeks of exhausting negotiations, Philippe Kirsch, the Canadian diplomat who served as chairman of the Rome Conference, called for a vote. The US tried to introduce a last-minute amendment to modify the ICC's jurisdiction, but other delegations quickly voted to table it and move ahead to the final vote. Following instructions from the White House, the American delegation in Rome voted against establishing the ICC. Nonetheless, the vote passed by an overwhelming margin of 120 to 7. The Americans sat quietly in the conference hall as most other delegations "erupted in applause that grew louder and louder, spilling over into rhythmic stomping and

---

[150] For legal analyses of such objections, see Wedgwood 2000; Cuéllar 2003. Some of the disagreement over the design of the ICC stemmed from differences in the legal systems of common law and civil law countries, ultimately yielding a Court that mixed elements of both systems. On the role of domestic legal traditions in the ICC negotiations, see Mitchell and Powell 2011.

[151] These other concerns were secondary in part because the US successfully lobbied for numerous concessions from other countries in Rome. Even as the US lost the crucial debates on the ICC's independent prosecutor and territorial jurisdiction, the US got its way on many of the details. One member of the US delegation, Theodor Meron, noted that "with just a few exceptions, America's concerns were accommodated." See Weschler 2000, 109. Another member, William Lietzau, similarly concluded that "many U.S. concerns were accommodated [but] the most significant ones were not." See Lietzau 2001, 124.

[152] Scheffer 2012a, 232.   [153] Scheffer 2012a, 192.
[154] Weschler 2000, 110.

hooting that lasted a good ten minutes."[155] The US delegation left Rome completely isolated, as not even one of its NATO allies was willing to join it in voting against the ICC. In fact, America's "no" vote put it in some dubious company: the other six countries opposing the ICC's creation were China, Cuba, Israel, Iraq, Syria, and Yemen.[156]

The US government faced harsh criticism over its decision to reject the ICC. Not surprisingly, the US was roundly condemned around the world.[157] More intriguing was the reaction within the US itself. The *New York Times* and the *Washington Post*, typically bellwethers for establishment foreign policy thinking, both denounced the string of decisions that led the US delegation to vote against the ICC's creation. In the *Times*, Pulitzer Prize-winning columnist Anthony Lewis argued that "the great disappointment at the Rome Conference was the performance of the United States."[158] In the *Post*, Thomas Lippman labeled American participation in the ICC negotiations a "diplomatic trainwreck in Rome."[159] To be fair to the US delegation, however, their hands were tied during the negotiations by inflexible instructions from Washington. At multiple points, Scheffer had to beg his superiors back in DC to allow him to make even minor concessions as the US delegation attempted (unsuccessfully, of course) to find common ground with the other delegations on the structure of the Court.[160] Even those who sparred with the Americans in Rome seemed to recognize this reality. One of Kirsch's deputies, despite his frustration with the intransigence of the American negotiators, noted, "In fairness, they seemed on an incredibly short leash. Clearly, they had their instructions from back home – and very little room to maneuver."[161]

---

[155] Weschler 2000, 108. [156] Scheffer 2012a, 224.
[157] See, for example, the harsh international reactions described in Bosco 2014a, 57.
[158] Anthony Lewis, "At Home Abroad: A Turn in the Road," *New York Times*, July 20, 1998.
[159] Thomas W. Lippman, "America Avoids the Stand," *Washington Post*, July 26, 1998.
[160] In his memoirs, Scheffer recounts seeking permission from White House and Pentagon officials to modify the delegation's negotiating stance. The officials ultimately agreed to Scheffer's request, but the reply from Washington was, "There was blood on the floor of the tank [the Pentagon conference room] over this David, and no one likes you anymore ... Do not even think about coming back to us with another compromise formula." See Scheffer 2012a, 219.
[161] Weschler 2000, 105.

After leading the US delegation in Rome, Scheffer returned home filled with disappointment that there had not been a way to salvage the negotiations and establish an ICC that the US could support.[162] He almost immediately was called to testify before the Senate Foreign Relations Committee. The bipartisan group of senators – in sharp contrast to the American media's harsh assessment of events in Rome – uniformly praised Scheffer and his team for their resolve in opposing the creation of an ICC that did not reflect American preferences. They then proceeded to bash the ICC. Republicans used harsher language, such as when Rod Grams labeled the ICC "a monster" with "no effective screen against politically motivated prosecutions."[163] Jesse Helms likewise insisted that the Court was "irreparably flawed" because it "represents a very real threat to our military personnel."[164] Democrats moderated their tone but shared the same concerns. Dianne Feinstein fretted about a prosecutor with "untrammeled authority" and "a court that frivolously prosecutes Americans or which acts with politics, not justice, as its motivating force."[165] Joe Biden warned that the ICC "raises serious concern about the US forces deployed overseas in countries which are parties to the Court" and declared that rejecting the Rome Treaty was "the right conclusion for our country."[166] Thus, there was a clear political center of gravity in the Senate, shared by Republicans and Democrats alike, that the US should oppose the ICC.

Throughout the entire process of negotiating the ICC, President Clinton – the person ultimately responsible for America's decision to vote against the Court – remained something of an enigma. Rather than engage directly in the process, he largely delegated the task to others. For example, when Scheffer went to the Oval Office to receive a final set of instructions before decamping for Rome, he ended up meeting with First Lady Hillary Clinton rather than the president.[167] Once in Rome, there "essentially was no leadership from President Clinton" to support the efforts of the US delegation during their five weeks of negotiations.[168] Like other veterans of the Clinton administration, Scheffer concluded that the president and his top advisors were distracted by the Clinton–Lewinsky scandal, which hit fever pitch in

[162] Scheffer 2012a, 227–231.   [163] Scheffer 2012a.
[164] Senate Committee on Foreign Relations 1998.
[165] Senate Committee on Foreign Relations 1998.
[166] Senate Committee on Foreign Relations 1998.   [167] Scheffer 2012a, 195.
[168] Scheffer 2012a, 229.

the summer of 1998 – the same time that the ICC negotiations reached their climax. As a result, the day-to-day domestic political churn of the scandal may have "overshadowed the endgame of the International Criminal Court negotiations."[169]

What is known is that Clinton was torn on the ICC. One the one hand, Clinton undoubtedly favored the creation of an ICC in the abstract. Before Rome, he was a strong advocate for the ICC's precursor ad hoc international tribunals for Yugoslavia and Rwanda, and he repeatedly voiced his support for the establishment of a permanent tribunal to carry on the tradition. Creating the ICC under American leadership would have been the crown jewel of his administration's many attempts to manage the world's problems via multilateralism. On the other hand, Clinton's general support for the idea of an ICC was tempered by the details of the ICC that emerged from Rome. Like so many others in Washington, his primary concern appears to have been the ICC's implications for America's global military presence. In his memoirs, Clinton recounts the widespread fear in foreign policy circles "that US soldiers sent to foreign lands would be hauled before the court for political purposes" and acknowledges that he was "concerned about that, too."[170] In line with this view, deeply sourced reporting from just before the Rome Conference suggests that Clinton gave his "blessing to the Pentagon to become the attack dog in the United States' campaign to create a court more to Washington's liking."[171] In other words, Clinton hoped to create an ICC – but only if it was the right kind of ICC from the American perspective.

Two years after the Rome Conference's conclusion, Clinton had another surprise in store for US–ICC relations. On December 31, 2000 – the day that the delegates in Rome had agreed would be the last possible chance for a state to sign the Rome Statute – Clinton decided the US ought to sign.[172] It is not entirely clear why Clinton changed his mind at the last minute. To be sure, he was conflicted about his earlier decision to vote against the ICC, but America's underlying issues with the Court had not been resolved. Clinton's memoirs are frustratingly vague on his decision-making process: "I

---

[169] Scheffer 2012a, 195.   [170] Clinton 2004, 942–943.
[171] Eric Schmitt, "Pentagon Battles Plan for International War Crimes Tribunal," *New York Times*, April 14, 1998.
[172] States would still be allowed to join the ICC after that date, but they would have to go through a separate process.

had been among the first world leaders to call for an international war crimes tribunal, and I thought the United States should support it."[173] One theory is that after reading a December 12, 2000 op-ed in the *New York Times* calling on him to "safeguard humankind" and "reaffirm America's inspiring role as leader of the free world" by signing the Rome Statute, Clinton was determined to end up on the right side of history with regards to the ICC.[174] The op-ed resonated with many in Washington because of the identity of its authors: former Secretary of Defense Robert McNamara and former Nuremberg prosecutor Benjamin Ferencz, who had become the moral authority of the international justice movement in the intervening years. This odd couple – one representing the US military perspective and the other the international law perspective – appears to have swayed Clinton.[175] Regardless of the precise motive, Clinton authorized Scheffer to sign the Rome Statute on behalf of the US at a hastily organized ceremony at UN headquarters in New York.[176]

In signing the Rome Statute, Clinton equivocated yet again. One might expect that America's signature would have been a cause for celebration, but Clinton immediately made it clear that he had no intention of actually joining the ICC. He explained in an official statement that his purpose in signing was instead to put the US in a better "position to influence the evolution of the court." Moreover, he used the occasion to lament the "significant flaws" in the ICC's jurisdiction and warn about the risk of "unfounded charges" against Americans. Clinton therefore would not submit the Rome Treaty to the Senate for possible ratification (with only twenty days left in his presidency, there was no time even if he had wanted to do so).[177] Moreover, Clinton warned future presidents about the risks of the

---

[173] Clinton 2004, 943.
[174] Robert S. McNamara and Benjamin B. Ferencz, "For Clinton's Last Act," *New York Times*, December 12, 2000.
[175] Scheffer 2012a, 237–238.
[176] Israel joined the US in signing the Rome Statute on the last day possible. Like the US, Israel never ratified it.
[177] Even if Clinton had sent the Rome Treaty to the Senate for advice and consent, there was no chance the Senate would have ratified it. As one journalist memorably summarized the situation, the Rome Treaty "faced certain rejection ... by a U.S. Senate where American sovereignty and the protection of U.S. troops are as sacred as motherhood and apple pie." See Thomas W. Lippman, "America Avoids the Stand," *Washington Post*, July 26, 1998.

ICC as it was presently constituted: "Given these concerns, I will not, and do not recommend that my successor submit the treaty to the Senate for advice and consent until our fundamental concerns are satisfied."[178]

Conclusion

This chapter set out to explain the origins of America's fears of the ICC. To do so, I revisited the diplomatic negotiations at the Rome Conference that created the Court. The US lost two key negotiating battles in Rome that convinced many in official Washington that the ICC was bound to become a new foreign policy threat. The first concerned the ICC's jurisdiction: The US wanted jurisdiction based on nationality alone, but most other countries wanted jurisdiction based on nationality and territory. As a result, the ICC gained automatic jurisdiction over all individuals – including those from states that, like the US, never joined the ICC – when they are on the territory of an ICC member. This was an alarming development to the US because its globe-spanning military presence means that American soldiers are uniquely exposed to the ICC's authority. The second concerned the ICC's prosecutor: the US wanted the Security Council to pick the prosecutor's investigations, but most other countries wanted an independent prosecutor. Consequently, the ICC prosecutor received the authority to open his or her own investigations without consulting powerful states. Taken together, these two institutional design choices – territorial jurisdiction and an independent prosecutor – convinced American officials that the ICC would initiate biased investigations and prosecutions that target US troops scattered across the world.

In Chapter 4, I shift my focus to American policy toward the ICC in the post-Rome period. I show that the same underlying issue – the desire to protect members of the US military from the ICC – has played an outsized role in explaining both the extent and the timing of American hostility toward the Court.

[178] Clinton 2000.

4 US Opposition to the ICC
Practice

After the US cast its controversial vote against the ICC in Rome, Canadian Foreign Minister Lloyd Axworthy remarked that the fledgling institution's future hinged in large part on American policy: "The question is whether the United States treats the Court with benign neglect or whether they are aggressively opposed."[1] As I document below, US policy toward the ICC has alternated between the possibilities that Axworthy identified. Aggressive opposition has often been the hallmark of American policy toward the Court, with many officials treating the ICC as a dire foreign policy threat. At other times, however, the US has displayed benign neglect toward the ICC, effectively ignoring the Court's decisions to open investigations or issue arrest warrants. At still other times, the US has even offered support to the ICC, such as after Sudan's genocide in Darfur and Russia's invasion of Ukraine. This suggests that even though American wariness of the ICC's potential to target its troops is a constant, American policy toward the ICC is a variable.

In this chapter, I provide a theoretical framework for understanding variation in US policy toward the ICC. I start by generating a typology of possible American responses to the Court's investigations. Building on Axworthy's assessment, I identify three broad strategies that the US might pursue vis-à-vis the ICC: opposition, assistance, and neglect. After introducing the typology's three strategies, I explain why the US might pick one over the others in response to an ICC investigation. My explanation focuses on two key variables: (a) whether the ICC investigation threatens US troops and (b) whether the ICC investigation advances broader US foreign policy goals. When an ICC investigation presents a conceivable threat to American servicemembers abroad, the US gravitates toward opposition. When an ICC investigation aligns with American foreign policy interests, the US is

---

[1] Senate Committee on Foreign Relations 1998.

predisposed toward assistance. However, reality is not always so straightforward: the two variables can interact in interesting ways to produce neglect or a more ambiguous situation where American officials must choose between competing priorities.

To evaluate the usefulness of the theoretical framework, I document US policy toward the ICC during each presidential administration since the Court opened its doors. The theory does a good job explaining the American approach to the ICC. Presidents Bush, Obama, Trump, and Biden each brought very different personalities and policy priorities into the White House. But they shared one thing in common: a commitment to protect American servicemembers from the ICC. All four of them demonstrated their willingness to oppose the ICC – sometimes subtly, sometimes explicitly – when they believed the Court presented a risk to US troops around the world. At the same time, none of them were inherently committed to opposition. Each president also showed a willingness to employ either neglect or assistance strategies in response to ICC investigations if the circumstances were right. As a result, my argument helps explain why the degree to which the US opposes the ICC waxes and wanes over time and across cases.

Explaining Variation in US Policy toward the ICC

This section provides a typology of potential American policy responses to the ICC.[2] At the outset, it is worth highlighting how my typology relates to the one David Bosco developed in his excellent book *Rough Justice*.[3] While both typologies are interested in describing and explaining the strategies that guide state policy toward the ICC, they do so in different ways. Most notably, our typologies operate at different levels of analysis. Bosco's typology operates at *the institutional level*: it is meant to capture the overall approach that major powers (including but not limited to the US) have toward the ICC. In Bosco's framework, major powers can choose between three broad strategies – marginalization, control, and acceptance – that govern their interactions with the ICC. Notably, states may only

---

[2] On the promise and pitfalls of typologies, see Elman 2005; Collier, LaPorte, and Seawright 2012.
[3] Bosco 2014a.

pursue one strategy at a time. It is not possible for a major power to condemn the Court to irrelevance (marginalization) while simultaneously submitting to the Court's authority (acceptance).

My typology, by contrast, operates at *the investigation level*: it is designed to capture how the US responds to specific ICC investigations. This is a crucial difference. By focusing on the investigation level, my typology allows the US to pursue multiple strategies at the same time depending on the circumstances of each investigation. As this chapter shows, the payoff to my approach is substantial because the US sometimes opposes one ICC investigation at the exact same time that it assists or neglects other ICC investigations. Blanket opposition to the ICC – that is, opposing everything the Court does anywhere in the world – is rare. In fact, blanket opposition only occurred during George W. Bush's first term, a unique period in which the ICC did not yet have an established track record. American officials therefore based their policy toward the ICC on worst case assumptions rather than ICC actions. But ever since Bush's second term – specifically, the opening of the ICC's Sudan investigation in 2005 – the US has responded to ICC investigations on a case-by-case basis.

Table 4.1 lists the three general strategies, as well as the more specific tactics associated with each of them, that the US might conceivably pursue in response to ICC investigations. Assistance is the first strategy.

Table 4.1 *Potential American responses to ICC investigations*

Strategy	Tactics
Assistance	• Enable new investigations: refer situations to ICC via Security Council
	• Support ongoing investigations: share information, enforce arrest warrants, enact pro-ICC domestic legislation, legitimize ICC with words and deeds
Opposition	• Direct attack: target ICC
	• Indirect attack: target states that support ICC
	• Velvet gloved opposition: block Security Council referrals, withhold information, decline to enforce arrest warrants, enact anti-ICC domestic legislation, delegitimize ICC with words and deeds
Neglect	• Neither help nor hinder ICC
	• Save political capital for other US foreign policy priorities

When the US pursues an assistance strategy, its overarching goal is either to grant the ICC the authority to open a new investigation or to help an ongoing investigation reach a successful outcome. Enabling new ICC investigations entails providing the Court with diplomatic support at the Security Council, where the US is invariably a key player given its veto power. The US can help orchestrate a referral of a situation to the ICC by explicitly voting in favor of the referral or at least by abstaining on the referral. To be sure, positive votes and abstentions may carry different meanings on a symbolic level. But they are functionally equivalent in the sense that US declines to use its veto power in each case, allowing the ICC to exercise jurisdiction in a situation where it otherwise would not have it.

To aid ongoing investigations, the US could grant the ICC precisely the same types of support that it gave to prior international tribunals. For starters, the US might use its unparalleled military and policing powers to help fill the ICC's enforcement gap by tracking down, apprehending, and transferring wanted fugitives – just as the US did for the tribunals at Nuremberg and Tokyo. It also might involve putting American pressure on other states to carry out arrests, such as when the US cajoled Nigeria into arresting exiled Liberian leader Charles Taylor and handing him over to the SCSL. Additionally, the US can share information – especially evidence derived from America's unique advantages in satellite, information, and communication technology – with ICC investigators and prosecutors in a fashion that mirrors its copious evidence sharing program with the ICTY. The US also could enact domestic legislation designed to support the ICC, not unlike how Congress passed the Cambodian Genocide Justice Act that provided vital support for the ECCC and Cambodia's broader efforts to reckon with the crimes of the Khmer Rouge period. Lastly, the US may seek to legitimize the ICC by publicly meeting with Court officials and praising their efforts to hold the world's most notorious war criminals accountable.

Opposition is the second strategy. When pursuing an opposition strategy, the US aims to undermine an ongoing ICC investigation or prevent the opening of a new investigation. Several different sets of tactics may be linked to an opposition strategy. Most controversially, the US can wield its military, economic, and diplomatic might to attack the ICC. There are two varieties of attack tactics: direct and indirect. The difference between a direct and an indirect attack lies with who, exactly, the US targets. In a direct attack, the US goes after the Court and its personnel. This might involve imposing economic sanctions or using military force (or at least threatening to do so) against the ICC itself. In such a case, the US attempts to manipulate the cost/benefit calculus of ICC personnel, especially those in the Office of the Prosecutor (OTP), as they make decisions about opening new investigations or issuing arrest warrants in ongoing investigations. In an indirect attack, by contrast, the US targets the ICC's state supporters. This might involve withholding foreign aid, blocking membership in US-dominated international organizations, or threatening to jeopardize the entire bilateral relationship if the state supports the ICC. Regardless of the details, indirect attack tactics are meant to manipulate the cost/benefit calculus of the ICC's backers and ultimately erode support for the ICC's work among states that would otherwise assist it.

In addition to attack tactics, the US also can oppose the ICC by relying on "velvet gloved" opposition tactics. Velvet gloved tactics generally are less aggressive and less controversial than attack tactics, but they nevertheless aim to thwart an ongoing ICC investigation or block the ICC from launching a new investigation. The American policies associated with velvet gloved opposition are often the inverse of the policies the US pursues with an assistance strategy. For example, the US can wield its veto power on the Security Council to block referrals to the ICC and prevent the Court from opening new investigations, withhold information that ICC investigators and prosecutors need to make a credible case in court, decline to use its military and policing powers to help the ICC apprehend suspects, enact anti-ICC domestic legislation, and delegitimize the ICC through its rhetoric and actions.

As I document later in the chapter, there often is a partisan divide in the tactics that presidential administrations employ while pursuing an opposition strategy. Conditional on the US deciding to oppose an ICC investigation, Democrats generally prefer more subtle velvet gloved tactics, whereas Republicans generally prefer more aggressive attack tactics. These different types of opposition tactics track with larger philosophical differences between the foreign policies of the two parties, especially in the post–Cold War period.[4] In general,

---

[4] On the divergent policy preferences of Democratic and Republican elites toward international institutions and the rules-based international order, see Busby and Monten 2012; Gries 2014; Jentleson 2023. On partisan differences in public opinion toward international institutions, see Zvobgo 2019; Brutger and Clark 2023.

Republicans tend to exhibit more skepticism toward international institutions (not just the ICC) and demonstrate a greater willingness to alienate American allies (who overwhelmingly are ICC supporters). Democrats, by contrast, tend to place more faith in international institutions and show higher levels of deference to US allies. The differences between attack tactics and velvet gloved tactics – and therefore between Republicans and Democrats – may seem significant enough to cast doubt on my decision to consider them both part of a broader opposition strategy. To be sure, withholding evidence from the Court is not the same thing as imposing sanctions on ICC personnel. Despite some obvious differences between the tactics, it is appropriate to consider them both part of an opposition strategy. In each case, the fundamental goal is the same: to undermine an ongoing ICC investigation or prevent a new one. The various tactics merely represent different means to the same end.

Neglect is the third strategy. When the US pursues a strategy of neglect, it neither helps nor hinders the ICC. In practice, this means that the US largely ignores an ICC investigation other than perhaps voicing general statements of concern about the unfolding situation of atrocity crimes that the ICC investigation is meant to address. The US simply gets out of the ICC's way as the Court pursues its investigation. A neglect strategy generally receives far less public attention than more high-profile cases of opposition or assistance, which is hardly surprising since one of the defining characteristics of a neglect strategy is *inaction* on the part of the US. Of course, the US might have a weak preference on whether and how the ICC gets involved in a particular case, but the key point is that the ICC investigation never rises to the level of importance where it becomes a salient issue for American foreign policy. As a result, the US does not expend meaningful political capital on responding to it. The neglected ICC investigation falls to the wayside of US foreign policy given the countless other challenges and opportunities that American officials must consider at any given time.

Why does the US select one strategy over the others? My explanation focuses on two key variables that jointly determine the American response to ICC investigations. First, does the ICC investigation present a threat to America's global military? Second, does the ICC investigation help advance broader US foreign policy goals? In what follows, I first describe each variable and then explain how they interact to produce the outcomes identified in my typology.

The first variable is whether the ICC investigation presents a conceivable threat to American troops scattered around the world. In the eyes of US officials, ICC investigations can threaten American soldiers on foreign soil in a pair of ways. Most obviously, the ICC can open an investigation in an ICC member state where US troops are present, putting the conduct of American servicemembers there directly under the harsh spotlight of an ICC investigation. This is the precise scenario that American politicians and policymakers fretted about during the Rome Conference when they tried (and failed) to scale back the Court's territorial jurisdiction. Less obviously, the ICC can present a threat – albeit a more distant one – to US troops when the Court opens an investigation into the conduct of forces from any nonmember state. The US worries about ICC attempts to exercise jurisdiction over individuals from *other* countries that never signed up for the Court because doing so creates a precedent that might be used to target Americans in the future.[5] Indeed, ICC investigations into other nonmember states are vexing to American officials since these investigations call into question the stance that every US president since Bill Clinton has taken: the ICC should never exercise jurisdiction over Americans because the US never joined the Court. In this subtle way, the desire to protect American troops can cast a long shadow over US policy toward the ICC even in situations that ostensibly do not concern the American military.

The second variable is whether the ICC investigation advances broader US foreign policy interests. Put simply, America's ICC policy does not exist in a vacuum. Regardless of underlying American concerns about the ICC unfairly targeting its troops, for instance, a belligerent ICC policy might undermine America's ability to realize its foreign policy goals on other fronts. In some cases, an ICC investigation may even help further American interests. US officials therefore must also consider how the ICC factors into their wider foreign policy objectives. These objectives may be altruistic or strategic.

On the altruistic side, the US might pursue justice for its own sake. From Nuremberg to the present day, Americans – policymakers and the public alike – generally want to see war criminals around the world

---

[5] To be clear, this concern applies to the ICC exercising jurisdiction over individuals from nonmember states because they are on the territory of member states (not because the Security Council referred a situation to the Court).

held accountable for committing deplorable crimes.⁶ To be sure, the US does not necessarily have to collaborate with the ICC to bring war criminals and genocidaires to justice. The US also has the option to support investigations in a different international tribunal,⁷ a newly created international tribunal,⁸ a foreign court exercising universal jurisdiction,⁹ or even US domestic courts.¹⁰ But as "the pinnacle" of the tribunal-building process and the lone permanent international court with broad jurisdiction over atrocity crimes, the ICC often is the natural starting point for conversations about legal accountability.¹¹ Moreover, the ICC sometimes is the only feasible legal venue for addressing atrocities due to jurisdictional hurdles and geopolitical realities – an issue that the US confronted in multiple cases discussed later in this chapter. When the ICC is the only game in town, American officials may set aside their reservations about the Court because they face the stark choice between pursuing justice at the ICC and not pursuing justice at all.

On the strategic side, there are times when the work of the ICC advances American geopolitical interests – even if that is not the Court's intention. In particular, the involvement of the ICC might help the US confront its adversaries around the world. The ICC is based on

---

⁶ Survey evidence indicates that a large majority of Americans (73 percent) believe that the US should participate in international organizations that hold individuals accountable for mass atrocities. See American Bar Association 2018.

⁷ An example is American support for the prosecution of Charles Taylor at the SCSL (discussed in Chapter 2).

⁸ Creating a new tribunal is always an option, but working through the ICC typically is more expedient since there is no need to wade through the tiresome diplomacy of building a new tribunal from the ground up. Nonetheless, the US considered this possibility on multiple occasions, as I describe later in this chapter.

⁹ Several European nations, for instance, have attempted to exercise universal jurisdiction over atrocity crimes committed in Syria. See Anthony Faiola and Rick Noack, "For Syrian Victims, the Path to Justice Runs through Europe," *Washington Post*, March 2, 2017.

¹⁰ The War Crimes Act of 1996 allowed US courts to exercise jurisdiction over war crimes committed abroad if the victim or perpetrator was an American citizen. With the Justice for Victims of War Crimes Act of 2023, Congress expanded the reach of US courts by granting them jurisdiction over all war crimes – regardless of the nationality of the victim or perpetrator – when the perpetrator is present on American territory. This ensures that the US will not become a safe haven for war criminals by eliminating the requirement of an American nexus to the crime (other than the perpetrator entering the US).

¹¹ Kersten 2016, 2.

Explaining Variation in US Policy toward the ICC 139

Table 4.2 *Determinants of American strategy toward ICC investigations*

		Investigation threatens US troops?	
		No	Yes
Investigation advances US interests?	No	*Neglect*	*Opposition*
	Yes	*Assistance*	*Competing priorities*

an attractive set of ideals, such as upholding the global rule of law and ensuring that the perpetrators of the world's worst crimes face accountability, that make it something of a moral authority in international politics.[12] This moral authority can be advantageous to the US because the targets of ICC scrutiny sometimes are also the targets of American foreign policy. When ICC action aligns with American interests, the US has a compelling reason to consider supporting the Court's investigations. A "war criminal" label from the ICC can spark international condemnation of American enemies and help the US build global consensus for diplomatic isolation, economic sanctions, or even military intervention.[13] The US, in other words, may have strategic incentives to aid the ICC for its own ends.

These two variables – whether the ICC threatens US troops and whether the ICC advances broader US interests – interact to determine the strategy that the US selects in response to a particular ICC investigation. This interaction is summarized in Table 4.2. The table's columns capture whether the ICC investigation presents a conceivable threat to American servicemembers abroad. The table's rows address whether the ICC investigation is a boon to more general US foreign policy goals. The cells inside the table represent the expected outcome – that is, the predicted American strategic response to the ICC investigation.

Neglect is likely when an ICC investigation neither threatens American troops nor advances American foreign policy interests. In other words, neglect occurs in situations where the US has nothing to fear from ICC involvement but also little to gain from supporting the Court. Given the relatively low stakes of such investigations for

---

[12] On the ICC's potential to exercise moral authority, see Struett 2012; Dobson and Stolk 2020.
[13] In contrast, America's geopolitical interests work in the opposite direction when the ICC investigates an American ally, an issue I discuss later in the context of the ICC's Palestine investigation.

American foreign policy, the US is unlikely to invest a significant amount of political capital responding to the ICC. The ICC's investigation into 2012 violence in the Central African Republic (CAR) illustrates the dynamics that produce a neglect strategy.[14] Consider my framework's two variables. First, the ICC investigation presented no conceivable threat to US servicemembers. The US did not maintain any military bases in the CAR, and, because the CAR was an ICC member, the investigation did not raise precedent setting concerns about the ICC exercising jurisdiction over nonmembers. Second, the ICC investigation into the CAR did not advance broader American foreign policy goals. The US had no major interests at stake in the CAR, an extremely poor land-locked country in the heart of Africa with a long history of political instability. As a result, the US largely ignored the ICC's CAR investigation.[15] Instead of focusing on the investigation, the US prioritized shutting down the American embassy in Bangui and evacuating American personnel to safety.[16]

Assistance is likely when an ICC investigation does not threaten US troops but does help advance American foreign policy goals. Indeed, this is the easiest set of conditions for American cooperation with the Court because the US has nothing to lose and much to gain when the ICC targets individuals Washington does not like. American policy toward the ICC's Libya investigation illustrates why the US sometimes assists the Court. Not only was there no American military presence on the ground in Libya to cause concern, but Muammar Gaddafi had also been one of the most prominent adversaries of American foreign policy for several decades by the time he initiated a campaign of killing against Arab Spring protestors in 2011. American officials quickly realized that an ICC investigation would be entirely consistent with American foreign policy objectives in Libya. The US therefore supported a UN Security Council referral of the Libyan situation to the ICC, a move that allowed the ICC to open an investigation and issue an arrest warrant for Gaddafi. The ICC's "war criminal" label for

---

[14] This was the ICC's second investigation in the Central African Republic. The Court opened another investigation in 2007 that addressed an earlier bout of violence in the country.

[15] The US did, however, provide funding to the Special Criminal Court, a hybrid tribunal established in the CAR.

[16] Nana Karikari-Apua, "US Diplomats Leave Central African Republic Amid Unrest," *CNN News*, December 28, 2012.

Gaddafi, in turn, helped the US build support for a larger campaign to isolate Gaddafi, impose sanctions on his regime, and ultimately oust him from power.

Opposition is likely, if not guaranteed, when an ICC investigation threatens US troops and does not advance other American foreign policy interests. In such an investigation, the US has nothing to gain but much to lose from ICC involvement. The prospect of an American soldier getting hauled before ICC judges at The Hague has been the nightmare scenario for US officials ever since the negotiations that produced the ICC first began in the 1990s. An example of how this long-standing fear informs the American response to the ICC comes from the Court's investigation in Afghanistan, which put US forces deployed there under the ICC's microscope. As I document later in the chapter, three different presidential administrations – Obama, Trump, and Biden – had to confront first the prospect and then the reality of the Afghanistan investigation. All three adamantly opposed it, though they used different tactics to do so.

Lastly, a more ambiguous scenario – which I label "competing priorities" in Table 4.2 – occurs when an ICC investigation presents a threat to the US military but also helps advance US foreign policy interests. From the US perspective, this sort of investigation presents a challenge because it is helpful in some ways and harmful in others. While many American officials instinctively oppose ICC investigations that could pose problems for the US military, the implications of an ICC investigation for other foreign policy priorities also matter. An investigation with negative ramifications for US troops might conceivably create a windfall for broader American interests. When this happens, the US is forced to weigh tough trade-offs. An example of the competing priorities dynamic emerged in the American response to the ICC's Ukraine investigation. On the one hand, the investigation – especially after the ICC issued an arrest warrant for Russian leader Vladimir Putin – was consistent with the big-picture American goal of punishing Russia for its invasion of Ukraine. On the other hand, the investigation created a troubling precedent for US troops abroad because it gave the ICC jurisdiction over Russian forces in Ukraine. Since Russia, like the US, never joined the ICC, the US worried that prosecuting Russians now might pave the way for prosecutions of Americans later. The Biden administration, as I explain in this chapter, eventually decided to assist the Court after struggling with these trade-offs for more than a year. But the key point is that the American choice of strategy is relatively indeterminate when competing priorities are at play. Whether the US ultimately settles on assistance, opposition, or neglect is a product of context-specific factors.

The rest of this chapter examines my theoretical framework's payoff by assessing the policies that each US presidential administration has pursued toward the ICC. As I document, the theory compellingly explains variation in America's strategic approach to the Court.

George W. Bush

Bill Clinton's decision to sign but not seek Senate ratification of the Rome Statute in the waning days of his presidency left US–ICC relations in the hands of his successor, George W. Bush. Fresh off a bruising presidential campaign and a controversial electoral recount in Florida, Bush focused the earliest days of his tenure on domestic policy, particularly the tax cuts that were the focal point of his campaign. On foreign policy, Bush was an unknown quantity since his only previous political post was the governorship of Texas. Given Bush's lack of experience in the foreign policy realm, many observers looked to his appointments for clues about his foreign policy preferences. Bush's decision to elevate John Bolton, a well-known critic of the ICC and international institutions more broadly, to the important position of Under Secretary of State for Arms Control and International Security, hinted that US–ICC relations were about to take a turn for the worse.[17] Bolton's views on the ICC were unambiguous. When he gave expert witness testimony at a congressional hearing shortly after the Rome Conference, Bolton did not hold back: "I propose for the United States policy ... the Three Noes: no financial support, directly or indirectly; no collaboration; and no further negotiations with other governments to improve the statute. This approach is likely to maximize the chances that the ICC will wither and collapse, which should be our objective."[18]

The Bush administration objected to the ICC for precisely the same reasons that the Clinton administration had done so previously. In a

---

[17] After several years at the State Department, Bush promoted Bolton to the role of US Ambassador to the UN in 2005.

[18] Senate Committee on Foreign Relations 1998.

speech at the Center for Strategic and International Studies, a Washington think tank, Under Secretary of State for Political Affairs Marc Grossman outlined the Bush administration's problems with the Court. The speech echoed the criticisms that Clinton administration officials made in Rome, especially when Grossman bemoaned the "enormous unchecked power in the hands of the ICC prosecutor," lamented that the ICC "dilutes the authority of the UN Security Council," and deplored how the Court "asserts jurisdiction over citizens of states that have not ratified the treaty."[19] The result of these flaws, according to Grossman, was that "our men and women in uniform" are "exposed to the prospect of politicized prosecutions and investigations."[20] President Bush himself shared this assessment. As White House spokesman Ari Fleischer described Bush's view of the Court, "The president thinks the ICC is fundamentally flawed because it puts American servicemen and women at fundamental risk of being tried by an entity that is beyond America's reach."[21] The ICC even made its way into presidential debates during the Bush years. During a nationally televised 2004 debate with challenger John Kerry, Bush voluntarily brought up the ICC and lambasted it as "a body based in The Hague where unaccountable judges and prosecutors could pull our troops, our diplomats up for trial."[22]

Given these sentiments, the Bush administration quickly settled on a strategy of opposition toward the ICC. However, unlike what came later, this opposition was not a response to any specific ICC action. The ICC did not even have a track record of investigations or prosecutions at this point. Instead, the Bush administration initially decided to pursue a strategy of blanket opposition aimed at undermining the perceived ICC threat in every way possible.

The Bush administration's first step in opposing the ICC began even before the new tribunal had opened its doors. In May 2002, the US "unsigned" the Rome Statute. Technically, there was no way to unsign the treaty, but Bolton sent a formal letter to UN Secretary General Kofi Annan informing him that the US had no intention of ever joining the ICC and declaring that the US had "no legal obligations arising from its signature on December 31, 2000."[23] The legal obligations in

[19] Grossman 2002.   [20] Grossman 2002.
[21] Tim Lister, "International Justice Works – but Maybe Not That Well," *CNN News*, May 28, 2011.
[22] Bush 2004.   [23] Boucher 2002.

question referred to the Vienna Convention on the Law of Treaties, which holds that states have an obligation to refrain from any actions that might undermine a treaty during the period where they have signed but not ratified it. By unsigning the Rome Statute, the US was effectively asserting that it was free to attack the ICC. It was a moment of triumph for Bolton and other ICC opponents in the US. In his memoirs, Bolton recounts that he "felt like a kid on Christmas Day" and that his "happiest moment at State was personally 'unsigning' the Rome Statute that created the International Criminal Court."[24]

The ICC officially came into existence later that summer, on July 1, 2002.[25] For the all-important role of prosecutor, the ICC's Assembly of State Parties selected Luis Moreno-Ocampo. The Argentine lawyer was a curious pick in the context of US–ICC relations: the State Department had advanced Moreno-Ocampo's name as a candidate for the prosecutor of the ICTY in the early 1990s (the job ultimately went to Richard Goldstone instead). Some hoped that Moreno-Ocampo's selection might assuage US concerns about the ICC prosecutor "going rogue" since American officials had already vetted him and concluded that he could make a good international prosecutor. In this spirit, Moreno-Ocampo reached out to US officials to try to schedule a meeting where he could explain why American fears of the ICC were overblown, but they refused to meet with him.[26] This window of opportunity to mend fences quickly passed as the US initiated a virulent campaign against the Court.

The centerpiece of American opposition to the ICC was the American Servicemembers' Protection Act (ASPA), a piece of Congressional legislation that Bush signed into law in August 2002. As the name suggests, the motivation behind the ASPA was to protect US troops from ICC investigation and prosecution. Incredibly, the ASPA managed to combine all three of the different tactics associated with an opposition strategy into a single piece of legislation: direct attack, indirect attack, and velvet gloved opposition.

Not surprisingly, the ASPA was an unpopular piece of legislation in most foreign capitals. Along with other Bush policies, most notably the

[24] Bolton 2007, 85.
[25] This date was the product of the timing of state ratifications of the Rome Statute, which held that the ICC would formally open after sixty states deposited their instruments of ratification with the UN.
[26] Bosco 2014a, 87.

war in Iraq, US hostility toward the ICC played an important role in sparking the transatlantic rift that developed between the US and its European allies in the early 2000s.[27] According to Stephen Rademaker, a Bush administration official who helped draft the ASPA, it was meant to stir controversy abroad: "It *was* an objectionable bill ... It was designed to be objectionable because we found the International Criminal Court objectionable and so we tried to deal with it in a way that others found objectionable."[28] There was one place, however, where the ASPA was popular: Congress. The ASPA passed with broad bipartisan support in a 75-19 vote in the Senate.[29] Not only did every Republican vote for it, but the majority of Democrats did too, including prominent Senators (and future presidential nominees) John Kerry and Hillary Clinton.[30]

As mentioned earlier, the ASPA contained a variety of opposition tactics. To start, it established policies of velvet gloved opposition that would survive well beyond the Bush years. Specifically, the ASPA banned all US government entities – not just Congress but also agencies, courts, and police at the local, state, and federal levels – from cooperating with the ICC. Among other things, this meant that the US was legally barred from sharing national security or law enforcement information with the ICC, appropriating funds for the ICC, or allowing ICC personnel to conduct any investigative activities on American soil. However, Senator Christopher Dodd introduced an amendment to the ASPA that created a carve-out for the US to assist the ICC under certain conditions if American officials are so inclined.[31] Dodd's amendment may have been partly a product of his family's history with international tribunals: his father, Thomas, was an attorney who served on Robert Jackson's staff at Nuremberg.

---

[27] Moravcsik 2002; Gordon 2003.   [28] Bosco 2014a, 71–72.
[29] The ASPA was passed as an amendment to the 2002 Supplemental Appropriations Act for Further Recovery from and Response to Terrorist Attacks on the United States.
[30] Senator (and future president) Joe Biden, however, voted against the ASPA even though he supported the US decision to vote against the ICC's establishment in Rome.
[31] The most relevant portion of the Dodd Amendment states that nothing in the ASPA "shall prohibit the United States from rendering assistance to international efforts to bring to justice Saddam Hussein, Slobodan Milosevic, Osama bin Laden, other members of Al Qaeda, leaders of Islamic Jihad, and other foreign nationals accused of genocide, war crimes or crimes against humanity."

The more controversial aspects of the ASPA involved attack tactics – an elaborate set of punitive measures aimed at both the ICC itself and the states that supported it. Two policies stand out in this regard. The first was a clause granting the president the authority to use "all means necessary" to free any American imprisoned at the ICC.[32] Given that the ASPA effectively authorized the president to use military force against the ICC, the legislation quickly became known around the world as "The Hague Invasion Act." To be sure, it was unlikely that a US president would ever order an invasion of The Hague – the text authorizing the president to do so was arguably more of a symbolic protest than a practical strategy. But it nonetheless alienated the US even further from ICC supporters, including many of its staunchest European allies. As one observer put it, "This administration never misses an opportunity to gratuitously antagonize its allies on the ICC."[33] Some, however, thought that the best response to American antagonism was parody. A group of pro-ICC activists, including Benjamin Ferencz, the elderly former Nuremberg prosecutor, manned sand bunkers along the Dutch coast near The Hague to "protect" the ICC against any looming American attack.[34]

The second was a devastating provision targeting state supporters of the ICC: The US would cut off military aid to states that joined the ICC unless they signed agreements pledging never to surrender Americans to The Hague.[35] These agreements, known as Article 98 agreements (or sometimes bilateral immunity agreements), took their name from Article 98 of the Rome Statute, which held that the ICC would not ask a state to arrest and transfer an individual if doing so would force the state to violate any of its other obligations under international law. The US therefore tried to convince other states, including ICC members, to sign Article 98 agreements since this would create a new legal obligation not to surrender Americans to the ICC. This conflicting obligation,

---

[32] For the full text of the American Servicemembers' Protection Act, see Bureau of Political-Military Affairs 2003.
[33] Human Rights Watch 2002.
[34] Chris Stephen, "International Criminal Court to Open in Face of US Opposition," *Irish Times*, March 8, 2003.
[35] NATO members and a handful of other key allies were exempt from this policy. A separate piece of Congressional legislation, the Nethercutt Amendment, also cut off economic development aid to ICC members who did not sign Article 98 agreements with the US.

at least in theory, could prevent the ICC from going after Americans in the first place.[36]

The American campaign to conclude Article 98 agreements was global. When discussing it, White House spokesman Ari Fleischer promised "that the issue of protecting U.S. persons from the International Criminal Court will be a significant and pressing matter in *our relations with every state.*"[37] The US campaign also included a healthy dose of pressure to sign the immunity agreements. According to one Colombian official, "We were made to understand indirectly that it wasn't only the military aid at risk, but also our close bilateral relations with the United States, which are crucial to us."[38] Similarly, Pierre-Richard Prosper, Bush's Ambassador-at-Large for War Crimes Issues, warned Eastern European countries seeking NATO membership that their candidacies might be jeopardized if they did not sign Article 98 agreements.[39] Several dozen countries, particularly those with strong domestic rule of law and normative commitments to the ICC, resisted the American pressure to sign and lost US military aid as a consequence.[40] By the end of Bush's presidency, however, the US had managed to sign Article 98 agreements with just over 100 countries.[41]

In addition to these provocative provisions in the ASPA, the US found other ways to demonstrate its blanket opposition to the Court early in Bush's tenure. Peacekeeping offered an easy way for the US to flex its diplomatic and military muscles. Much to the chagrin of the United Nations, American officials warned before the ICC opened that "if there is not adequate protection for US peacekeepers, there will be no US peacekeepers."[42] The US soon proved that it was willing to

---

[36] Many countries and human rights groups pushed back against the American logic. See Johansen 2006, 311–313. In addition to Article 98 agreements, the US has several other legal tools – such as status of forces agreements and extradition treaties – that might conceivably block the surrender of Americans to the ICC. See Putnam 2020.
[37] Elizabeth Becker, "US Suspends Aid to 35 Countries over New International Court," *New York Times*, July 2, 2003. Emphasis added.
[38] Letta Tayler, "US at Odds over World Tribunal," *Newsday*, October 17, 2004.
[39] Julian Borger and Ian Black, "America Attacked for ICC Tactics," *The Guardian*, August 26, 2002.
[40] For analyses of which countries resisted American pressure to sign Article 98 agreements, see Kelley 2007; Nooruddin and Payton 2010.
[41] Buchwald and Van Schaack 2021, 10.
[42] Serge Schmemann, "US Links Peacekeeping to Immunity from New Court," *New York Times*, June 19, 2002.

follow through on its threat and began withdrawing its forces from UN peacekeeping missions in countries that refused to shield American soldiers from the ICC with Article 98 agreements.[43] At other times, American opposition to the ICC stooped to the level of mere pettiness. In August 2003, the US threatened to veto a proposed UN Security Council resolution condemning attacks on foreign aid workers that was introduced after a truck bomb killed several UN employees in Iraq. Why? The resolution referred to the ICC a potential venue where attacks on aid workers might someday be prosecuted as war crimes. The resolution only passed after the reference to the ICC was deleted at the insistence of American officials.[44]

After such a hostile start to its relationship with the ICC, the US shifted away from blanket opposition during Bush's second term. Instead, the US moved toward case-by-case evaluations of the challenges and opportunities that specific ICC investigations create for American foreign policy. Three reasons prompted this shift in American thinking about the Court.

First, the genocide in Darfur created a dilemma for America's policy of blanket opposition toward the ICC. Starting in 2003, Omar Bashir's Sudanese government and its militia ally, the Janjaweed, began a scorched earth counterinsurgency campaign in Darfur, a region in western Sudan. Pro-government forces killed hundreds of thousands of Darfuri civilians and displaced millions more. To their credit, members of the Bush administration – first Secretary of State Colin Powell and then President Bush himself – took an interest in the conflict and were among the first world leaders to label Darfur a genocide.[45] As a non-ICC member committing crimes entirely within its own borders, Sudan remained outside the Court's jurisdiction absent a referral from the UN Security Council. Given the horrific nature of the crimes in Darfur and the pressure to do something, most Security Council members appeared open to a referral. At least initially, though, the US was unwilling to go along. While the Bush administration very much favored the idea of prosecuting Sudan's leaders, it refused to help

---

[43] The US also pressured the UN Security Council into granting peacekeepers from nonmember states immunity for the ICC's first two years, but the US eventually abandoned this strategy when other Security Council members pushed back.
[44] "U.N. Makes Attacks on Workers a War Crime," *CNN News*, August 26, 2003.
[45] Straus 2005; Hamilton 2011, 37–39.

the ICC do so. As Pierre-Richard Prosper explained, "We don't want to be party to legitimizing the ICC."[46] The Bush administration instead tried to drum up support for a new ad hoc tribunal for Sudan, but American officials quickly discovered there was no enthusiasm for its plan at the Security Council.[47] According to John Bellinger, the State Department's legal advisor, the administration eventually came to accept the reality that the ICC was "the only game in town for bringing accountability for the atrocities in Darfur."[48]

The US therefore had to reconcile its opposition to the ICC with its support for bringing Sudan's leaders to justice. This was not an easy task. John Danforth, who served as Bush's special envoy for Sudan before becoming US Ambassador to the UN, described it in a now-declassified cable to Washington as a looming "train wreck."[49] On the one hand, the US could veto a UN Security Council referral of Sudan to the ICC as part of its broader campaign against the Court, but the optics of this strategy were terrible. As Danforth asked, "Do we really want to raise, yet again, our objection to the ICC – even on a situation we have called genocide?"[50] On the other hand, the US could join other Security Council members in voting to refer the violence in Sudan to the ICC, but that would signal American approval of the Court and directly contradict the policies of Bush's first four years in office. In the end, the Bush administration tried to find the middle ground. On March 31, 2005, it abstained on UN Security Council Resolution 1593, a move that allowed the ICC to open an investigation in Sudan without the US explicitly voting in favor of it.[51] This abstention marked a turning point in the US–ICC relationship, moving the US away from uniform hostility and toward occasional cooperation if the circumstances were right. But it also highlighted just how much the US still worried about the ICC targeting its troops. In exchange for its willingness to abstain, American officials negotiated language into the Security Council resolution that any peacekeepers deployed to Sudan

---

[46] Jonathan F. Fanton, "US Obstructs Global Justice," *Los Angeles Times*, March 29, 2005.
[47] Hamilton 2011, 61–67.
[48] Neil MacFarquhar, "Security Council Members Push to Condemn Sudan," *New York Times*, June 6, 2008.
[49] Danforth 2005. [50] Quoted in Hamilton 2011, 58.
[51] By not vetoing the resolution, the US allowed the other members of the Security Council to refer the situation in Sudan to the ICC for a potential investigation. China also abstained on Resolution 1593.

from states that had not joined the ICC (i.e., American troops) would be exempt from the Court's jurisdiction.

Second, the US slowly realized that the punitive parts of the ASPA were backfiring. Most notably, the decision to suspend military assistance to countries that refused to sign Article 98 agreements hurt the US nearly as much as the countries that lost American aid. The countries that declined to sign Article 98 agreements with the US generally were democracies,[52] which produced a self-defeating dynamic for the US because other democracies tend to be American allies. During a 2006 tour of Latin America, a region where a dozen countries lost US military aid, Secretary of State Condoleezza Rice admitted that cutting off assistance to friendly countries who otherwise would help the US fight terrorists and arrest drug traffickers was "sort of the same as shooting ourselves in the foot."[53] American military leaders, despite their extreme wariness of the ICC, agreed with Rice's assessment. The cutoffs in the ASPA not only suspended financial assistance but also participation in programs that produced mutually beneficial military-to-military ties such as the International Military Education and Training (IMET) program. General Bantz Craddock, the Combatant Commander of US Southern Command, warned Congress in 2005 that sacrificing IMET for the sake of undermining the ICC could "have negative effects on long-term US security interests in the Western Hemisphere, a region where effective security cooperation via face-to-face contact is absolutely vital to US security interests."[54] By the end of Bush's presidency, the US had eliminated all of the ASPA's restrictions on military assistance to countries that declined to shield Americans from the ICC. The other parts of the ASPA, however, remained on the books and continued to prohibit many forms of US cooperation with the ICC.

Third, America's worst fears of the ICC had not come to fruition. When the ICC opened its doors in 2002, the Bush administration's default option was to view the ICC as an inherently threatening institution because of its potential to investigate and prosecute US troops while they were on the territory of ICC members. With no track record to suggest otherwise, it was almost impossible to move US officials away from this viewpoint. By the end of Bush's tenure, however, US

---

[52] Kelley 2007.
[53] Steven R. Weisman, "U.S. Rethinks Its Cutoff of Military Aid to Latin American Nations," *New York Times*, March 12, 2006.
[54] Craddock 2005.

threat perceptions of the ICC had started to moderate. The American fear of a rogue ICC prosecutor that initiated investigations targeting US troops around the world no longer seemed as realistic as it once did. There had been no ICC attempts to "get" American soldiers in Iraq, Afghanistan, or anywhere else the US stationed its troops. Furthermore, ICC Prosecutor Luis Moreno-Ocampo looked nothing like the "international Ken Starr" that American officials worried about in Rome: the ICC did not initiate a single *proprio motu* investigation during Bush's presidency.[55] In fact, the processes leading to the four investigations that started during the Bush years were all unthreatening to the US. Three of them – Uganda, the Democratic Republic of the Congo, and the Central African Republic – occurred when governments asked the ICC to help investigate violence that had occurred on their own territory. The fourth – Sudan – was the result of a UN Security Council referral, which was exactly how the US had wanted ICC investigations to work all along. As Bellinger, the State Department attorney, acknowledged in an interview, the ICC "hadn't done anything threatening to us."[56] As a result, a shift away from the blanket opposition of Bush's first term became palatable to US officials even though they remained skeptical of the Court. Going forward, American presidents – Democrats and Republicans alike – would respond to the ICC on a case-by-case basis.

Barack Obama

The thaw in American hostility toward the ICC that started during Bush's second term continued during Barack Obama's presidency. The fact that ICC investigations had not threatened the US during the Bush years opened up the political space for Obama to assist the Court more deeply than the US had ever done before. As I describe below, the Obama administration notched several "firsts" in America's cooperative relations with the ICC. Nonetheless, the same fears about the ICC that animated the Clinton and Bush administrations lingered during Obama's tenure. Above all, the US continued to worry about the potential for politicized investigations and prosecutions of American troops around the world. Obama's assistance to the Court

---

[55] The first time the ICC independently opened an investigation occurred in Kenya in 2010.
[56] Quoted in Bosco 2014a, 112.

consequently had sharp limits. It only applied in cases where ICC involvement aligned with American interests and presented no conceivable threat to American soldiers. As my theoretical framework expects, the Obama administration's support quickly dried up – or even turned to opposition, albeit a more subtle form of opposition than Bush's aggressive attack tactics – when the ICC appeared to pose a threat to American servicemembers.

As the Obama administration took shape, there were early signs that US–ICC relations were set to shift in a positive direction. Most notably, many of Obama's high-level foreign policy appointments went to individuals who had previously advocated for more constructive American engagement with the Court. Several hailed from the ivory tower: Samantha Power, a Harvard professor, worked on Obama's campaign and then joined the National Security Council; Harold Koh, the dean of Yale Law School, became the State Department's legal advisor; and Anne-Marie Slaughter, the dean of Princeton's School of Public and International Affairs, was tapped for the role of policy planning director at the State Department. Some American officials referred to these new Obama appointees collectively as the "ICC glee club" given their well-known preference for closer US–ICC ties.[57] This enthusiasm for the ICC, to be clear, did not translate to the whole of the US government. Wariness about the Court remained the norm in the halls of the Pentagon, State Department, and Congress. But relative to the ICC skeptics in powerful roles in the Bush administration, it was noteworthy that ICC supporters now held key positions of influence under Obama.

Once in office, the Obama administration wasted no time signaling its openness to a better relationship with the ICC. Stephen Rapp, Obama's new Ambassador-at-Large for War Crimes Issues, announced in 2009 that the US would for the first time attend the ICC's annual Assembly of State Parties meeting as a nonvoting "observer state."[58] In making the announcement, Rapp cautioned that the US was not preparing to join the ICC and that potential flashpoints in the relationship persisted. Echoing earlier statements from officials in the Clinton and Bush administrations, he noted, "There remain concerns

---

[57] Bosco 2014a, 154.
[58] All states that have signed but not ratified the Rome Statute are invited to attend the Assembly of State Parties as nonvoting observer states. The Bush administration consistently declined to do so.

about the possibility that the United States ... and its servicemembers might be subject to politically inspired prosecutions."[59] But at the same time, Rapp's primary message to the ICC and its supporters around the world was clear: "Our government has now made the decision that Americans will return to engagement with the ICC."[60]

This willingness to engage translated into an American strategy of assistance for several ICC investigations. To start, the US helped enable new investigations by providing the ICC with crucial diplomatic support at the UN Security Council. After Libyan leader Muammar Gaddafi initiated a brutal crackdown on protestors during the Arab Spring, Libya descended into a bloody civil war where atrocity crimes were widespread. But the ICC lacked jurisdiction to investigate because (a) Libya had not joined the Court and (b) the crimes occurred entirely within Libya's territory. The US helped the ICC get jurisdiction by joining the rest of the Security Council in passing Resolution 1970. Among other measures targeting the Gaddafi regime, this resolution referred the situation in Libya to the ICC and allowed the Court to open an investigation. This was a watershed moment because it marked the first time that the US explicitly voted in favor of referring a situation to the ICC.[61] As US Ambassador to the UN Susan Rice stated after Resolution 1970 passed, "We are pleased to have supported this entire resolution and all of its measures including the referral to the ICC. ... We think it is a very powerful message to the leadership of Libya that this heinous killing must stop and that individuals will be held personally accountable."[62] Only three years later, the Obama administration once again voted in favor of referring a situation to the ICC. This time, the referral concerned Syria, another case where Arab Spring protests eventually morphed into government repression and civil war, though the Syrian referral arguably was more of a token gesture than a realistic policy proposal since Russia and China both made it clear they would veto the resolution before the vote occurred.[63]

---

[59] "US to Resume Engagement with ICC," *BBC News*, November 16, 2009.
[60] Ibid.
[61] Recall that the Bush administration abstained when the Security Council referred Sudan to the ICC in 2005.
[62] Rice 2011.
[63] Ian Black, "Russia and China Veto UN Move to Refer Syria to International Criminal Court," *The Guardian*, May 22, 2014.

The US also assisted ongoing ICC investigations by enforcing the Court's arrest warrants for the first time. Specifically, the US played a pivotal role in the apprehension and transfer of two wanted fugitives to the ICC during the Obama years. One case concerned Bosco Ntaganda, a leader of the M23 rebel group in the Democratic Republic of the Congo. The ICC issued an arrest warrant for Ntaganda in 2006 for war crimes and crimes against humanity committed during the Congolese wars. Seven years later, Ntaganda shocked the world when he simply walked into the US embassy in Kigali, Rwanda in 2013 and asked to be transferred to The Hague.[64] The US obliged, and the ICC sentenced Ntaganda to thirty years in prison after finding him guilty. The other case involved Dominic Ongwen, a top commander in Joseph Kony's notorious Lord's Resistance Army (LRA). In 2005, the ICC issued an arrest warrant for Ongwen for a litany of abuses, including his role in abducting children in northern Uganda for use as soldiers and sexual slaves. After falling out with Kony in 2014, Ongwen went into hiding. American special forces operating in the region took him into custody shortly thereafter and helped facilitate his transfer to the ICC.[65] The Court found Ongwen guilty and sentenced him to twenty-five years behind bars.

These positive developments during the Obama administration seemed to herald a new era in US–ICC relations, producing a celebratory atmosphere on both sides. At a 2013 conference at the Brookings Institution, for example, officials from the US and the ICC not only shared a stage but also publicly traded compliments in what one observer labeled "an outright lovefest."[66] Fatou Bensouda, who succeeded Luis Moreno-Ocampo as ICC prosecutor, toasted Washington for helping to bring war criminals to justice at The Hague. On the American side, Stephen Rapp reciprocated by calling Bensouda a "good friend" and proclaiming that "every one of the situations in

---

[64] There was rampant speculation on why Ntaganda gave himself up to the US embassy and asked for a transfer to the ICC, but the leading theory is that he was convinced another M23 faction would kill him if he remained at large. In other words, he may have preferred risking a trial at the ICC to risking an untimely death in Africa. See, for example, Max Fisher, "Why Did Infamous War Criminal Bosco Ntaganda Just Surrender at a US Embassy?" *Washington Post*, March 18, 2013.

[65] "LRA Rebel Dominic Ongwen Surrenders to US Forces in CAR," *BBC News*, January 7, 2015.

[66] Kaye 2013.

which arrest warrants have been issued [by the ICC] merit the support of the United States."[67] Around the same time, David Scheffer, who had left government service for a teaching post at Northwestern University, cheered the US for effectively becoming a "de facto member" of the ICC and argued that the Obama administration "engaged the International Criminal Court on so many levels that the days of Washington seeking to undermine the ICC are over."[68]

On the one hand, these celebratory reactions were merited. The Obama administration's assistance led directly to tangible successes for the ICC, such as opening a new investigation and ensuring that wanted war criminals ended up behind bars. On the other hand, the celebrations were premature. The Obama administration's support for the ICC, as my theory predicts, was limited to a very specific set of conditions. The US only assisted investigations when there was no threat to American troops and the Court's intervention aligned with American interests.

American efforts to refer situations to the ICC, for example, were about promoting US foreign policy objectives as much as assisting the Court. Consider the Libya referral.[69] To start, the US was able to assist the ICC in Libya with no risk to its own troops.[70] One of Muammar Gaddafi's earliest acts after taking power in a coup in 1969 was to close Western military bases in Libya, including America's massive Wheelus Airbase.[71] Moreover, Gaddafi had been an American adversary since the 1970s, when the Jimmy Carter administration elevated Libya to the US list of state sponsors of terrorism.[72] Over the ensuing decades, multiple American presidents initiated not only economic

---

[67] Brookings Institution 2013.   [68] Scheffer 2012b.
[69] The unsuccessful Syria referral featured a similar set of dynamics. Specifically, an ICC investigation in Syria could have helped marginalize Bashar Assad, an American adversary, without imperiling US troops.
[70] Moreover, the US did not need to worry about exposing American soldiers to ICC jurisdiction on Libyan soil because Obama borrowed from the Bush playbook and inserted language into the Libya referral that effectively created a carve-out for any US peacekeepers who might be deployed there in the future.
[71] Vandewalle 2012, 79.
[72] This adversarial relationship largely continued until Gaddafi's demise in 2011, though the period after the 9/11 attacks provided an interlude during which Gaddafi rehabilitated his international image to some degree. Gaddafi did this by sharing counterterrorism information with the Western governments and dismantling his weapons of mass destruction program. See Jentleson and Whytock 2005.

sanctions but also bombing campaigns against Libya, most notably the Ronald Reagan administration's targeting of Gaddafi's Bab al-Aziziya residential compound in retaliation for Gaddafi's role in an attack at a Berlin discotheque that killed two American servicemembers.[73] When the Obama administration faced a decision in 2011 on whether to support a UN Security Council referral of the Libyan situation to the ICC, US officials moved quickly to aid the Court and undermine an adversary. The ICC investigation – and the accompanying "war criminal" label that came after the ICC issued an arrest warrant for Gaddafi – isolated the Libyan ruler and cast the conflict as a battle of good (the rebels) versus evil (the Gaddafi regime).[74] Indeed, referring Libya to the ICC was just one part of a much broader American campaign against Gaddafi. Obama also imposed sanctions against the Gaddafi regime, armed the Libyan rebels seeking Gaddafi's ouster, supported a NATO bombing campaign against Gaddafi's forces, and demanded that Gaddafi must "go" several times.[75] Overall, the absence of any threat to American troops and the possibility of advancing American interests in the region spurred the US toward assisting the ICC in Libya.[76]

Similarly, the US decision to assist with the apprehension and transfer of ICC fugitives certainly helped the ICC – but it was also consistent with American interests. Consider the case of LRA commander Dominic Ongwen.[77] At the domestic level, there was tremendous

---

[73] For a history of modern Libya, see Vandewalle 2012.

[74] Kersten 2016, 118–125.

[75] Mark Lander, "Obama Tells Qaddafi to Quit and Authorizes Refugee Airlifts," *New York Times*, March 3, 2011; Barack Obama, David Cameron, and Nicolas Sarkozy, "Libya's Pathway to Peace," *New York Times*, April 14, 2011.

[76] The campaign against Gaddafi culminated with his ouster and death at the hands of the NATO-backed Libyan rebels. Gaddafi's demise prompted a celebratory mood in official Washington. Most famously, Secretary of State Hillary Clinton reportedly quipped: "We came, we saw, he died!" See Scott Shane and Jo Becker, "A New Libya, with Very Little Time Left," *New York Times*, February 27, 2016.

[77] The case of Bosco Ntaganda played out in a different fashion. Unlike Ongwen, the US never had a policy to pursue Ntaganda. Instead, he forced America's hand when he unexpectedly showed up at the US embassy in Kigali and asked for a transfer to the ICC. Ntaganda's actions surprised American policymakers as much as they did outside observers. As State Department spokesperson Victoria Nuland described it, "I don't think that we had any advance notice that he would plan to walk in ... it was something that just happened this morning." See Nuland 2013.

pressure on the US to do something about the LRA, especially after the viral success of the "Kony 2012" movement.[78] At the same time, there was a clear geopolitical motive: The US viewed Ongwen, Kony, and other LRA leaders as a major threat to American security interests in central Africa. The US military was worried enough about the LRA to launch Operation Observant Compass in 2011, which sent American special forces to the region to help the Ugandan military and African Union forces remove Kony and his top lieutenants from the battlefield. In 2013, the US also placed a bounty on Ongwen when it used the War Crimes Rewards Program to offer up to $5 million for information leading to his capture.[79] The following year, Ongwen spilt from Kony after an intra-LRA dispute and fled the group's remote bush hideout.[80] Not long after, American special forces operating in the region apprehended Ongwen.[81] Transferring him to the ICC was a "win-win" for both sides: the ICC got to put a wanted fugitive on trial, and the US got a (legal) way to remove an LRA commander from the battlefield.

When circumstances were less favorable to an assistance strategy – that is, when helping the ICC did not also help the US – the Obama administration's enthusiasm for supporting for the Court waned. The US pursued a neglect strategy in response to five investigations the ICC opened during Obama's tenure: Kenya, the Ivory Coast, Mali, the Central African Republic, and Georgia. Consistent with my typology, the US never made helping or hindering these investigations a priority. While the details surrounding these investigations vary considerably, they all share crucial similarities. Most notably, the ICC investigations neither threatened America's global military nor did the Court's involvement tangibly advance American foreign policy interests. With

---

[78] Schomerus, Allen, and Vlassenroot 2012.
[79] The US offered a similar reward for information leading to the capture of Joseph Kony or Okot Odhiambo, another LRA commander.
[80] By this point, the LRA had largely been forced out of Uganda and into remote parts of South Sudan, the Central African Republic, and the Democratic Republic of the Congo.
[81] There is some dispute over exactly how Ongwen ended up in American custody. The US government provided scarce details beyond describing Ongwen as an LRA "defector" who surrendered to American forces. But independent reporting suggests that a faction of the Seleka, a rebel group operating in the region, initially captured Ongwen. Shortly thereafter, the US collected Ongwen in a military helicopter and flew him to Uganda before his eventual transfer to the ICC. See "LRA's Dominic Ongwen Capture: Seleka Rebels Want $5m Reward," *BBC News*, January 9, 2015.

little to gain *and* little to fear from these investigations, the US was not willing to expend significant political capital on them, prodding Washington toward neglect. To be clear, the point is not that US officials cared nothing about events in these countries but rather that the ICC investigations themselves did not move the needle for the US. Given the multitude of other priorities competing for the attention of Obama administration officials, these ICC investigations were largely ignored.

The Obama administration's ICC strategy shifted toward opposition when the Court's mandate to investigate the world's worst abuses conflicted with America's foreign policy interests or its desire to protect its troops. This pattern is seen most clearly in the two instances during the Obama administration where the ICC conceivably represented a threat to American servicemembers on foreign soil.

The first concerned ICC jurisdiction over the crime of aggression. During the Rome Conference in 1998, delegates punted on the issue of defining the crime of aggression because a handful of powerful states – including the US – objected to giving the ICC jurisdiction over the crime.[82] To prevent quibbling over the crime of aggression from derailing the entire Rome Conference, the participants decided to delay the issue until a future "review conference" that would define aggression and specify when the ICC would have jurisdiction over it. This review conference eventually was scheduled for Kampala, Uganda in the spring of 2010. In anticipation of the Kampala Conference, government officials and legal experts from many states had been meeting informally for several years, often at Princeton University, to craft a draft definition of aggression. The Bush administration, as part of its broader effort to delegitimize the Court, declined to participate in the so-called Princeton process.[83] This left the Obama administration in a difficult position because the US had squandered any opportunity it might have had to influence the terms of the debate heading into Kampala. By contrast, the governments that participated in the Princeton process entered Kampala as a united front that had already settled on a definition of aggression even before the conference opened.

Despite their late start, the Obama administration invested a significant amount of time and energy in the Kampala Conference. The US

---

[82] Scheffer 1999.
[83] On the Princeton process on the crime of aggression, see Barriga, Danspeckgruber, and Wenaweser 2009.

sent one of the largest national delegations to Kampala: representatives from the Departments of State, Defense, and Justice were included, as were members of the Joint Chiefs of Staff and the National Security Council, in addition to Congressional lawyers.[84] Even though it was merely an observer state with no formal power, the US hosted dozens of meetings and emerged as a leader in the conference negotiations.[85] This might, on the surface, sound like an example of American assistance to the Court. But upon closer inspection, the American goal in Kampala was self-interested: to limit the ICC's reach. As Harold Koh and Todd Buchwald, two leaders of the American delegation in Kampala later described it, US officials believed they needed to participate in the conference because they "feared that the Kampala conference might produce an outcome with which the United States fundamentally disagreed."[86]

American fears in Kampala, like in Rome, related to the protection of American servicemembers and political leaders from potentially biased ICC investigations and prosecutions. But the specifics of the debate were different this time. The crux of the issue in Kampala revolved around how to define aggression – essentially starting an unprovoked and unjust war – as a crime. The challenge, as Noah Weisbord pithily summarized, is that "just as one nation's terrorist is another nation's freedom fighter, one state's just war is bound to be another state's unjust war."[87] American officials consequently worried that the definition of aggression emerging from the Princeton process was too vague, leaving room for political biases to creep into the ICC's work.[88] Allowing this to happen, US officials warned, might jeopardize the Court's future just as the US was finally warming to it. Speaking at the American Society of International Law shortly before the Kampala

---

[84] Koh and Buchwald 2015, 294. [85] Weisbord 2019, 106.
[86] Koh and Buchwald 2015, 260.
[87] Noah Weisbord, "Who Started the Fight?" *New York Times*, May 3, 2010.
To this point, the 2003 American invasion of Iraq weighed on the participants in Kampala. Iraq was a poignant reminder that what the US considered a legitimate use of force could very well be interpreted as an illegitimate act of aggression in the eyes of others.
[88] Some legal experts warned that "the definition's ambiguity broadens its potential reach to the point that, had it been in effect for the last several decades, every U.S. President since John F. Kennedy, hundreds of U.S. legislators and military leaders, as well as innumerable military and political leaders from other countries could have been subject to prosecution." See Glennon 2010, 73. For a counterpoint, see Trahan 2012.

Conference, Koh expressed concern that criminalizing aggression could "politicize and weaken this young institution ... If you think of the Court as a wobbly bicycle that is finally starting to move forward, is this frankly more weight than the bicycle can bear?"[89] For many participants at Kampala, Koh's comments were interpreted as a warning that contained both "a carrot and a stick."[90] In particular, future American assistance to the ICC under Obama might be conditional on finding a way to shield Americans from potentially facing investigations and prosecutions for the crime of aggression.

To protect itself from the alleged vagueness in the crime of aggression, the US delegation in Kampala borrowed a page from America's Rome Conference playbook: it argued that the UN Security Council should have the authority to determine whether an act of aggression had taken place.[91] Only then would the ICC be allowed to investigate aggression as a crime. When taking this position, which the other members of the Security Council largely shared, the US had a fair point. The UN Charter already gave the Security Council responsibility for the maintenance of international peace and security, including determining when aggression occurred. But just as in Rome, the American position "scandalized" most of the world because it created a set of double standards.[92] The US and other permanent members of the Security Council, armed with their veto power, would effectively have immunity from ICC scrutiny on the crime of aggression. The rest of the world would not. Many of the Kampala Conference participants, led by the Princeton group, made it clear to the US and other Security Council members that they had the superior numbers and would roundly reject any attempt to give the Security Council control of aggression investigations at the ICC.

With the US position losing out on both the definition of aggression and the role of the Security Council, the ICC's jurisdiction over the crime became the final battle in the negotiations. This time, the American position prevailed. Delegates from small and middling powers, afraid that they might inadvertently create a modern-day League of Nations if they antagonized the major powers any further, agreed to the "Kampala compromise."[93] This compromise sharply

---

[89] Koh 2010.   [90] Weisbord 2019, 106.   [91] Koh and Buchwald 2015, 262.
[92] Weisbord 2019, 103.   [93] Weisbord 2019, 107.

limited ICC jurisdiction over the crime of aggression in two ways. First, it guaranteed that ICC jurisdiction over the crime of aggression would not extend to individuals from nonmember states. This meant that the Court could not investigate Americans for aggression – even if the US invaded an ICC member state. Second, it offered ICC member states a way to opt out of ICC jurisdiction for the crime of aggression. Taken together, the terms of the Kampala compromise ensured that ICC jurisdiction over aggression is considerably more limited than its jurisdiction over genocide, war crimes, and crimes against humanity. For many international justice advocates, the concessions offered to the US and other major powers in Kampala were painful, though it was generally acknowledged that they "were necessary for a law on the crime of aggression to exist."[94] From the American perspective, the concessions in Kampala were a cause for celebration, effectively a "win for the United States [and] a loss for the ICC."[95] At least with respect to the crime of aggression, the Obama administration succeeded in ensuring that the US would remain above the law.

The second instance where the Obama administration opposed the ICC concerned possible ICC scrutiny of American forces in Afghanistan. To be clear, the ICC did not open an investigation into alleged crimes committed on Afghanistan's territory until after Obama left office. The most explicit American hostility toward the Court, as I describe in the following section, took place during the Donald Trump administration. But hints emerged near the end of Obama's time in office that the ICC might soon open an Afghanistan investigation that would put US troops, among other actors, under the Court's microscope.

Afghanistan joined the ICC in 2003, a move that granted the Court jurisdiction to investigate any atrocity crimes that occurred on its territory regardless of the perpetrator's nationality. Afghanistan's decision to become an ICC member meant that Afghanistan's military and police forces, the Taliban, Northern Alliance militias, and American security and intelligence personnel deployed to Afghanistan could all theoretically face ICC scrutiny for their actions. This territorial jurisdiction over Americans on foreign soil was exactly what the US had unsuccessfully fought against during the Rome Conference.

In 2006, the ICC opened a preliminary examination, the information gathering process that can eventually lead to an investigation, into

[94] Weisbord 2019, 109.   [95] Zvobgo 2023.

alleged war crimes and crimes against humanity committed on Afghanistan's territory. The preliminary examination moved extremely slowly. The remainder of Bush's presidency and the majority of Obama's presidency passed without meaningful developments. For their part, US officials in both the Bush and Obama administrations remained relatively quiet about the preliminary examination because they thought there was little chance that it would progress to an investigation. In fact, Obama administration officials reportedly believed the preliminary examination in Afghanistan was merely a "box-checking exercise" intended to prove that the Court was willing to show interest in atrocity crimes outside Africa.[96]

During the final years of Obama's tenure, however, ICC Prosecutor Fatou Bensouda began asking uncomfortable questions. It started with a private letter from Bensouda requesting additional information from US officials about America's controversial detention policies for enemy combatants in Afghanistan. This hint that the prosecutor might someday try to open a wide-ranging investigation in Afghanistan that could sweep up US forces "set off alarm bells in Washington."[97] Obama administration officials rushed to The Hague to attempt to dissuade Bensouda from pursing this line of inquiry, but the bad news continued for the Americans. The ICC's 2014 end-of-year report on preliminary examinations mentioned that the prosecutor was reviewing allegations that American forces abused detainees and engaged in torture in Afghanistan during the Bush years. Even though the report was couched in neutral, bureaucratic language, it nonetheless was a bombshell as it represented the first time the ICC explicitly acknowledged the possibility of investigating American forces.[98] The ICC's 2015 report also mentioned civilian deaths stemming from US bombing techniques in Afghanistan, particularly the bombardment of a Doctors without Borders hospital in October 2015 that killed forty-two people, as possible war crimes.[99] The 2016 report went further still and identified the American practice of transporting captured Taliban and Al Qaeda fighters from Afghanistan to "black sites" in Poland, Lithuania, and Romania, where additional war crimes may have occurred.[100] By the time Obama left office, both public and private statements from ICC officials had "generated significant concern within the Obama

---

[96] Bosco 2014b.   [97] Bosco 2013.   [98] Office of the Prosecutor 2014.
[99] Office of the Prosecutor 2015.   [100] Office of the Prosecutor 2016.

Administration" that an investigation in Afghanistan was imminent.[101]

While the Obama administration had been eager to support some ICC investigations and willing to tolerate others, its response was fundamentally different when the ICC turned its gaze toward a war zone with American troops present. The mere possibility of an investigation prompted Obama to pursue an opposition strategy. As part of its preliminary examination, the ICC asked all countries with armed forces present in Afghanistan for the information relating to civilian deaths and other potential atrocity crimes. The US, its NATO partners, and the US-backed Afghan government all greeted the request with silence.[102] For the Obama administration, declining ICC requests for information offered a subtle but powerful way to use velvet gloved opposition tactics to undermine the Court in Afghanistan. To open a *proprio motu* investigation,[103] the prosecutor would first have to persuade the judges in the ICC's pretrial chamber that there was a reasonable basis to believe an investigation was warranted. Convincing the judges would require high-quality evidence. But with the US, NATO, and Afghanistan all refusing to cooperate with the ICC, the prosecutor was sure to face an uphill battle in convincing the judges to move forward. The US strategy to oppose the ICC in Afghanistan, albeit in an understated way, fit with Obama's general preference to move on from Bush-era abuses without pursuing legal accountability. As Obama put it, "I don't want [Americans responsible for post-9/11 abuses] to suddenly feel like they've got to spend all their time looking over their shoulders."[104]

Overall, American policy toward the ICC during Obama's tenure is consistent with my theoretical framework. The US did not hesitate to assist the Court when its investigations advanced American interests and avoided American troops. But the US otherwise employed strategies of neglect or even opposition. The Obama administration was quite candid about its desire to work only selectively with the ICC and to use the Court as a tool of American foreign policy. The

---

[101] Buchwald and Van Schaack 2021, 28. [102] Bosco 2014a, 163.
[103] Triggering an investigation with a state party referral or a Security Council referral were unlikely options since Afghanistan and the US both opposed ICC involvement.
[104] David Johnston and Charlie Savage, "Obama Reluctant to Look into Bush Programs," *New York Times*, January 11, 2009.

administration's 2010 National Security Strategy stated, "Although the United States is not at present a party to the Rome Statute of the International Criminal Court (ICC), and will always protect US personnel, we are engaging with State Parties to the Rome Statute on issues of concern and are supporting the ICC's prosecution of those cases *that advance U.S. interests and values.*"[105] This conditional approach to the Court produced several instances of meaningful cooperation when US interests aligned with the ICC taking action. But the fundamental American objections to the ICC – most importantly, the risk the Court posed to American soldiers abroad – never disappeared either. Under Obama, the US continued to insist the ICC should not have jurisdiction over Americans, never seriously considered joining the ICC, did not revoke the Article 98 agreements negotiated under Bush, insisted on limiting the ICC's jurisdiction over the crime of aggression in such a way that it could never apply to Americans, and undermined the ICC's attempts to gather information about possible war crimes in Afghanistan. In this sense, there arguably was more continuity than change in US policy toward the ICC during the transition from Bush's second term to Obama's presidency even though the Obama administration's rhetoric toward the Court was undeniably more positive.[106]

Donald Trump

The ICC's decision to open an investigation in Afghanistan dominated US–ICC relations during the Donald Trump administration. The hypothetical scenario that US officials had feared since the Rome Conference – American forces facing ICC scrutiny for their actions on a foreign battlefield – finally became a reality. The Trump administration responded by attacking the Court with an unprecedented level of enmity. Actions that seemed unthinkable during the heyday of US–ICC cooperation just a few years prior, such as American sanctions against ICC personnel and open discussion of destroying the Court, quickly became the norm during the Trump years. As a result, the US relationship with the ICC and its member states sank to a nadir

---

[105] The White House 2010.
[106] On the broader phenomenon of continuity between the foreign policies of Bush and Obama, see Kreps 2009.

unmatched even in the dark days after Clinton's decision to vote against the ICC in Rome or during the hostilities of Bush's first term.

With the benefit of hindsight, a conflict between the Trump administration and the ICC may seem like an inevitable outcome. But that oversimplifies a US–ICC relationship that was very much in flux in 2016. On the campaign trail, Trump famously promised to put "America first." While the precise meaning of this promise was not always clear, the overarching themes of the America First movement were skepticism of international institutions and disengagement from global affairs.[107] Attacking the ICC could be seen consistent with an America First policy, but so could ignoring the Court entirely – which is exactly what Trump did during his first year in the White House. Rather than wage war on the ICC, the Trump administration's initial instinct was to deprioritize the role of international justice and human rights in American foreign policy. For example, the Trump administration nearly shuttered the entire Office of Global Criminal Justice in the summer of 2017 as part of Secretary of State Rex Tillerson's cost-saving initiative, though the office was eventually spared the chopping block.[108] The initial consequences of America First for US policy toward the ICC were therefore modest. There was no meaningful American cooperation with the ICC as the US awaited Bensouda's decision on possibly opening an Afghanistan investigation, but there was not yet overt hostility either.

The US–ICC relationship fundamentally changed in November 2017. After a preliminary examination that spanned more than a decade, Bensouda formally announced her intention to open an ICC investigation in Afghanistan. Bensouda's application to open an investigation focused the majority of its attention on the Taliban's alleged crimes, which were more numerous and severe than those of any other actor. But she also made it clear that nobody would get a

---

[107] Trump either withdrew from or considered curtailing US participation in numerous international treaties and international organizations that his predecessors supported. Examples include the North Atlantic Treaty Organization (NATO), the North American Free Trade Agreement (NAFTA), the Trans-Pacific Partnership (TPP), the World Health Organization (WHO), the Paris Climate Accords, and the Iran Nuclear Deal, among others.

[108] Michael R. Gordon and Marlise Simons, "War Crimes Office May Be Closed in State Dept. Reorganization," *New York Times*, July 18, 2017; and David Scheffer, Clint Williamson, and Stephen Rapp, "The State Department's Retreat in the Fight against Genocide," *The Hill*, July 19, 2017.

pass from ICC scrutiny. Most notably, Bensouda's application stated that she planned to investigate the conduct of American forces in Afghanistan, particularly allegations that CIA and Defense Department personnel committed war crimes as part of their detention and interrogation programs.[109]

The investigation, however, did not begin immediately. Since Bensouda was attempting to open the Afghanistan investigation using her *proprio motu* authority, she needed to wait for authorization from the judges in the ICC's pretrial chamber before proceeding. Despite this delay, Bensouda's decision marked a milestone in the evolution of international justice. The US, despite being a leading promoter of international justice around the world, never wanted international justice applied to itself. This policy of promoting international justice selectively – a double standard in the eyes of much of the world – was a long-standing American tradition that stretched all the way back to Nuremberg, where the US ensured that the IMT's jurisdiction would not cover Allied conduct during World War II. But Bensouda's decision meant that American forces, and perhaps American political leaders too, would for the first time face a real risk of investigation and prosecution at an international tribunal for allegedly committing war crimes.

The prosecutor's request for authorization to open an investigation in Afghanistan appeared to catch the Trump administration flat footed. Some US officials trotted out the old argument, which the Court and all of its member states rejected, that the ICC should not have jurisdiction over Americans since the US was not a member. Beyond questioning the ICC's territorial jurisdiction over Americans in Afghanistan, the Trump administration did not initially have a meaningful ICC policy.[110] The Trump administration was caught unprepared in part because it did not have an Ambassador-at-Large for Global Criminal Justice, the person responsible with navigating the day-to-day US relationship with the ICC and other international justice institutions. When the Trump administration nearly closed the Office

---

[109] Office of the Prosecutor 2017.
[110] Trump administration officials initially turned to banal rejections of the ICC. This reaction from the Pentagon spokesman is representative: "Our view is clear: An ICC investigation with respect to U.S. personnel would be wholly unwarranted and unjustified." See Merrit Kennedy, "ICC Prosecutor Calls for Afghanistan War Crimes Investigation," *NPR News*, November 3, 2017.

of Global Criminal Justice in the summer of 2017, it relieved Todd Buchwald, a holdover from the Obama administration, from his duties as Ambassador. When Bensouda announced her plans to open an investigation in Afghanistan in November 2017, the Trump administration still had not gotten around to nominating a permanent replacement.[111]

While the Trump administration struggled to find its footing, a more forceful response came from outside the government: John Bolton, the ICC's old foe. Recall that Bolton had led the American attack on the ICC during Bush's first term, a period that included the "unsigning" of the Rome Statute, the global campaign for Article 98 agreements, and threats to invade The Hague. Now a fellow at the American Enterprise Institute, Bolton published an op-ed in the *Wall Street Journal* shortly after Bensouda's request to open the Afghanistan investigation. Bolton reiterated the warning that he and other ICC critics had advanced since the Rome Conference: The Court was unable to resist "going rogue" to target American servicemembers. He then extolled the virtues of a belligerent opposition strategy that would allow the US "to strangle the ICC in its cradle."[112] President Trump apparently liked what he read: He appointed Bolton as his National Security Advisor a few months later.

Bolton used his first major address as National Security Advisor to attack the ICC. Speaking to the Federalist Society in Washington, DC, Bolton's speech foreshadowed many of the policies that Trump would later follow vis-à-vis the ICC, even after Bolton left the administration. Concerns about protecting American soldiers were paramount. Bolton described the potential targets of an ICC investigation in Afghanistan as "American patriots, who voluntarily went into harm's way to protect our nation, our homes, and our families in the wake of the 9/11 attacks." In the speech, he also increased the vitriol of the rhetoric that US government officials directed at the ICC, setting a tone that would soon become common throughout the Trump administration and among some Democrats as well. Specifically, Bolton promised, "We will not cooperate with the ICC. We will provide no assistance to the ICC. And we certainly will not join the ICC ... for all intents and

---

[111] Trump did not nominate a replacement until April 2019, when he selected law professor Morse Tan for the role.

[112] John Bolton, "The Hague Aims for U.S. Soldiers," *Wall Street Journal*, November 20, 2017.

purposes, the ICC is already dead to us." Bolton went on to describe a host of policies that the US would pursue "if the Court comes after us," including banning its prosecutors and investigators from entering the US, imposing financial sanctions on its staff, and even using US courts to prosecute ICC personnel who took part in any investigation of Americans.[113]

The Trump administration's opening shot in its attack on the ICC was to revoke Bensouda's visa, effectively barring her from entering the US. This policy, however, was more symbolic than practical. Given the preexisting restrictions on assisting the ICC contained in the ASPA, it was exceedingly unlikely that Bensouda would have been able to obtain evidence pertaining to the Afghanistan investigation from official Washington anyway. Moreover, the revocation of the visa did not block her travel to UN headquarters in New York City, where she occasionally traveled to brief the Security Council on the Court's ongoing investigations, because access to UN headquarters is governed by a separate agreement between the US and the UN. The visa ban nevertheless was a potent symbol. It put the US in some dubious company – Sudan and Burundi had previously blocked ICC staff from entering their countries – and signaled how far the US would go to protect its troops from the ICC. The US also hinted that there was more to come. Mike Pompeo, who had replaced Rex Tillerson as secretary of state and competed with Bolton for the harshest anti-ICC stance in the Trump administration, promised the US was "prepared to take additional steps, including economic sanctions, if the ICC does not change its course."[114]

As the US was ramping up its war on the ICC, the judges in the Court's pretrial chamber continued to weigh Bensouda's request to open an investigation in Afghanistan. After more than a year of deliberation, they finally reached a decision. In a move that shocked much of the world, the judges rejected Bensouda's request on April 12, 2019. The American forces who allegedly committed war crimes in Afghanistan, at least for the time being, would not face ICC scrutiny. Trump administration officials took a victory lap and insisted that the pretrial chamber's decision validated their claims that the ICC never

---

[113] Bolton 2018.
[114] Marlise Simons and Megan Specia, "U.S. Revokes Visa of I.C.C. Prosecutor Pursuing Afghan War Crimes," *New York Times*, April 5, 2019.

should have tried to assert jurisdiction over Americans in the first place.[115]

A closer reading of the pretrial chamber's decision, however, is at odds with the Trump administration's interpretation.[116] To start, the judges reaffirmed that the ICC had jurisdiction over all parties – including Americans – while they were on the territory of Afghanistan. Furthermore, the pretrial chamber did not dispute Bensouda's assertion that there was a reasonable basis to believe that American military and intelligence personnel in Afghanistan may have committed war crimes. Disputing Bensouda's assessment would have been difficult given that American officials themselves had previously admitted to much of the behavior Bensouda hoped to investigate. President Obama, for example, publicly acknowledged that "we tortured some folks."[117] The Senate Select Committee on Intelligence produced a report of over 6,000 pages, commonly known as "the torture report," on the CIA's detention and interrogation programs that provided evidence supporting Obama's off-the-cuff admission. The full report remains classified, but a declassified summary demonstrates the US routinely engaged in torture as part of its War on Terror, including in Afghanistan.[118] The US military also implicitly acknowledged its responsibility for a substantial number of civilian deaths in Afghanistan stemming from American bombing techniques, such as when it offered condolence payments of $6,000 to the families of each person killed when the US bombed the Doctors without Borders hospital.[119]

The pretrial chamber also rejected the argument that Americans in Afghanistan should be shielded from the ICC under the principle of complementarity. Recall that the ICC is a court of last resort that is supposed to back off whenever national courts initiate genuine

---

[115] Trump personally hailed the decision – perversely, in the eyes of his critics – as "a major international victory, not only for [American] patriots, but for the rule of law." See Carol Morella, "Trump Administration Applauds International Court's Decision to Abandon Afghan War Crimes Probe," *Washington Post*, April 12, 2019.
[116] Pre-Trial Chamber 2019.
[117] Paul Lewis, "Obama Admits CIA 'Tortured Some Folks' but Stands by Brennan over Spying," *The Guardian*, August 1, 2014.
[118] Senate Select Committee on Intelligence 2014.
[119] Laura Wagner, "16 U.S. Service Members Disciplined in Mistaken Airstrikes on Afghan Hospital," *NPR News*, April 28, 2016.

investigations or prosecutions.[120] But the US only prosecuted a handful of soldiers for abuses related to its controversial detention and interrogation system. More often than not, the US military justice system proved reluctant to punish its own forces, even in cases that resulted in the death of detainees.[121] Trump further undermined the complementarity defense by torpedoing some of the few attempts that US military tribunals did, in fact, make to prosecute their own soldiers for war crimes in Afghanistan. Specifically, Trump pardoned two members of the Army, Clint Lorance and Matthew Golsteyn, who the US military justice system had already charged with war crimes for shooting unarmed Afghan civilians.[122] Trump's pardons were egregious enough that his own appointees to Secretary of Defense and Army Secretary pushed back against his decision on the grounds that the pardons clashed with the military code of justice and set a poor precedent for other troops.[123]

Given all this, why did the pretrial chamber judges reject Bensouda's request? The judges relied on a contested concept known as the interests of justice. They concluded that the Afghanistan investigation was "doomed to failure" because all the relevant parties – the Afghan government, the Taliban, and above all the US – staunchly opposed it.[124] Since the investigation was unlikely to produce any convictions, it would not serve the interests of justice to approve Bensouda's application. The ICC, they reasoned, would be better off devoting its limited resources to other investigations that had better prospects for putting criminals behind bars. The pretrial chamber's decision sparked

---

[120] In an interview, ICC President Chile Eboe-Osuji reiterated that the Court was willing to step back if the US proved willing to investigate its own abuses:

> If the U.S. considers that it is adequately addressing the allegations of crimes through its own courts, or that they have done that already, then this is the moment to inform the Court and bring that question before the judges. There is a clear legal mechanism for doing that, and so far the United States has not availed itself of that path.

See Tom O'Connor, "ICC President Condemns 'Unprecedented' US Attack on International Court," *Newsweek*, June 22, 2020.

[121] Tim Golden, "In US Report, Brutal Details of 2 Afghan Inmates' Deaths," *New York Times*, May 20, 2005.

[122] Trump also reversed the demotion of Edward Gallagher, a Navy SEAL, after his trial for allegedly committing war crimes in Iraq.

[123] Dave Philipps, "Trump Clears Three Service Members in War Crimes Cases," *New York Times*, November 15, 2019.

[124] Pre-Trial Chamber 2019.

controversy. On the one hand, many in the human rights community castigated the ICC for caving to the Trump administration's threats.[125] On the other hand, some legal scholars saw merit in the decision. Alex Whiting, for example, argued that the decision wisely recognized the "growing consensus that the ICC is stretched too thin and that it should consider ways to focus its energies and resources in places where it could succeed."[126]

Bensouda promptly appealed the pretrial chamber's decision. On March 5, 2020, the ICC's appeals chamber sided with Bensouda after ruling that the pretrial chamber erred in its reasoning about the interests of justice.[127] The appeals chamber therefore authorized the prosecutor to launch an investigation covering crimes committed in Afghanistan since May 1, 2003, the date that Afghanistan joined the Court. After a long and winding road, the ICC's Afghanistan investigation was finally open.

The US responded by accusing the ICC of anti-American bias. John Bolton was out of the Trump administration by this point due to his disagreements with the president on American policy toward Iran, North Korea, Cuba, and Venezuela, among others. But there were many other officials in the Trump administration who were eager to carry on the attacks against the ICC that Bolton had set in motion. Just hours after the appeals chamber permitted the ICC's Afghanistan investigation to commence, Secretary of State Mike Pompeo denounced the decision as a "truly breathtaking action by an unaccountable, political institution masquerading as a legal body" and warned that the ICC was nothing more than "a vehicle for political vendettas."[128] Ambassador-at-Large for Global Criminal Justice Morse Tan labeled Bensouda "a renegade prosecutor" and described the ICC as "corrupt" and "politicized."[129] Attorney General William Barr argued that the investigation "validates our longstanding concern [that] the ICC" would pursue "politically motivated investigations of American servicemembers."[130] If these critiques sound familiar, it is

---

[125] Amnesty International 2019.   [126] Whiting 2019.
[127] The appeals chamber concluded that the pretrial chamber should leave determinations about the interests of justice to the prosecutor.
[128] Pompeo 2020a.
[129] Edith M. Lederer, "Over 70 ICC Nations Support Court and Oppose US Sanctions," *Associated Press*, November 2, 2020.
[130] Department of State 2020.

because American officials had been making similar arguments ever since the Clinton administration lost control of the negotiations at the Rome Conference.

On June 11, 2020, the American attack on the ICC reached a new level when President Trump issued an executive order to sanction the Court's personnel. Invoking national emergency authority, Trump determined that the Afghanistan investigation "constitutes an unusual and extraordinary threat to the national security and foreign policy of the United States." The executive order's goal was straightforward: to "impose tangible and significant consequences on those responsible for the ICC's transgressions."[131] While Trump's executive order created a legal basis for the US to impose sanctions, no sanctions were implemented until the Secretary of State identified specific targets. Secretary Pompeo soon made the sanctions a reality by listing Fatou Bensouda and one of her top staffers, Phakiso Mochochoko, as "specially designated nationals" on the Treasury Department's Office of Foreign Assets Control (OFAC) registry. The consequences of such a designation include asset freezes, visa restrictions, and the risk of designation for anyone else who materially assists the designated individual.

When announcing the sanctions, Pompeo left no doubt that the imperative of protecting US troops around the world from the ICC was the primary cause of America's vitriol toward the Court. Speaking to the press, Pompeo remarked:

> As many of you know, I have an important affection for our servicemen and women – I'm a veteran myself – and here's a scenario that I think about a lot: Imagine an American soldier, sailor, airman, Marine, or an intelligence officer is on leave with his or her family, maybe on a beach in Europe. And over the course of two decades or more, this soldier honorably defended America in Anbar Province, in Kandahar, taking down terrorists. Then suddenly, that vacation turns into a nightmare. The European country's national police takes that soldier into custody, detaining him or her on politically motivated charges. A prison sentence abroad is a distinct possibility. A spouse behind bars for defending freedom. A son or daughter robbed of their mom or dad, all on the initiative of some prosecutor in the Netherlands.[132]

The fact that the ICC had never done anything similar in any of its other investigations – such as requesting the arrest of a vacationing soldier – did not assuage the Trump administration's concerns.

[131] Office of the President 2020.   [132] Department of State 2020.

The global reaction to America's sanctions on the ICC was fiercely negative. The overwhelming majority of ICC member states issued at least one, if not multiple, statements in support of the Court and/or in opposition to the US.[133] The sanctions also drove a wedge between the US and its allies, who were incensed enough to ignore standard diplomatic niceties when discussing the sanctions. For example, the European Union's highest ranking foreign policy official criticized America's policy as "unacceptable and unprecedented" and promised that Europeans would "resolutely defend [the ICC] from any attempts aimed at obstructing the course of justice."[134] For their part, dozens of NGOs signed a joint letter expressing their "deep concern" over the sanctions and urging the White House to reverse course. The letter went on to note that the American attack on the ICC was "so alarming" because the US had turned a weapon designed for terrorists, drug cartels, and war criminals on legal professionals at the very institution meant to prosecute those bad actors.[135] Even America's adversaries used the sanctions against it. China, for example, described the US sanctions as "bullying practices" that are "inconsistent with international law."[136] While not typically known for defending the ICC, Chinese leaders were locked in a fierce trade war with the Trump administration and recognized that the unpopular sanctions offered an easy way to level criticism at American foreign policy.

The Trump administration hoped its sanctions would force the ICC to back off its Afghanistan investigation, but Bensouda promised to "stand firm" in the face of American pressure.[137] In response, US officials signaled that even more attacks might be on the way. Ambassador Tan vowed that the Trump administration would "do anything necessary to ensure that American personnel are not hauled before the International Criminal Court" and threatened to "seek the dissolution of the Court itself."[138] Precisely how the US planned to dissolve the ICC remained unclear, but it nonetheless was an ominous development. The US, however, never followed through on Tan's threat. Only a few days later, Americans headed to the polls for the

---

[133] Broache and Reed 2023, 2.   [134] Borrell 2020.
[135] Human Rights Watch 2020.   [136] Bing 2020.
[137] Salem Solomon, "Facing US Sanctions, ICC Prosecutor Pledges to Continue 'Without Fear or Favor,'" *Voice of America*, June 17, 2020.
[138] Edith M. Lederer, "Over 70 ICC Nations Support Court and Oppose US Sanctions," *Associated Press*, November 2, 2020.

2020 presidential election and voted Joe Biden into the White House. The Trump administration devoting its waning days to contesting the election results, a diversion that likely spared the ICC another American onslaught.

In conclusion, one of the challenges that the Trump presidency presents to scholars of foreign policy is untangling Trump's idiosyncratic personality from broader political forces in the US.[139] On the one hand, Trump brought a unique worldview into the White House, making him something of an outlier in terms of his preferences for how America engaged with the rest of the world.[140] On the other hand, even some of Trump's harshest critics have acknowledged that his first term did not alter US foreign policy as drastically as they initially feared.[141] In terms of the US–ICC relationship, Trump may have been unique in the specific means – particularly the aggressive sanctions and the extreme rhetoric – that he used to oppose the ICC. But the general strategic decision to oppose the ICC had little to do with Trump's individual foibles. In fact, there are three compelling reasons to think that American opposition to the ICC's investigation in Afghanistan was not just about Trump.

First, Trump and his America First supporters were not alone in opposing the Afghanistan investigation. Republicans and Democrats alike found the ICC's decision to open an investigation in Afghanistan objectionable. For example, in May 2020 – just before Trump signed the executive order that authorized sanctions – members of the House of Representatives penned a public letter denouncing the ICC's Afghanistan inquiry.[142] The letter warned that the investigation served as a powerful example of "how politics have been infused into the judicial process and distorted the purposes for which the Court was established." It then urged Secretary Pompeo to "marshal a diplomatic initiative with likeminded countries who are members of the ICC to

---

[139] On the challenge of isolating the effects of individual leaders in a world full of structural forces, see Krcmaric, Nelson, and Roberts 2020.
[140] Schake 2016.
[141] Cohen 2024. The early days of Trump's second term, however, appear on track to reshape American foreign policy dramatically, especially in the economic realm.
[142] The letter also warned the ICC against opening an investigation in Palestine that would scrutinize the actions of America's ally, Israel. I discuss this investigation later in this chapter.

call on the ICC to cease its politically motivated investigations."[143] The letter was wildly popular in the halls of Congress as 262 House members signed it. It also was a bipartisan affair: 93 Democrats and 169 Republicans added their names. After the Trump administration imposed sanctions, politicians on both sides of the aisle cheered the decision. Elaine Luria, a Democratic member of the House who co-sponsored the letter, took credit for her role in organizing opposition to the ICC, noting, "It's hard to get two members of Congress to agree on anything, let alone more than 260."[144] Likewise, Tom Cotton, a Republican member of the Senate, gleefully noted that "Trump lowered the boom on them [the ICC]."[145] Even in an era of extreme partisanship, opposing the ICC's Afghanistan investigation was one area where Republicans and Democrats could still find common ground.

Second, if someone other than Trump had been president, the broad counters of US policy toward the Court would have been similar. The Afghanistan investigation was the precise scenario that every American president had fretted about since Rome. An opposition strategy was virtually guaranteed regardless of who was in the White House. Indeed, it is hard to imagine any presidential administration employing a neglect or assistance strategy in response to an ICC investigation that directly threatened American troops. Imagine, for example, a counterfactual in which Hillary Clinton defeated Donald Trump in the 2016 election. Clinton had a long history of worrying about the ICC's potential to target American soldiers around the world. As the first lady, she reportedly expressed her amazement during the negotiations in Rome that other members of the UN Security Council did not find the ICC as "abhorrent" as the US did.[146] Years later, as a senator, Clinton voted in favor of the American Servicemembers' Protection Act, which authorized the president to invade The Hague in response to a scenario like Afghanistan. A Clinton presidential administration therefore would likely have responded forcefully to the ICC's Afghanistan probe. To be sure, the details of Clinton's response may have been different than Trump's in the sense that she might have favored velvet gloved tactics over attack tactics. But the broader

---

[143] Luria and Gallagher 2020.   [144] Office of Representative Elaine Luria 2020.
[145] Marc A. Thiessen, "It's Not Just Netanyahu. The ICC Wants to Prosecute U.S. Lawmakers Too," *Washington Post*, May 24, 2024.
[146] Scheffer 2012a, 196.

strategy of opposing the ICC in Afghanistan almost certainly would have been the same.

Third, Trump's attacks on the ICC were confined to the specific circumstances where my theory expects American opposition. In this sense, the Trump administration followed the case-by-case evaluations of US policy toward ICC investigations established in Bush's second term and continued during Obama's tenure.[147] Two key pieces of evidence – over-time variation and cross-case variation – both show that Trump was not inherently committed to attacking the ICC. First, the Trump administration effectively ignored the ICC during its first year in office and only attacked the ICC after the Court opened an investigation that put US troops at risk. Second, Trump neglected the other two investigations the ICC opened during his tenure. Specifically, the ICC opened investigations in response to Myanmar's violence against its Rohingya population and Burundi's attacks on civilians protesting the ruling regime's abolition of term limits. These investigations – which neither threatened US troops nor advanced American interests in a meaningful way – never became salient foreign policy issues like the Afghanistan investigation. As a result, the Trump administration did not expend political capital helping or hindering the ICC in these cases. Overall, this pattern suggests that the difference in the ICC policies of Trump and his predecessors was more about style than substance.[148]

Joe Biden

When Joe Biden entered the White House in January 2021, he inherited a US–ICC relationship in disarray over the Afghanistan investigation. But the tumult in the relationship did not stop there: the ICC opened four new investigations during Biden's first fourteen months in office. By the time he left the White House, the Court had

---

[147] In the Trump administration's waning days, American officials flirted with the idea of returning to a blanket opposition strategy akin to Bush's first term, such as when Ambassador-at-Large for Global Criminal Justice Morse Tan threatened to seek the dissolution of the ICC. But these ideas never translated into policy because Trump lost the 2020 presidential election to Biden only a few days later.

[148] Trump's second term, however, may represent a more substantive shift away from the policies of his predecessors. I return to this issue in the conclusion.

made two of the largest gambits in its history by going after Russia's Vladimir Putin and Israel's Benjamin Netanyahu. Though only a single term, Biden's presidency packed in a remarkable number of twists and turns for the US–ICC relationship. Biden's tenure not only witnessed the full gamut of American responses – opposition, assistance, and neglect – but it also exposed American double standards more profoundly than any other president's time in office.

Biden's initial task was crafting a strategy to manage the fallout from the sanctions Trump imposed on the ICC as retaliation for the Afghanistan probe. The American sanctions on ICC personnel, as described previously, were wildly unpopular around the world. Just days after entering the White House, the Biden team issued a statement indicating that it was reviewing whether the sanctions policy should continue, noting, "Much as we disagree with the ICC's action ... the sanctions will be thoroughly reviewed as we determine our next steps."[149] After a review that lasted many months – too long in the eyes of some ICC supporters – Biden finally revoked Trump's executive order and the accompanying sanctions. The decision to terminate the sanctions was cheered around the world, including at The Hague, where Bensouda spoke of a potential "reset" in the US–ICC relationship.[150] At the same time, however, Biden made it abundantly clear that his administration still opposed the Court's investigation in Afghanistan. When announcing the removal of the sanctions, Biden stressed that the US "continues to object to the International Criminal Court's assertions of jurisdiction over [Americans] and ... will vigorously protect current and former United States personnel from any attempts to exercise such jurisdiction."[151] In other words, the difference between the policies of Biden and Trump was at the tactical, not the strategic, level.

Biden's decision to withdraw the sanctions reflected a pair of political dynamics. To start, the sanctions were a poor mechanism for protecting American servicemembers from the ICC. The sanctions not only failed to convince the ICC to drop the Afghanistan investigation – the Trump administration's original goal – but they also

---

[149] Simon Lewis, "Biden Administration to Review Sanctions on International Criminal Court Officials," *Reuters*, January 26, 2021.
[150] Mike Corder, "ICC Prosecutor Sees 'Reset' under Biden," *Associated Press*, June 14, 2021.
[151] Office of the President 2021b.

hampered American foreign policy across the board. Several observers anticipated this outcome almost as soon as the US decided to target the Court. The editorial board of *The Guardian*, for instance, warned that America's standing in the world would be the ultimate victim of the sanctions, correctly predicting that "this attack may be more damaging to America's reputation and authority than it will be to the Court's."[152] Likewise, an open letter from 175 international law experts described the sanctions as "wrong in principle, contrary to American values, and prejudicial to U.S. national security."[153] Another letter, this one signed by several former US policymakers in the international justice space from both Republican and Democratic administrations – including some who had sparred with the ICC in the past – labelled the sanctions "reckless" and argued that there were "far better" ways to protect Americans from unwanted ICC investigations.[154] The Biden administration agreed with these outside assessments. In his first comments after the sanctions were removed, Secretary of State Anthony Blinken called them "ineffective."[155]

The other dynamic that prompted Biden to discard the sanctions was his goal of rebuilding American alliances in the post-Trump era. Repairing alliances was a key theme of both Biden's inaugural address and his first major foreign policy speech, where he proclaimed that "America's alliances are our greatest asset."[156] Given that most of America's allies were steadfast ICC supporters, revoking the sanctions was an easy way for Biden to win back some goodwill. In fact, Biden had a long history of balancing his personal concerns about the ICC with his desire to respect the wishes of American allies. Recall, for example, that Biden supported the decision to vote against the ICC's creation in 1998, calling it "the right conclusion for our country."[157] When the Senate debated the anti-ICC measures contained in the ASPA in 2002, Biden again voiced his displeasure with the Court, calling ICC jurisdiction over Americans "wrong" and asserting that the US "must

---

[152] Editorial Board, "The Guardian View on Trump and the International Criminal Court: An Attack on Human Rights," *The Guardian*, June 21, 2020.
[153] Ellen Nakashima and Carol Morello, "Lawyers Urge Trump to Rescind Sanctions and Travel Bans for International Criminal Court," *Washington Post*, June 29, 2020.
[154] Buchwald et al. 2020. [155] Blinken 2021b.
[156] Office of the President 2021a.
[157] Senate Committee on Foreign Relations 1998.

protect our servicemen from the jurisdiction of this tribunal."[158] Despite his objections to the ICC, Biden ultimately ended up in the minority of senators who voted against the ASPA and its threats to invade The Hague. Why? In Biden's own words: "Many of our closest allies in Europe are strong supporters of this Court. This legislation will further complicate our relationship with those friends."[159] When Biden had to choose between keeping or discarding US sanctions against the ICC in 2021, he once again deferred to American allies by pulling back from direct attacks on the Court. American opposition to the Afghanistan probe, Biden signaled, would rely on velvet gloved tactics instead.

The ICC, like the US, experienced a change of leadership in 2021: Bensouda's nine-year term as prosecutor ended in June. Her replacement, Karim Khan, brought a new perspective to the role, arguing that the "time for change [at the ICC] is ripe" and pledging to refocus the Court on cases where the chances of successful prosecution were relatively high.[160] As one of his first major decisions, Khan announced that his office would modify the parameters of its Afghanistan investigation.[161] Specifically, the Court would "deprioritize" the alleged crimes of American personnel and Afghan governmental forces so that it could devote its "limited resources" to investigating the more severe crimes of the Taliban and the Islamic State.[162] Like the commentary that surrounded the pretrial chamber's initial decision to reject Bensouda's request to open an investigation in 2019, observers debated whether Khan made a mistake by letting the US "off the hook" or a smart choice by allocating the Court's scarce resources in the most efficient manner.[163] Whatever the merits of Khan's decision, both the ICC and the US seemed eager to move on from the hostilities that emerged out of the Afghanistan investigation. With the Afghanistan standoff over, the key question was what came next for American policy toward the Court. The Biden administration's answer

---

[158] Congressional Record – Senate 2002.
[159] Congressional Record – Senate 2002.
[160] "ICC Prosecutor Defends Dropping US from Afghan War Crime Probe," *Al Jazeera*, December 6, 2021.
[161] The investigation was briefly put on hold as Afghanistan requested that the ICC defer to its national courts. Khan rejected this request and resumed the investigation at the same time he announced its more limited scope.
[162] Office of the Prosecutor 2021.   [163] See, for example, Zvobgo 2021b.

came from Linda Thomas-Greenfield, the new US Ambassador to the UN: "There may be exceptional cases where we consider cooperating with the Court as we sometimes have in the past. We will weigh the interests at stake on a case-by-case basis."[164] In other words, Biden planned to continue the policy of his predecessors by making case-by-case assessments of whether the US should assist, oppose, or neglect ICC investigations.

A crucial test for Biden's ICC policy emerged in late February 2022. Vladimir Putin announced a "special military operation" as Russian troops poured across the border into Ukraine and Russian airstrikes targeted Ukrainian cities, setting off the largest interstate war in Europe since World War II. On March 2, only a week into the hostilities, Khan announced that the ICC was opening an investigation into potential atrocity crimes committed on the territory of Ukraine. Notably, neither Ukraine nor Russia was an ICC state party.[165] The ICC nonetheless had jurisdiction over atrocity crimes in Ukraine because Ukraine made an Article 12(3) declaration after Russia's prior incursion into Crimea and eastern Ukraine in 2014. This declaration, named after Article 12(3) of the Rome Statute, allows non-state parties to grant the ICC jurisdiction over crimes committed on their territory without going through the standard ratification process. In effect, it made Ukraine a de facto member of the ICC.[166]

The Ukraine investigation created a dilemma for the US. For the first time, an ICC investigation advanced America's broader foreign policy interests while it simultaneously created a potential threat to US troops – the "competing priorities" scenario in my theoretical framework. On the one hand, the Ukraine investigation would help the US punish a longtime American adversary, Vladimir Putin, for launching Russia's unprovoked attack on Ukraine. The case for supporting the ICC became even more compelling after the ICC sent shockwaves around the world by issuing an arrest warrant for Putin, among other Russian officials. The ICC's decision to go after Putin bolstered attempts from the Biden administration to cast Putin as a "war

---

[164] Senate Committee on Foreign Relations 2021.
[165] Ukraine formally joined the ICC as a state party on January 1, 2025.
[166] Technically, Ukraine made a pair of Article 12(3) declarations, one in 2014 and another in 2015. The 2015 declaration was for an infinite duration, providing the ICC jurisdiction when Russian invaded in 2022.

criminal," "murderous dictator," and "pariah" while the US sought to build a global coalition to push back against Russian aggression.[167]

On the other hand, the Ukraine investigation raised uncomfortable implications for America's attempts to shield its own troops from the ICC. For more than two decades, every presidential administration and a large bipartisan majority of Congress asserted that the ICC should not be able to investigate or prosecute individuals from states that never joined the Court. The problem was that Russia, like the US, never joined the ICC. Any American support for the ICC's investigation of Russian forces in Ukraine would therefore undercut the longstanding American position and set a precedent that might pave the way for the ICC to target American forces in the future. Moreover, assisting the ICC's attempts to hold Russians accountable in Ukraine would expose the US to charges of double standards. Given the recent US reaction to the Afghanistan probe, it would reek of hypocrisy for American officials to claim that the ICC can investigate the nationals of one nonmember state (Russia) but not another nonmember state (the US) even though both stood accused of committing war crimes on the territory of a country where the ICC had jurisdiction.

The Biden administration tried to find a way out of this conundrum. As much as American officials wanted Putin and his allies to face justice for their crimes in Ukraine, the investigation did not necessarily have to happen at the ICC. For example, when National Security Advisor Jake Sullivan was asked whether Biden's decision to call Putin "a war criminal" meant that the US would support the ICC's investigation, Sullivan hinted that the US preferred to find an alternative venue for holding Putin accountable. Specifically, Sullivan replied, "Obviously, the ICC is one venue where war crimes have been tried in the past, but there have been other examples in other conflicts of other mechanisms being set up."[168] Sullivan went on to express his admiration for "creative solutions to the question of accountability."[169] Similarly, Ambassador-at-Large for Global Criminal Justice Beth Van Schaack noted that "everything's on the table" as the Biden administration considered "all the various options for accountability."[170]

---

[167] David E. Sanger, "By Labeling Putin a 'War Criminal,' Biden Personalizes the Conflict," *New York Times*, March 17, 2022.
[168] The White House 2022.   [169] The White House 2022.
[170] Department of State 2022.

In exploring an alternative to the ICC, the Biden administration borrowed from the playbook of the Bush administration. Recall that in 2005, Bush tried to garner international support for a new ad hoc tribunal for Sudan, which would have allowed the US to support prosecutions of Sudan's leaders without lending legitimacy to the ICC. But Biden's plans, like Bush's, were unsuccessful. Setting up a new ad hoc tribunal for Russian crimes likely would have meant working through the UN Security Council, where Russia – armed with its veto power – was sure to quash such plans. Even outside the Security Council, small and middling powers saw little reason to go through the complex process of building a new tribunal when the ICC was standing at the ready.[171] In response, American officials dropped plans for an alternative tribunal and accepted the reality that the ICC was "the only venue that works" for prosecuting Putin and his henchmen.[172] The US therefore had to reconcile its desire to punish Putin with its concerns about the Ukraine investigation setting a worrisome precedent for American troops abroad.

Different branches of the US government approached this trade-off in different ways. In Congress, enthusiasm for prosecuting Putin outweighed fears about the threat that the Ukraine investigation might someday pose to American soldiers. There was a shocking amount of Congressional support for the Ukraine probe – including from some of the very same politicians who had just led the charge against the Court's investigation in Afghanistan. In fact, the Senate *unanimously* passed Resolution 546, which encouraged American assistance to the Ukraine investigation and described the ICC in a positive light, calling it "an international tribunal that seeks to uphold the rule of law, especially in areas where no rule of law exists."[173] While the resolution did not commit the US to any specific course of action, it nonetheless marked a dramatic shift in Washington's tone toward the Court. A bipartisan Congressional delegation also made a visit to The Hague, an unmistakable public signal of support for the ICC, where

---

[171] In fact, several dozen countries asked the ICC to open an investigation in Ukraine shortly after Russia's invasion and then pledged to give the ICC extra money, technology, and legal expertise after the investigation began. See Vasiliev 2022.

[172] Charlie Savage, "U.S. Weighs Shift to Support Hague Court as It Investigates Russian Atrocities," *New York Times*, April 11, 2022.

[173] United States Senate 2022.

they met with Khan to "discuss how the United States can better support [ICC] efforts to deliver justice to the people of Ukraine."[174] This level of Congressional goodwill was unimaginable just two years prior, but the Ukraine investigation rapidly altered the counters of US–ICC relations in Congress for a simple reason: an investigation of Russian conduct in Ukraine served American foreign policy interests. As Senator Lindsey Graham, not typically a friend of the ICC, summarized, "This is one of Putin's bigger accomplishments. I didn't think it was possible, but he did it – and that's for him to rehabilitate the ICC in the eyes of the Republican Party and the American people."[175]

In this spirit, Congress enacted new domestic legislation to support the Ukraine investigation. Laws from the late 1990s and early 2000s that banned US assistance to the ICC, including the ASPA, were still on the books. This old legislation prevented the US from providing funding, sharing intelligence, or offering most other forms of assistance to the ICC. To be sure, there were a few carveouts – such as the Dodd Amendment and a 2010 memo from the Justice Department's Office of Legal Counsel – that provided a legal basis for the US to offer occasional support to the Court.[176] But this nebulous patchwork of rules left even Biden administration attorneys wondering how much "wiggle room" they had in their efforts to help the ICC hold Russians accountable.[177] Against this backdrop, Congress passed a new bill in December 2022 that removed all ambiguity. Congress explicitly declared that ASPA restrictions on American aid to the ICC no longer applied "to investigations and prosecutions of foreign persons for crimes within the jurisdiction of the International Criminal Court related to the Situation in Ukraine."[178] In other words, Congress gave the Biden administration carte blanche to assist the Ukraine investigation.

The Pentagon emerged as the strongest voice against US cooperation with the ICC. From the beginning, the Defense Department signaled its opposition to Congress removing legal barriers on American aid to the

---

[174] Office of Senator Chris Coons 2022.
[175] Charlie Savage, "U.S. Weighs Shift to Support Hague Court as It Investigates Russian Atrocities," *New York Times*, April 11, 2022.
[176] The 2010 Office of Legal Counsel memo was not publicly disclosed until it leaked to the press shortly after the ICC opened its Ukraine investigation.
[177] Charlie Savage, "U.S. Weighs Shift to Support Hague Court as It Investigates Russian Atrocities," *New York Times*, April 11, 2022.
[178] Congress of the United States of America 2022.

Ukraine investigation. Even after Congress passed the legislation and Biden signed it into law, the Pentagon worked behind the scenes to limit any cooperation between the Biden administration and the Court. This move infuriated many of the ICC's newfound supporters in Congress. Lindsey Graham, who had improbably emerged almost overnight as the ICC's leading Congressional cheerleader, labeled the Department of Defense a "problem child" for its attempts to stymie US support for the Ukraine investigation. Military officials, Graham complained, "opposed the legislative change – it passed overwhelmingly – and they are now trying to undermine the letter and spirit of the law."[179] Pentagon leaders, however, made no apologies as they repeatedly indicated that they were willing to trade away a potential prosecution of Putin and other Russians in order to avoid setting a precedent that might come back to haunt American troops. As Secretary of Defense Llyod Austin told Congress, "I will always prioritize the protection of U.S. military personnel."[180]

The White House and other executive branch agencies initially took a more middle-of-the-road approach. Administration officials were willing to offer general rhetorical support for ICC attempts to hold Russians accountable in Ukraine, but Biden was hesitant to assist the ICC directly. Instead, the administration focused on helping Ukraine prepare for any future trials that might take place – be it at the ICC or elsewhere. For example, Attorney General Merrick Garland made a surprise trip to Ukraine in June 2022 where he met with his Ukrainian counterpart near the Polish border. Garland offered American forensic and legal support to Ukraine and pledged that Russian perpetrators would have "no place to hide."[181] Garland also announced that Eli Rosenbaum – the former director of the Justice Department's Office of Special Investigations, a group famous for hunting Nazis that had snuck into the US after World War II – would lead a new unit coordinating American and Ukrainian efforts to bring Russian war criminals to justice.[182] American support to Ukraine, to be sure, helped the ICC

---

[179] Charlie Savage, "Pentagon Blocks Sharing Evidence of Possible Russian War Crimes with Hague Court," *New York Times*, March 8, 2023.
[180] Phil Stewart and Idrees Ali, "US Senators Accuse Pentagon of Hindering War Crimes Prosecution of Russia," *Reuters*, May 11, 2023.
[181] Glenn Thrush, "Garland, Visiting Ukraine, Names Prosecutor to Investigate Russian War Crimes," *New York Times*, June 21, 2022.
[182] Ibid.

indirectly because Ukrainian officials were cooperating with the Court. But the Biden administration generally struggled to decide which of the Ukraine investigation's competing priorities – punishing an adversary or protecting US troops – should come first. Biden himself spoke to this awkward tension after the ICC issued an arrest warrant for Putin in March 2023. In response to a reporter's question about the warrant, Biden's reply captured the muddled American response: "Well, I think it's justified. But the question is, [the ICC] is not recognized internationally by us either. But I think [the arrest warrant] makes a very strong point."[183]

These competing priorities came to a head in the summer of 2023 as American officials debated arguably the most consequential thing they could do to help the Ukraine investigation: sharing classified intelligence with the ICC. Both before and during the war, American military and intelligence agencies proved that they had high-quality intelligence concerning Russian military plans. Before the conflict, this allowed the US to predict that Russia would, in fact, invade Ukraine even as much of the world interpreted Putin's mobilization as a bluff.[184] Most relevant to the ICC investigation was American intelligence showing that Russian officials deliberately chose to target civilians and civilian infrastructure in Ukraine. The key question was whether the US would share this evidence of Russian war crimes with the Court. The Pentagon stood firm in its position that nonmember states like Russia and the US should remain above the law and that any support for prosecuting Russian forces now might harm American forces later.[185] But most other parts of the government – Congress, the State Department, the Justice Department, and US intelligence agencies – preferred to share the evidence. The gains from providing proof of Russian malfeasance to the ICC, they believed, outweighed the downside risk of hypothetical future prosecutions of US soldiers.[186]

---

[183] The White House 2023.
[184] Shane Harris, Karen DeYoung, Isabelle Khurshudyan, Ashley Parker, and Liz Sly, "Road to War: U.S. Struggled to Convince Allies, and Zelensky, of Risk of Invasion, *Washington Post*, August 16, 2022.
[185] Charlie Savage, "Pentagon Blocks Sharing Evidence of Possible Russian War Crimes with Hague Court," *New York Times*, March 8, 2023.
[186] Ambassador Van Schaack captured this viewpoint when she testified before the Senate Foreign Relations Committee. When questioned on whether transferring evidence to the Court would set a dangerous precedent that undermined the protection of American troops, she replied, "I do not think that that is an acute

After letting the issue linger for over a year, Biden finally resolved the internal divisions in July 2023: He overruled the Pentagon and ordered the government to start sharing evidence of Russian war crimes in Ukraine with the ICC. Biden never publicly explained his decision, but two factors appeared to have tipped his hand toward an assistance strategy. First, Congress steadily increased pressure on the Biden administration. In the days before Biden made his decision, a Senate committee approved a new funding bill that contained a clause stipulating that the president "shall provide information" to the ICC for its Ukraine investigation.[187] Moreover, Congress demonstrated that it was willing to play hardball with the administration on ICC policy. A letter from a bipartisan group of senators to President Biden – which conveniently leaked to the press on the day it was penned – questioned his lack of support for the Court. After reminding Biden that Congress had recently removed all restrictions on assistance to the Ukraine probe, the senators lamented that "months later, as the ICC is working to build cases against Russian officials, including Putin himself, the United States ... has not yet shared key evidence that could aid in these prosecutions."[188] Second, Ukraine wanted the US to aid the ICC. Ukrainian officials repeatedly praised the Court to their American counterparts in a charm offensive that culminated with a surprise visit from President Volodymyr Zelensky, who had achieved hero status in Washington, to The Hague.[189] At one point, Ukraine's prosecutor general even bluntly told American officials, "If you support the ICC, you are supporting us."[190] Given that Biden staked his foreign policy legacy on supporting Ukraine against Russian aggression, these sentiments likely played a role in his ultimate decision to assist the ICC.

Both the US and the ICC refused to comment on the specifics of the intelligence sharing program, but there is good reason to think the American assistance was crucial to the Ukraine investigation. Before

risk at this time." See Dan De Luce and Abigail Williams, "Pentagon Is Blocking U.S. Cooperation with International Investigations of War Crimes in Ukraine," *NBC News*, May 31, 2023.

[187] Charlie Savage, "Biden Orders U.S. to Share Evidence of Russian War Crimes with Hague Court," *New York Times*, July 26, 2023.

[188] Charlie Savage, "Senators Urge Biden to Send Evidence of Russian War Crimes to the ICC," *New York Times*, March 24, 2023.

[189] Phil Stewart and Idrees Ali, "US Senators Accuse Pentagon of Hindering War Crimes Prosecution of Russia," *Reuters*, May 11, 2023.

[190] Breedlove, Clark, and Hodges 2023.

the Biden administration decided to share evidence with the ICC, the Court had only issued two arrest warrants – for Putin and Maria Lvova-Belova, his Commissioner of Children's Rights – for the specific charge of abducting children from occupied Ukraine and transferring them to Russia. This charge was the proverbial low-hanging fruit for the Court because Putin and Lvova-Belova openly discussed the deportation policy on Russian television.[191] But the ICC had yet to issue any arrest warrants connected to Russia's broader campaign of attacks on civilians in Ukraine. That changed after the US began sharing evidence. The Court quickly issued arrest warrants for four senior Russian military leaders: Defense Minister Sergei Shoigu, Army Chief of Staff Valery Gerasimov, Aerospace Force Commander Sergei Kobylash, and Black Sea Fleet Commander Viktor Sokolov. The common factor linking these four men was their role in selecting civilian targets in Ukraine for missile and drone strikes – exactly the sort of intelligence that the Biden administration reportedly shared.[192] While it is not possible to prove definitively that American evidence led to their arrest warrants, both the timing of the warrants and the nature of the charges against them suggest that American assistance to the Court may have been vital.

ICC supporters around the world applauded Biden's decision to assist the Court in Ukraine.[193] American assistance not only helped the Ukraine investigation in the short term, but it also seemed to signal a shift in US thinking on the ICC that boded well for long-term cooperation. If the US officially recognized ICC jurisdiction over Russians in Ukraine, then the long-standing US objection to the Court exercising jurisdiction over nonmembers appeared to be a relic of the past. Abandoning this objection could open up a new range of possibilities for the US to assist the ICC in other circumstances. Along these lines, Human Rights First, a prominent NGO, commended the Biden administration for "setting aside an old policy position that stood in the way of U.S. backing for the court, not just in Ukraine

---

[191] Marc Santora and Emma Bubola, "Russia Signals It Will Take More Ukrainian Children, a Crime in Progress," *New York Times*, March 18, 2023.
[192] Charlie Savage, "Pentagon Blocks Sharing Evidence of Possible Russian War Crimes with Hague Court," *New York Times*, March 8, 2023.
[193] Natasha Bertrand and Jennifer Hansler, "Biden to Allow US to Share Evidence of Russian War Crimes with International Criminal Court," *CNN News*, July 27, 2023.

but in other crises."[194] However, this optimism that American support for the Ukraine investigation would translate into support for the Court's activities elsewhere was soon dashed. Another ICC investigation during Biden's tenure – this one in Palestine – exposed the double standards in America's ICC policy yet again.

The ICC investigation in Palestine was the culmination of a lengthy process that spanned the tenures of three American presidents and three ICC prosecutors.[195] The saga began in 2009 when Palestine submitted an Article 12(3) declaration – the same process Ukraine used – to grant the ICC jurisdiction over crimes committed on its territory. ICC Prosecutor Luis Moreno-Ocampo opened a preliminary examination but ultimately declined to move ahead with an investigation on the grounds that the ICC lacked jurisdiction because Palestine was not a state. In making this determination, Moreno-Ocampo deferred to the UN's position that Palestine did not enjoy statehood. But the calculus changed when the UN General Assembly passed Resolution 67/19 and officially recognized Palestine as a state in 2012. Palestine submitted another Article 12(3) declaration as well as its instrument of ratification for the Rome Statute in 2015, a move that allowed it to become an ICC member. In response, ICC Prosecutor Fatou Bensouda opened another preliminary examination. But Bensouda proceeded with caution. Even though the UN had apparently resolved the issue of Palestinian statehood, Bensouda asked the judges in the ICC's pretrial chamber to confirm that her office had jurisdiction given Palestine's unique history and disputed borders. In February 2021, the pretrial chamber ruled that Palestine was a legitimate state party and that the Court had jurisdiction over Palestinian territories including Gaza, the West Bank, and East Jerusalem. The next month, Bensouda formally opened an investigation and signaled that she planned to focus primarily on alleged crimes committed by both Palestinians and Israelis in the context of the 2014 Gaza conflict.

As this process played out, the Obama, Trump, and Biden administrations all took the same position and claimed that the ICC had no jurisdiction to investigate Israelis. American officials made two arguments against the Court's jurisdiction. The first was that Palestine was

---

[194] Human Rights First 2023.
[195] On Palestine's long and winding path to the ICC, see Bosco 2016.

not a state and therefore was not eligible to join the ICC. To be sure, the credibility of this position suffered after the UN recognized Palestine as a state in 2012, but the US clung to it regardless. For example, Jen Psaki, who served in the Obama and Biden administrations, responded to Palestine's decision to join the Court in 2015 by declaring, "It doesn't qualify to join the ICC."[196] The second American argument was that even if Palestine was a state, the ICC should not have jurisdiction over Israelis on Palestinian territory because Israel had not joined the Court. This was, of course, a restatement of the familiar American position that the ICC should not be allowed to exercise jurisdiction over individuals from nonmember states while they were on the territory of member states. In this regard, Republican and Democratic foreign policy officials who typically struggled to find common ground were in perfect alignment.

The US opposed the Palestine investigation every step of the way. In 2015, after Palestine joined the ICC and Bensouda opened a preliminary examination, the Obama administration pushed back. A State Department spokesman announced that the administration "strongly disagree[d] with the ICC prosecutor's action today" and pledged to "oppose actions against Israel at the ICC."[197] A bipartisan group of seventy-five senators penned an open letter urging the administration to go even further by cutting off American foreign aid to the Palestinian Authority – some $400 million annually – as punishment for joining the ICC.[198] In 2020, after rumors began swirling that the Court was on the verge of opening an investigation,[199] the Trump administration sought to delegitimize any inquiry into Israeli conduct, with Secretary Pompeo declaring, "It's clear the ICC is only putting Israel in its crosshairs for nakedly political purposes."[200] Once again, a large

---

[196] Michael Wilner, Herb Keinon, and Yonah Jeremy Bob, "US: Palestine Not a State, Does Not Qualify for ICC Membership," *Jerusalem Post*, January 7, 2015. Several other officials from the Obama, Trump, and Biden administrations made similar statements.
[197] Rathke 2015.
[198] Jessica Schulberg, "75 Senators Want to Punish Palestine before It Can Accuse Israel of War Crimes," *The New Republic*, February 3, 2015.
[199] Israeli officials knew an investigation was coming because Israeli intelligence agencies spied on ICC personnel, including Bensouda and Khan. See Harry Davies, Bethan McKernan, Yuval Abraham, and Meron Rapoport, "Spying, Hacking and Intimidation: Israel's Nine-Year 'War' on the ICC Exposed," *The Guardian*, May 28, 2024.
[200] Pompeo 2020b.

bipartisan group of senators – including soon-to-be vice president Kamala Harris – released a statement encouraging the Trump administration to come out in "full force" against any ICC investigation of Israeli actions in Palestine.[201] In 2021, after the ICC finally opened the investigation, the Biden administration immediately signaled its displeasure, with Secretary Blinken reiterating that the US "firmly oppose[d]" the inquiry.[202] Thus, three different presidential administrations all unambiguously opposed an ICC investigation in Palestine, but the US also stopped short of direct attacks on the Court. Washington settled into something of a cold war with The Hague over the investigation since the ICC had not yet targeted any Israelis with arrest warrants.

Everything changed on October 7, 2023. Hamas, a Palestinian militant group based in Gaza, launched a brutal surprise attack against Israel, killing over 1,000 Israelis – mostly civilians – and capturing more than 200 for use as hostages. The October 7 attacks were frequently described as "Israel's 9/11" and, in the words of President Biden, represented "the deadliest day for Jews since the Holocaust."[203] Israel responded to the Hamas attack by initiating a massive bombing campaign against Gaza followed by a ground invasion. While the Israeli response was ostensibly meant to punish Hamas specifically and not Gazans in general, the words and deeds of Israeli officials sometimes crossed the line into collective punishment of Palestinian civilians in Gaza. Most notably, Israeli Defense Minister Yoav Gallant announced that he had "ordered a complete siege on the Gaza Strip. There will be no electricity, no food, no fuel, everything is closed," before adding, "We are fighting human animals [and] are acting accordingly."[204] As a result of Israel's military campaign, Gaza has been rendered uninhabitable. The Gaza health ministry estimates that over 40,000 Palestinians have died since the Israeli attack began, though the precise numbers are disputed.[205] In response to the violence perpetrated by both sides, ICC Prosecutor Khan announced on

---

[201] Cardin and Portman 2020.   [202] Blinken 2021a.
[203] "Hamas Attack 'Deadliest Day for Jews since the Holocaust', Says Biden, As Israeli Jets Pound Gaza," *The Guardian*, October 12, 2023.
[204] "Defense Minister Announces 'Complete Siege' of Gaza: No Power, Food or Fuel," *Times of Israel*, October 9, 2023.
[205] Miriam Berger, "More than 40,000 Killed in Israel's War in Gaza, Health Ministry Says," *Washington Post*, August 15, 2024.

May 20 that he had asked judges in the ICC's pretrial chamber to issue arrest warrants for senior Israeli and Hamas leaders. Specifically, he requested arrest warrants for Netanyahu and Gallant on the Israeli side as well as Yahya Sinwar, Mohammed Deif, and Ismail Haniyeh on the Hamas side.

The US responded furiously when Khan sought arrest warrants for Israeli officials. President Biden denounced Khan's decision as "outrageous" and insisted that "whatever this prosecutor might imply, there is no equivalence – none – between Israel and Hamas."[206] Congress, fresh off its unprecedented support for the Court's Ukraine investigation, put direct attack tactics against the ICC back on the table. In the Senate, a bipartisan group called on Biden to "fully implement" the provisions of the ASPA, a thinly veiled reference to the ASPA's authorization for the president to invade The Hague.[207] Other senators proposed issuing tit-for-tat arrest warrants for ICC personnel, vowing that Khan "should get a taste of his own medicine" and threatening that he "might find himself in an American prosecutor's crosshairs."[208] In the House, a bipartisan majority passed the "Illegitimate Court Counteraction Act," a bill that would once again impose sanctions on ICC personnel if it became law.[209] The Biden administration initially signaled openness to sanctioning the ICC – for example, Secretary Blinken said he "would welcome" the chance to work with Congress on a bipartisan sanctions package – though Biden ultimately decided against it.[210] The US also found more subtle ways to thumb its nose at the Court's inquiry in Palestine. Not long after Khan's request for arrest warrants, the US feted the two Israelis facing ICC scrutiny: Blinken shook hands with Gallant at a photo-op, and Congressional leaders from both parties invited Netanyahu to visit Washington and address a joint session of Congress.[211]

---

[206] The White House 2024.   [207] Rubio and Rosen 2024.
[208] Marc A. Thiessen, "It's Not Just Netanyahu. The ICC Wants to Prosecute U.S. Lawmakers Too," *Washington Post*, May 24, 2024.
[209] United States House of Representatives 2024.
[210] Simon Lewis, Humeyra Pamuk, and Patricia Zengerle, "Blinken Says He'll Work with US Congress on Potential ICC Sanctions," *Reuters*, May 21, 2024.
[211] While Republicans and mainstream Democrats overwhelmingly opposed the ICC investigation and supported the targeted Israelis, some progressive Democrats in Congress supported the Court's attempts to investigate Israeli leaders. For example, Representative Mark Pocan asserted, "If Netanyahu comes to address Congress, I would be more than glad to show the ICC the way

On November 21, 2024, the ICC's judges granted the arrest warrants that Khan previously requested, including the warrants for Netanyahu and Gallant.[212] Republicans and Democrats alike rushed to condemn the ICC in the harshest terms possible. Senator Tom Cotton, a Republican who clashed with the ICC a few years earlier over its Afghanistan investigation, implicitly threatened an invasion: "The ICC is a kangaroo court and Karim Khan is a deranged fanatic. Woe to him and anyone who tries to enforce these outlaw warrants. Let me give them all a friendly reminder: the American law on the ICC is known as The Hague Invasion Act for a reason. Think about it."[213] Democrats did not hold back their vitriol for the ICC either. Representative Ritchie Torres asserted the arrest warrants represented "the weaponization of international law at its most egregious" and argued that the ICC "should be sanctioned not for enforcing the law but for distorting it beyond recognition."[214] Senator John Fetterman offered the most succinct response to the Court's arrest warrants: "Fuck that."[215] The White House joined Congress in vociferously opposing the Court. President Biden repeated his claim that any ICC arrest warrants for Israeli officials were "outrageous."[216] White House Press Secretary Karine Jean-Pierre defended the government's harsh response by reiterating the old American argument that the ICC should not have jurisdiction over individuals from countries (e.g., Israel) that did not join the Court.[217]

---

to the House floor to issue that warrant." See John Parkinson, Lauren Peller, Mariam Khan, and Ivan Pereira, "Speaker Johnson Moving Ahead on Netanyahu Invite to Address Congress in Wake of Possible ICC Warrant," *ABC News*, May 21, 2024.

[212] Israel reportedly assassinated all three of the wanted Hamas leaders before the ICC's judges decided whether to issue the arrest warrants. The ICC nonetheless issued a warrant for one of them – Deif – because the Court was unable to confirm his death.

[213] Senator Tom Cotton, X (formerly Twitter), November 21, 2024, https://x.com/SenTomCotton/status/1859608976389714045.

[214] Representative Ritchie Torres, X (formerly Twitter), November 21, 2024, https://x.com/RitchieTorres/status/1859601113370005667.

[215] Senator John Fetterman, X (formerly Twitter), November 21, 2024, https://x.com/SenFettermanPA/status/1859582592183566697.

[216] Julian Borger and Andrew Roth, "ICC Issues Arrest Warrant for Benjamin Netanyahu for Alleged Gaza War Crimes," *The Guardian*, November 21, 2024.

[217] "How US Politicians Responded to Netanyahu's ICC Arrest Warrant," *Al Jazeera*, November 21, 2024.

The American decision to oppose the Court's probe in Palestine is consistent with my theoretical framework. The US and Israel represent one of the few "special relationships" in world politics, and US officials had no desire to witness their most reliable friend in the Middle East face the scrutiny of an ICC investigation. But American opposition was about more than just protecting a friend – it also was about protecting itself. Since the Palestine investigation involved the ICC exercising jurisdiction over individuals from a nonmember state, precedent setting concerns were at play once again. American officials worried that an ICC investigation into Israeli conduct on Palestinian territory would establish a dangerous pattern that might eventually harm Americans deployed abroad. As Speaker of the House Mike Johnson described it, if the ICC investigation of Israeli conduct succeeded, then the Court could "assume unprecedented power to issue arrest warrants against American political leaders, American diplomats, and American military personnel."[218] Hence, both of my theory's two variables – whether the investigation threatens US troops and whether the investigation advances broader US interests – suggested the US would oppose the ICC in Palestine.[219]

Overall, the greatest casualty of the Biden's administration's ICC policy may have been the credibility of American legal objections to the Court. Every US president since Bill Clinton had taken the position that the ICC should never have jurisdiction over individuals from countries that had not joined the Court (unless, of course, there was a Security Council referral). This legal position was controversial – all of the ICC's members rejected it – but it also was consistent. The Biden

---

[218] Patrick Wintour and Julian Borger, "ICC Urged to Delay Possible War Crimes Charges against Israel and Hamas," *The Guardian*, April 29, 2024. Likewise, when Trump returned to the White House in 2025 and imposed new sanctions against ICC personnel as punishment for the arrest warrants for Israeli leaders, he left no doubt that precedent setting concerns were paramount for the US. In particular, Trump's executive order authorizing sanctions stated that the ICC's probe into Israeli conduct "set a dangerous precedent, directly endangering current and former United States personnel, including active service members of the Armed Forces." See Office of the President 2025.

[219] Also consistent with my theory, the US largely neglected ICC investigations in the Philippines and Venezuela during Biden's presidency. In each case, the ICC investigation neither implicated American servicemembers nor advanced American foreign policy interests in meaningful way. Consequently, these investigations never became salient foreign policy issues like the investigations in Afghanistan, Ukraine, and Palestine.

administration, however, departed from this long-standing position when it threw its support behind the Ukraine investigation. While there may be compelling reasons to celebrate American assistance to the ICC in Ukraine, the totality of Biden's ICC policy unambiguously revealed a set of double standards.[220] Biden's presidency coincided with several investigations – Afghanistan, Ukraine, and Palestine – that all involved the ICC exercising jurisdiction over individuals from nonmember states. Even though the legal principles at stake were comparable, the political calculations were not: The US supported ICC jurisdiction over Russians in Ukraine but not over Americans in Afghanistan or Israelis in Palestine. In other words, the US wanted its adversary to face justice at the ICC at the same time that it insisted its ally – and, most importantly, itself – should be above the law.

Conclusion

As documented in this chapter, American policy toward the ICC has enough of a "Jekyll and Hyde" quality to compete with Robert Louis Stevenson's famous character. Though American politicians and policymakers have consistently worried about the ICC's potential to target American troops, there is remarkable variation in how the US responds to the Court's investigations. At multiple points in the US–ICC relationship, the US has cooperated with one ICC investigation at the exact same time that it sought to undermine another one of the Court's investigations. To make sense of this variation, I offered a theory of how the US selects between three broad strategies – opposition, assistance, and neglect – as well as a discussion of the specific tactics associated with each strategy.

The empirical record is consistent with the theory. Even though Bush, Obama, Trump, and Biden were very different presidents in

---

[220] To be sure, Congress joined the Biden administration in promoting a set of double standards. Many members of Congress went from supporting sanctions on the ICC in response to the Afghanistan inquiry to hailing the Ukraine investigation and back to threatening sanctions again for the Palestine probe. For example, just months after leading Congressional efforts to assist the Court's investigation into Russian crimes in Ukraine, Lindsey Graham promised to "levy damning sanctions against the ICC" in retaliation for its attempts to investigate Israeli crimes in Palestine. See Alexander Bolton, "Graham Rips 'Outrageous' ICC Prosecutor Request for Israel Arrest Warrants," *The Hill*, May 20, 2024.

most respects, their strategic approaches to the ICC were similar. As my theory expects, all four presidents stood ready to oppose the Court when its investigations threatened American troops. But none of them were committed to an opposition strategy under every set of circumstances. When ICC investigations did not pose a risk to US servicemembers, all were willing to neglect or even assist the ICC. To be sure, there were notable differences in the rhetoric that the presidents used to discuss the ICC as well as the specific tactics their administrations employed when opposing the Court. Most notably, Republican administrations favored more aggressive attack tactics when opposing ICC investigations, whereas Democratic administrations preferred more subtle velvet gloved opposition tactics. But at the level of big-picture strategy, both Democrats and Republicans agreed on when to oppose, assist, and neglect the Court. Indeed, opposing the ICC when it is perceived to threaten American troops is one of the last remaining areas of bipartisanship in US foreign policy.

5 | The ICC's Track Record

The desire to shield American troops from the Court has shaped every facet of the US–ICC relationship. As demonstrated in Chapter 3, the US voted against the ICC in Rome – despite being a traditional leader in the creation of international tribunals and an early backer of the movement to build a permanent court in the 1990s – because it feared the ICC would unfairly target American servicemembers scattered across the world. As shown in Chapter 4, the ramifications of ICC investigations for America's global military go a long way toward explaining both the extent and the timing of US opposition toward the Court. While these chapters illuminated the dynamics driving the American side of US–ICC relations, they said less about the ICC side of the relationship. In particular, one of the fundamental questions about the ICC has not yet been answered: Does the ICC, in fact, target the American military?

In this chapter, I perform a statistical analysis to evaluate whether the empirical record supports the allegations of bias that American policymakers frequently lob at the ICC. As described in the book's introduction, my goal is not to make a judgment call on whether the ICC was "right" or "wrong" to open certain high-profile investigations. Instead, my goal is to address the issue of anti-American bias by systematically examining whether ICC investigations are disproportionately likely in countries where the US military is present. Put another way, out of all the situations around the world that the ICC might conceivably investigate, does it gravitate toward those that have the potential to imperil US troops? This approach to the statistical analysis has a pair of advantages. First, it examines the entirety of the ICC's track record and prevents cherry-picking unrepresentative cases. Second, it allows me to include non-investigations in the analysis as well as investigations. As I explain later, the situations the ICC declined to investigate are just as important as the investigations it initiated when it comes to assessing bias.

Finally, a word of caution is warranted on the interpretation of the statistical tests presented in this chapter: They should be understood less as an exercise in proving causality and more as an effort to see whether a significant correlation exists in support of America's long-standing accusations of bias against the ICC.

In what follows, I first explain why the Court's investigations – rather than other actions the ICC can take – are the most appropriate place to look for the presence or absence of anti-American bias. I then describe how I constructed a sample of cases that approximates the universe of situations the ICC might potentially investigate. Next, I provide an overview of the data used in the statistical analysis. I finish by presenting and discussing the quantitative results. My conclusions are unambiguous: There is no evidence to suggest that ICC investigations disproportionately target the American military.

Looking for Bias

To evaluate whether the ICC targets the American military, we must examine the Court's actions. But which ICC actions, specifically, are most relevant for assessing potential anti-American bias? There are three main possibilities: preliminary examinations, investigations, and arrest warrants. In what follows, I explain why the investigation stage is the right place to evaluate American allegations about the ICC "going rogue" and injecting political biases into its decision-making.

The primary advantage of examining investigations is that the ICC prosecutor enjoys a tremendous amount of discretion when it comes to opening investigations. This is a crucial point: We can only assess potential bias for outcomes where the ICC has a significant degree of control. Examining an outcome where the ICC's freedom to make independent decisions is circumscribed would be a flawed research strategy. Investigations, as described in Chapter 3, represent an area where the ICC enjoys plenty of latitude. The ICC prosecutor – assuming basic jurisdictional requirements are met – can choose to open an investigation entirely on his or her own volition (the prosecutor's *proprio motu* authority). It was precisely this broad discretion for the ICC prosecutor to open investigations around the world that so worried American policymakers at the Rome Conference. Moreover, even when ICC member states or the UN Security Council refer situations to the ICC, the prosecutor must agree to pursue the investigation. The prosecutor does not take direction from states and is not bound to proceed with an investigation following a referral. This means that an investigation only goes forward when the ICC prosecutor wants it to do so. For this reason, the ICC's investigation stage is perfect for assessing the extent, if any, of anti-American bias.

There are two alternative ICC actions – one occurring before investigations and the other occurring after investigations – that might initially seem like reasonable places to look for ICC biases. Upon closer examination, however, neither is the ideal place to assess the degree of anti-American bias at the ICC.

The first is the preliminary examination stage. A preliminary examination is the period that precedes an investigation. It effectively is an information gathering exercise in which the Court determines whether or not there is a compelling reason – based on the strength of the available evidence suggesting atrocity crimes may have occurred and the rules governing the ICC's jurisdiction – to open an investigation. As a report from the Office of the Prosecutor puts it, the "goal [of a preliminary examination] is to collect all relevant information necessary to reach a fully informed determination of whether there is a reasonable basis to proceed with an investigation."[1] In the context of my study, there is a notable downside to focusing on preliminary examinations: the ICC has less discretion over them relative to investigations.[2] Indeed, the aforementioned report on preliminary examinations notes that the Court's policy is to open "a preliminary examination of all situations that are not manifestly outside the jurisdiction of the Court."[3] This means that if a state refers a situation to the Court – even if it has little chance of progressing to an investigation – the ICC will often open a preliminary examination as a matter of process. Hence, preliminary examinations may tell us more about the preferences of the states making the referrals than about the biases of the ICC prosecutor. The prosecutor's biases, to the extent they exist, should come into play as the Court moves from the preliminary

---

[1] Office of the Prosecutor 2013, 2.
[2] There is another downside to examining preliminary examinations: The ICC sometimes keeps secret the date on which it opens preliminary examinations. In these cases, the ICC merely shares when preliminary examinations are "made public." This leaves some ambiguity about when preliminary examinations started and makes statistical modeling more difficult than it is for investigations.
[3] Office of the Prosecutor 2013, 2.

examination phase to the investigation phase. Indeed, many preliminary examinations never led to investigations precisely because the ICC prosecutor uses his or her discretion and decides not to proceed. Preliminary examinations therefore are not the optimal place to test for the presence of bias, though I confirm later in the chapter that my results are similar when I examine preliminary examinations as an alternative dependent variable.

The other option is the arrest warrant stage. The ICC issues arrest warrants after investigations are underway and marks a shift in the ICC's focus from general situations (e.g., an investigation in Libya) to particular individuals (e.g., an arrest warrant for Muammar Gaddafi). It also is an area where the ICC has a substantial amount of discretion: the prosecutor and judges alone are responsible for deciding who should be prosecuted for atrocity crimes. Specifically, the prosecutor makes a request for an arrest warrant, and the judges in the pretrial chamber decide whether to grant it. While examining which individuals face ICC arrest warrants is interesting in its own right, it is not an effective measure in the context of my analysis for a simple reason: the ICC has never issued an arrest warrant for an American (soldier or civilian).[4] To whatever extent anti-American bias exists at the ICC, it most definitely is not occurring at the arrest warrant stage.

Overall, this discussion implies that if there is anti-American bias at the ICC, it should be found at the investigation stage. I therefore examine ICC investigations as the dependent variable in my statistical analysis. To date, the ICC has opened investigations into seventeen situations, which are listed in Table 5.1. Readers may notice that over half of them have been located on the African continent. However, this statistic masks some stark temporal variation: the ICC's first nine investigations were all in Africa.[5] But in more recent years, the ICC has generally avoided investigations in African countries: seven of its past eight investigations have been outside Africa. As a result, ICC

---

[4] At the time of writing, it appears highly unlikely that any Americans will be charged in the ICC's Afghanistan investigation. Prosecutor Khan signaled his intention to focus his limited investigative resources on Taliban and Islamic State abuses shortly after taking office.
[5] Not surprisingly, the Court's early pattern of investigations prompted accusations of anti-African bias. While the issue of anti-African bias at the ICC is not my primary focus, I empirically evaluate this possibility later in the chapter.

Table 5.1 *ICC investigations*

Situation	Year
Uganda	2004
Democratic Republic of the Congo	2004
Sudan	2005
Central African Republic	2007
Kenya	2010
Libya	2011
Ivory Coast	2011
Mali	2013
Central African Republic II	2014
Georgia	2016
Burundi	2017
Bangladesh/Myanmar	2019
Afghanistan	2020
Palestine	2021
Philippines	2021
Venezuela	2021
Ukraine	2022

investigations now span the globe and include not only Africa but also Europe, Asia, the Middle East, and the Americas.

It is worth emphasizing that ICC investigations, like many other important outcomes in world politics, are relatively rare events. With only seventeen investigations to date, any statistical analysis of ICC investigations should be concerned about the possibility of rare events bias, an issue I return to later in the chapter.

Sample of Cases

The ICC made headlines in 2020 when it opened an investigation into possible war crimes committed on the territory of Afghanistan. The ICC's decision put American troops in Afghanistan, along with Afghan security forces and Taliban fighters, under the Court's microscope. As described earlier in the book, many US officials interpreted this investigation as indisputable proof that the ICC is politically motivated to target the US military. Secretary of State Mike Pompeo captured the conventional wisdom when he bluntly stated, "Our fears [about the

ICC] were warranted."⁶ This sort of thinking is misguided. It is impossible to determine whether the ICC is biased by examining only one of its investigations. In fact, examining investigations alone – even if all of them are considered – is problematic. A study that includes just investigations samples on the dependent variable and therefore has an indeterminate research design. When it comes to assessing anti-American bias at the of ICC, the situations the ICC decided *not* to investigate matter every bit as much as the situations the ICC did decide to investigate. Therefore, the sample of cases in a systematic analysis must include all situations where investigations were possible even if they ultimately did not occur.

In theory, identifying the appropriate sample of cases is straightforward: the ICC might plausibly investigate any situation involving genocide, war crimes, and crimes against humanity. In practice, however, identifying clear-cut cases of these crimes is difficult because their legal definitions are vague and their application to real-world situations is fiercely contested.

Genocide's definition has received the most attention.⁷ The Rome Statute's definition of genocide borrows from the 1948 Genocide Convention, which refers to genocide as "acts committed with intent to destroy, in whole or in part, a national, ethnical, racial or religious group."⁸ Determining whether a specific case meets the legal definition of genocide is difficult because doing so requires making assumptions about the ultimate goals of the perpetrators of the violence. In particular, genocide requires that acts of violence are committed with the "intent to destroy" a targeted group. Identifying cases of genocide therefore requires tough judgment calls on the motives of the perpetrators (e.g., was the killing meant to destroy the targeted group or merely meant to coerce it?). In the context of Russia's war on Ukraine, for example, there are good faith disagreements on whether a genocide is unfolding because the intentions of Putin's regime are open to multiple interpretations even if the conduct of Russian forces is

---

⁶ Rick Noack, "Why Does the Trump Administration Hate the ICC So Much?" *Washington Post*, April 5, 2019.
⁷ Power 2003; Shaw 2015.
⁸ Raphael Lemkin, a Polish lawyer who fled to the US during World War II, first coined the term "genocide" and later played a key role in the creation of the Genocide Convention.

unambiguously barbaric.[9] Furthermore, an act does not qualify as genocide if the targeted group is political in nature because only "national, ethnical, racial or religious" groups are included in the definition. This means that mass violence against the political opponents of an incumbent regime – which includes some of the worst violence in modern history, ranging from Joseph Stalin's "Great Terror" in the Soviet Union to Bashar Assad's brutal crackdown in Syria – does not meet the legal definition of genocide.

The definition of war crimes is vexing as well. The Rome Statute starts by defining war crimes as "grave breaches" of the Geneva Conventions, the post–World War II treaties that sought to protect civilians caught in the midst of fighting by establishing the laws of war. This notion of war crimes may seem straightforward in the abstract, but the matter quickly becomes more confusing as the Rome Statute devotes an additional 1,600 words to providing examples of acts that may conceivably count as war crimes. Not surprisingly, legal scholars continue to debate basic questions about the nature of war crimes. For example, Oona Hathaway and several coauthors recently asked:

What is a war crime? The question appears to have a simple answer: a war crime is a violation of the law of war. But do all violations of the law of war qualify as war crimes? And are all war crimes violations of the law of war? These questions are not new. In 1942, Hersch Lauterpacht, a leading international lawyer who assisted the prosecution of the Nazis for war crimes at the International Military Tribunal (IMT) in Nuremberg, wrote a memo in which he asked, "Is there a definition of war crimes?" More than seven decades later, the answer to his question remains unsettled.[10]

The ambiguity of war crimes is not just a point of academic debate but instead has implications for who ends up behind bars at international tribunals. As one commentator notes, war crimes charges "have often been too slippery to stick, with obvious offenders sometimes escaping conviction."[11]

---

[9] See, for example, Philippe Sands, "What the Inventor of the Word 'Genocide' Might Have Said about Putin's War," *New York Times*, April 28, 2022; and Eugene Finkel, "What's Happening in Ukraine Is Genocide: Period," *Washington Post*, April 5, 2022.
[10] Hathaway et al. 2019, 54.
[11] Joseph Gedeon, "Why Prosecuting Russian War Crimes in Ukraine Could Be Complicated," *Politico*, April 13, 2022.

Crimes against humanity, in the words of the Rome Statute, are acts "committed as part of a widespread or systematic attack directed against any civilian population, with knowledge of the attack." This definition makes crimes against humanity the broadest category of international crime. Unlike genocide, there is not a specific list of potential target groups (crimes against humanity can occur against any civilian population, including political groups). Unlike war crimes, crimes against humanity can occur at any time, not just during a state of war. The first crimes against humanity prosecutions occurred at the Nuremberg Tribunal, where Hannah Arendt famously noted that the judges left the new crime in a "tantalizing state of ambiguity."[12] Time has not resolved this state of affairs. More recent legal scholarship notes that the term remains "shrouded in ambiguity"[13] and is a source of "chronic definitional confusion."[14] This confusion makes its way into public discourse as well. For instance, politicians and pundits tend to label nearly any policy they dislike – such as requiring the COVID vaccine – as a crime against humanity.[15]

As this section demonstrates, applying the legal definitions of genocide, war crimes, and crimes against humanity to real-world cases is a fraught exercise. Moreover, the excessive parsing of words associated with these atrocity crimes is frequently a source of frustration. Reflecting on his time as the US Ambassador-at-Large for War Crimes Issues, David Scheffer laments the "judicial hairsplitting in the face of sheer evil. Was it genocide or just mass murder in Rwanda? Did civilians in Sierra Leone suffer from war crimes or crimes against humanity? Were women and girls in Darfur victims of mass rape as a war crime or as a genocide?"[16] Since international tribunals and academics alike have long struggled to establish a coherent, consistent, and uncontroversial set of standards for identifying these crimes, I do not attempt to do so here. An alternative approach is required.

How, then, is it possible to identify a sample of cases that the ICC might plausibly investigate? My solution is to use a more objective

---

[12] Arendt 1977, 257. [13] Orentlicher 1991, 2585.
[14] Van Schaack 1998, 791.
[15] Mark Kersten, "Calling COVID-19 Vaccine Mandates a 'Crime against Humanity' Isn't Just Wrong, It's Dangerous," *The Globe and Mail*, February 2, 2022.
[16] Scheffer 2012a, 428.

indicator to identify situations the ICC may choose to investigate: the killing of a large number of civilians. This is admittedly a somewhat blunt indicator for the commission of genocide, war crimes, and crimes against humanity. The nuanced and case-specific information that goes into the "judicial hairsplitting," to borrow Scheffer's phrase, of making determinations about international crimes is clearly absent. But that is, in fact, an advantage of my indicator. The goal is not to construct a case-specific indicator but rather one that is general enough to make comparisons across cases. The killing of civilians – a variable that is objective and quantifiable in different country-level contexts – meets this criterion. To be clear, my coding decision does not require an assumption that genocide, war crimes, or crimes against humanity definitely occurred whenever a substantial number of civilians are killed. Instead, it merely requires the assumption that it is plausible for the ICC to believe that an investigation might be warranted in response to such violence.

This is a reasonable assumption because the ICC itself acknowledges using information on civilian killings when selecting investigations. At one point, the Office of the Prosecutor attempted to create an in-house methodological ranking of the gravest situations over which the Court had jurisdiction to help guide its investigations. The OTP developed "a chart that included major conflict zones, drawing on information from the United Nations and leading human rights groups. ... The key metric was violent deaths in the last several years."[17] Furthermore, this sort of thinking is not confined to behind-the-scenes discussions at the Court. ICC prosecutors have not been shy about publicly discussing the role that civilian fatalities play in the ICC's decision-making. Luis Moreno-Ocampo, for instance, noted in a speech at the United Nations that while many factors are relevant for selecting investigations, the "most obvious of these is the number of persons killed."[18]

To identify civilian killings, I examine cases of "one-sided violence" in the Uppsala Conflict Data Program's (UCDP) Georeferenced Event Dataset.[19] A one-sided violence event occurs whenever any organized political actor, such as the government or a rebel group, directly and deliberately kills at least twenty-five civilians in a given year.[20] For my

---

[17] Bosco 2014a, 90.   [18] Moreno-Ocampo 2005, 6.
[19] Sundberg and Melander 2013.   [20] Eck and Hultman 2007.

purposes, the UCDP dataset has several advantages. First, it includes both state and rebel group violence against civilians, making it possible to capture the full universe of cases the ICC could conceivably investigate. Many other datasets of civilian killings focus on only one actor, typically the state.[21] While examining the violence of just one actor is appropriate for many research questions, it is problematic in the context of my project because it risks missing situations where the ICC could open investigations. Second, it is a georeferenced dataset. It therefore is possible to match the location of violent events with ICC investigations and US military deployments.[22] Third, it codes the precise number of civilians killed. Many other datasets of violence against civilians only code (a) a dummy variable for whether a civilian killing event (however defined) occurred or (b) a wide range capturing the upper and lower bounds of the death toll. While one can fairly quibble with UCDP's arbitrary threshold of twenty-five civilian deaths (or, for that matter, any other threshold) needed to qualify as a one-sided violence event, the precise death tolls make it possible to control in the statistical models for the gravity of violence in each country. This allows me to differentiate between cases that barely met threshold and those that greatly exceeded it.

Given these advantages, I use the UCDP Georeferenced Event Dataset to create the sample of cases for my study. The study window begins in 2002, the first year of the ICC's temporal jurisdiction. A country enters my sample after its first instance of one-sided violence, putting it "at risk" of an ICC investigation. The country exits the sample if and when the ICC opens an investigation (observations are right censored after 2023). A total of sixty-one different countries are included in my sample of cases over the 2002–2023 time period.

Note that I include all countries with one-sided violence in the sample, not just those that ratified the ICC's Rome Statute.

---

[21] See, for example, Harff 2003; Valentino 2004; Downes 2008; Uzonyi et al. 2021.

[22] This is especially important in the context of actor-based datasets since some actors commit violence in multiple countries (e.g., transnational rebel groups or terrorist groups). For example, UCDP's standard one-sided violence dataset is not geocoded. As a result, the authors warn that it should not be used for analyses with a geographic component because it simply lists every country where the violent actor is responsible for any deaths. See Eck and Hultman 2007. By contrast, the georeferenced version of the UCDP dataset provides the distribution and magnitude of violence for each country.

My reason for doing so is straightforward: The ICC can and does investigate violence in countries that are not ICC state parties. In fact, five of the ICC's investigations involve violence on the territory of non-state parties. Two of these investigations, Sudan and Libya, were the result of high-profile UN Security Council referrals. Two more, the Ivory Coast and Ukraine, were made possible because governments accepted the ICC's jurisdiction under Article 12(3) declarations (a legal mechanism that gives the ICC jurisdiction on an ad hoc basis) even though they had not ratified the Rome Statute. The fifth investigation, Bangladesh/Myanmar, occurred because the ICC took a new and somewhat controversial approach to interpreting its rules of territorial jurisdiction. The investigation concerns Myanmar's violence against the Rohingya population. Myanmar is not an ICC state party, but the Court asserted that it has jurisdiction because Bangladesh (where many Rohingya have fled) is a state party. The ICC's logic was that it could open an investigation into Myanmar's "clearance operations" because at least some of the crimes occurred as the Rohingya crossed the border into Bangladesh. Overall, these examples show how the ICC unambiguously has the ability to investigate non-state parties under certain circumstances, so all countries that experience one-sided violence are included in the sample.[23]

America's Global Military Presence

To test whether ICC investigations unfairly target the American military, it is necessary to know where the US military is located. To be clear, the variable I want to measure is whether US forces are present in a particular country, not whether those forces are necessarily committing abuses there. American military presence is the appropriate concept to measure because, as documented in Chapters 3 and 4, the persistent concern of American officials has been that US troops deployed abroad would unfairly get dragged into politicized ICC investigations *even when they were not responsible for atrocity crimes*. Recall, for example, Bill Richardson fretting at the Rome Conference that US soldiers stationed abroad could get entangled in ICC

---

[23] To be clear, including non-ratifiers in the sample does not mean that I ignore the issue of Rome Statute ratification. To the contrary, I control for it in the statistical analysis.

proceedings for merely "doing their jobs"[24] and John Bolton worrying that they would be "used as scapegoats simply because they were Americans."[25] Hence, the key issue I examine is whether ICC investigations are disproportionately likely in situations where American troops are present.[26]

This raises the question: where in the world is the US military? Answering this question is not as straightforward as it might initially seem. The Department of Defense's Base Structure Report, a publicly available document that provides an inventory of US military bases around the world, is a natural place to start.[27] However, the Pentagon's reporting on its overseas military presence is often incomplete and, at times, highly dubious. There are at least three reasons to doubt the veracity of official Department of Defense data on American military bases abroad. First, the Pentagon employs a plethora of euphemisms to avoid using the "base" label, even when the facility in question is a military base according to any reasonable definition. These euphemisms – such as "mission support site," "contingency location," and "forward operating site," among others – allow the Pentagon to maintain the stance, at least in a strict technical sense, that it does not have bases in some countries that would be unpopular or might create operational security concerns.[28]

Second, even when the Pentagon is willing to acknowledge that bases exist, it sometimes insists the bases do not belong to the US. Instead, it argues that the American forces there are simply "guests" at a base formally belonging to the host country's military. The Soto Cano Air Base in Honduras (also known as Palmerola Air Base) provides an example. American officials have long clung to the argument that there is not an American military base in Honduras because its forces there are classified as guests of the Honduran air force academy. Richard Armitage, a leading Department of Defense official during the Reagan administration, made the case in the 1980s that it

---

[24] Alessandra Stanley, "US Argues against Strongly Independent War Crimes Prosecutor," *New York Times*, June 18, 1998.
[25] Bolton 2007, 86.
[26] My *American Political Science Review* article addresses the same issue but covers a slightly different time period. See Krcmaric 2023.
[27] For the most recent report, see Department of Defense 2023.
[28] Nick Turse, "The Pentagon Won't Acknowledge Hundreds of Military Bases," *The Nation*, November 6, 2019.

was a mistake to consider Soto Cano an American base because the US military presence there was of "a temporary but indefinite nature" rather than a permanent one.[29] But nearly four decades later, the US military presence remains. In fact, there are now far more Americans than Hondurans at the base. While it is stretches credulity to insist that there is not an American military base in Honduras, there is a compelling reason for the obfuscation: the Honduran constitution's prohibition against the permanent stationing of foreign troops on its territory.[30]

Third, the US military can use a cut-out to try to mask its presence, although doing so is not easy. For instance, the Royal Thai Navy rented a base to a private company called Delta Golf Global, who then rented the base to the US Air Force. As journalist Robert Kaplan summarized the arrangement, "The US military was here, but it was not here. After all, the Thais did no business with the US Air Force. They dealt only with a private contractor."[31] In other cases, the cut-out exists primarily for the sake of public opinion in the host nation. Pakistan, for example, leased a base to Abu Dhabi, who then leased it to the US, so that the Pakistani government could claim the US military was not present and thereby disassociate itself from the unpopular American drone strikes program.[32] In such cases, the US military – at least officially – does not possess foreign bases, allowing host nations to mitigate the perception that the US is infringing on their sovereignty.[33]

The bottom line is that the data contained in the official Base Structure Reports are an unreliable measure of America's overseas military presence. The Pentagon refuses to acknowledge many – literally hundreds – of its own bases that are publicly known and widely verified.[34] It is a telling sign of the poor quality of the Department of Defense data that even some government-funded research reports on America's foreign military presence choose *not* to use the Pentagon's own list of bases.[35]

---

[29] Lawrence L. Knutson, "U.S. Troop Presence in Honduras Called Temporary but Indefinite," *Associated Press*, April 6, 1987.
[30] Vine 2015, 54. [31] Kaplan 2008, 80. [32] Woods 2011.
[33] Vine 2015, 58.
[34] Nick Turse, "The Pentagon Won't Acknowledge Hundreds of Military Bases," *The Nation*, November 6, 2019.
[35] O'Mahony et al. 2018. This report, produced by the RAND Corporation for the US Army, instead relies on David Vine's dataset, which I describe momentarily.

A better alternative is the list of American overseas bases compiled by David Vine, an anthropologist of the US military.[36] To avoid becoming bogged down in linguistic debates about the euphemisms the Pentagon sometimes uses for its military bases, Vine employs a simple definition of a base: "any place, facility, or installation used regularly for military purposes of any kind."[37] Defined this way, bases come in all sizes. At one extreme is the massive Ramstein Air Base, effectively a self-contained American city in the heart of Germany that houses up to 50,000 US troops and family members, along with shopping malls, schools, fast-food joints such as Taco Bell and Popeyes, and even a golf course. At the other extreme are much smaller and less elaborate installations – sometimes nicknamed "lily pads" after the plants enabling frogs to hop across ponds – that may house limited numbers of special forces, drones, and other prepositioned military equipment. An example is the spartan facility in Niger that gained widespread attention in 2017 after four American soldiers died in an Islamic State ambush.[38] Hence, Vine's dataset attempts to capture the universe of all known US military bases around the world, regardless of how the Pentagon officially classifies them.

A major advantage of Vine's dataset is that it uses both government and nongovernment sources. In practice, this means that Vine's dataset includes the bases that the Pentagon publicly acknowledges in its Base Structure Reports *and* several hundred additional bases that do not make it into official Department of Defense statistics but have been credibly reported by other government, academic, or media sources. In total, Vine's dataset identifies nearly 800 American overseas military bases.[39] For each of these bases, Vine provides the most precise geographic location information possible using specific latitude and longitude coordinates. Using this data, I map the global distribution of America's military presence in Figure 5.1, where each dot represents a US base.[40] In the statistical analysis reported later in this chapter,

---

[36] Vine 2019.   [37] Vine 2015, 4.
[38] Rukmini Callimachi, Helene Cooper, Eric Schmitt, Alan Blinder and Thomas Gibbons-Neff, "An Endless War: Why 4 U.S. Soldiers Died in a Remote African Desert," *New York Times*, February 20, 2018.
[39] If anything, this number may be an undercount since at least some bases presumably remain secret.
[40] There appear to be fewer than 800 points on the map because many of them overlap. That is, many of America's bases are clustered closely together.

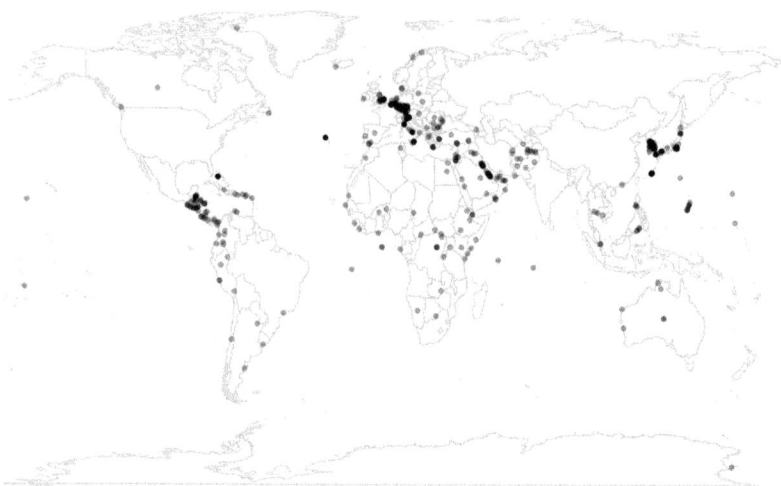

Figure 5.1 American military bases abroad

I use Vine's dataset to create a dummy variable that equals 1 for states that have a US military base on their territory. According to Vine's data, there are seventy-eight countries or dependencies that have at least one American base.

Despite its many advantages, there is one downside to Vine's dataset: it is not an annual time-series dataset. Rather, it provides snapshots of America's foreign military bases at a few discrete points in time (specifically, 1939, 1945, 1989, 2015, and 2021). Given my study's time frame, I use the 2015 snapshot. Hence, my main US military presence variable codes whether a country had an American military base on its territory in 2015. While annual data would be ideal, there is little reason to think that using the 2015 snapshot of America's foreign military bases is problematic. Put simply, US military presence in a country is a "sticky" variable. By their very nature, military bases are fixed and immobile assets. While bases are sometimes closed, the US more frequently holds onto its bases and repurposes them as foreign policy threats change. This dynamic has a long history. As early as 1970, a Senate Committee on Foreign Relations Report concluded, "Once an American overseas base is established it takes on a life of its own. Original missions may become outdated but new missions are developed, not only with the intention of keeping the facility going, but often to actually enlarge it."[41] For instance, bases that were initially created for post–World War II occupations in Europe and Asia later became bulwarks in America's Cold War containment strategy. When the Soviet Union collapsed, many of these bases nonetheless persisted and once again were reinvented as tools of the global war on terror after the 9/11 attacks. Even today, eighty years after the conclusion of World War II, a large portion of America's overseas bases are located where they are because of patterns of World War II conquest. No less an authority than Mark Milley, Chairman of the Joint Chiefs of Staff, acknowledged that the American military may have "too much infrastructure overseas" and that "much of [it] is a derivative of where World War II ended."[42] Thus, even if Vine's dataset had annual observations, my US military presence variable would change very slowly.[43] While the number of troops at each military base may vary considerably over time, whether or not a given country has any US military bases on its territory is relatively static.

For these reasons, Vine's dataset on America's overseas military bases represents the best available indicator of US military presence. Nonetheless, I employ an alternative measure later in the chapter to ensure that my results are robust to different ways of measuring the presence of the American military in a given country.

Covariates

The presence or absence of the US military in a country is not the only factor that might influence ICC investigations. I therefore control for several other variables that may shape the likelihood that the Court opens an investigation into a given situation. These additional covariates fall into two general categories: legal and political.

Legal Covariates

One group of covariates captures legal factors. To start, I control for whether a country has ratified the ICC's Rome Statute. As mentioned

---

[41] Quoted in Johnson 2004, 152.
[42] "Milley Urges 'Relook' at Permanent Overseas Basing of Troops," *The Independent*, December 3, 2020.
[43] Similarly, when discussing America's global military presence in the post–Cold War period, one analyst notes that "the broad contours of the US presence have been more notable for what has remained steady than for what has changed." See O'Hanlon 2008, 47–48.

earlier, I include non-ratifiers in the sample of cases for my analysis because the ICC can (and does) investigate violence in countries that are not ICC state parties. UN Security Council referrals are particularly noteworthy in this regard because they allow the ICC to open investigations into situations that are beyond its standard jurisdiction. This wide reach prompted David Bosco to marvel, "A leader whose country has not signed onto the Rome Statute, and who is committing crimes entirely within his own borders, could still find himself in the Court's crosshairs."[44] Nonetheless, investigations may be more likely when the ICC automatically has jurisdiction. I therefore control for Rome Statute ratification to capture the degree to which there are jurisdictional barriers that must be overcome before an investigation is opened.

I also account for a pair of legal principles – gravity and complementarity – that are meant to guide the ICC's selection of investigations. The gravity principle holds that the ICC should prioritize pursuing accountability for the world's gravest abuses. The Court lacks the time and resources to investigate every crime that might fall under its jurisdiction, so the Rome Statute tasks the ICC with investigating the "most serious" crimes of concern to the international community. Hence, if the ICC is following its mandate, the likelihood of an investigation should increase in tandem with the severity of the atrocity crimes. To address this dynamic, I proxy the gravity of each situation by controlling for the cumulative number of civilians killed in one-sided violence on a country's territory since the ICC's temporal jurisdiction began in 2002.[45] Of course, gravity is more than just a number, but there is no consensus on exactly what else it entails.[46] The Rome Statute never explicitly defines gravity, though the Office of the Prosecutor published a paper in 2013 that attempted to clarify which factors influence its assessments of gravity other than the number of people killed.[47] However, the paper's criteria "are not easy to apply"

---

[44] Bosco 2014a, 55.   [45] Sundberg and Melander 2013.
[46] According to Margaret deGuzman, "In light of the serious repercussions of labeling an international crime 'grave,' one might expect the concept of gravity to have reasonably well-defined and accepted content in international law. In fact, the opposite is true. Individuals who craft, apply, and write about international criminal law invariably reference the seriousness of the crimes at issue but rarely specify what they mean." See deGuzman 2012, 21.
[47] Office of the Prosecutor 2013.

and "provide scant insight into how one might, in a tangible way, compare two situations to determine which is of greater gravity."[48] Given this, I rely on cumulative deaths because this indicator (a) allows for comparisons across situations given its quantifiable nature and (b) is, in the words of one former ICC prosecutor, the "most obvious" metric for assessing gravity.[49]

The complementarity principle holds that the ICC is a "court of last resort" that should only get involved when national courts do not make a genuine effort to address crimes committed on their country's territory.[50] When national courts are willing and able to handle investigations of genocide, war crimes, and crimes against humanity on their own, the ICC should back off and allow the domestic investigations to proceed on their own. Hence, if the Court adheres to the complementarity principle, the likelihood of an ICC investigation should decrease as the quality of a country's domestic courts increases. To proxy the quality of national legal systems, I include a rule of law index from the Varieties of Democracy project, a dataset that surveys thousands of country experts. The rule of law variable captures the extent to which laws are "transparently, independently, predictably, impartially, and equally enforced."[51]

Political Covariates

Another group of covariates captures political factors that might shape investigations. Even though ICC officials repeatedly stress their apolitical nature, a wide range of political incentives and biases could conceivably influence the Court. For example, my book focuses on the possibility of anti-American bias at the ICC, but that is not the only potential type of ICC bias. In fact, some have suggested that the ICC

---

[48] Buchwald 2020.   [49] Moreno-Ocampo 2005, 6.
[50] On the complementarity principle, see El Zeidy 2002; Nouwen 2014.
[51] Coppedge et al. 2024. This rule of law index admittedly has a shortcoming in the context of my project. It describes the quality of a country's judicial system in general, not whether the country is willing and able to investigate atrocity crimes in particular. While these two things often go hand-in-hand, there are exceptions (e.g., the US and Israel have high-quality judicial systems, but both have been reluctant to investigate atrocity crimes allegedly committed by their armed forces). Despite this shortcoming, the rule of law index remains the best available indicator for making cross-national comparisons.

may be biased against the global south, especially Africa.[52] Given that the ICC's first nine investigations all were in African countries, allegations of Africa bias were rampant during the ICC's early years (though such accusations have become less common over time as the ICC moved its focus beyond Africa). Many political elites in Africa – especially those most likely to face investigations and arrest warrants – have led the charge against the Court. To give just a few examples, one African Union official lambasted the ICC's "glaring practice of selective justice."[53] Rwanda's prime minister warned that "Westerners who don't understand anything about Africa should stop trying to import their solutions."[54] Gambia's information minister claimed that the ICC actually is "an International Caucasian Court for the persecution and humiliation of people of color, especially Africans."[55] To address the possibility of anti-African bias at the ICC, I include a dummy variable for countries in Africa.

I also account for the dynamics of the UN Security Council. Recall that the Security Council can refer situations to the ICC that are outside of the Court's standard jurisdiction, giving the ICC potentially global reach. Referrals from the UN Security Council, for instance, granted the ICC jurisdiction to open investigations in Sudan and Libya, two states that never signed up for the ICC. However, Security Council referrals to the ICC are uncommon because it requires the unanimous consent of the Security Council's permanent five members (the "P5"). That is, the path to an ICC investigation in a nonmember state closes if only one member of the P5 is willing to veto the referral. This dynamic explains why the ICC has never been able to open an investigation in Syria despite the horrific violence there: Russia and China vetoed a Security Council resolution supported by the US, the UK, and France in 2014 that would have granted the ICC jurisdiction over atrocity crimes committed on Syrian territory.[56] As this example illustrates, the P5 can

---

[52] David Bosco, "Why Is the International Criminal Court Picking Only on Africa?" *Washington Post*, March 29, 2013.
[53] "African ICC Members Mull Withdrawal over Bashir Indictment," *Voice of America News*, November 2, 2009.
[54] Alfred de Montesquiou, "African Leaders Denounce International Court," *Associated Press*, July 3, 2009.
[55] "The Gambia joins African Queue to Leave ICC," *BBC News*, October 26, 2016.
[56] Ian Black, "Russia and China Veto UN Move to Refer Syria to International Criminal Court," *The Guardian*, May 22, 2104.

effectively shield their allies from at least some ICC investigations by vetoing Security Council referrals. I therefore add a dummy variable for states that have a formal alliance with any P5 member.[57]

Another factor that might influence the ICC's decision to open an investigation relates to the prospects of the investigation ultimately yielding successful convictions. That is, the Court may be unlikely to open investigations into situations where geopolitical realities make obtaining evidence or apprehending suspects difficult. Even when the Court has jurisdiction, it still needs at least some level of cooperation from the state on whose territory the alleged crimes occurred. A proper investigation is not feasible if the state refuses to grant ICC investigators access to crime scenes, witnesses, or other evidence. Anticipating that an investigation will go nowhere without state support, the ICC might be reluctant to open investigations into such situations and instead may devote its scarce resources elsewhere.[58] Along these lines, ICC prosecutor Karim Khan acknowledged that the Court "cannot act like an NGO nor as a university, only producing long interesting academic or policy papers which shine a light on atrocities but with no real ability to take action against those crimes. It must make an impact and make inroads in terms of accountability."[59] Concerns about the feasibility of conducting investigations may be especially acute in situations involving the American military. As mentioned in Chapter 4, the US signed about 100 "Article 98 agreements" in which partner countries pledged not to cooperate with the ICC in situations involving Americans.[60] I therefore include a dummy variable for states that signed Article 98 agreements since this variable serves as a proxy for the difficultly of pursuing investigations in countries where US military forces are present.

Lastly, I account for the fact that some US presidents have been more combative toward the ICC than others. As described previously, Bush, Obama, Trump, and Biden all pursued similar big-picture strategies toward the ICC in terms of when they decided to oppose, assist, or neglect the Court's investigations. However, once a decision was made to oppose an investigation, the presidents relied on different tactics to undermine the Court. The Republican presidents used aggressive

---

[57] Gibler 2009. The dataset includes mutual defense pacts, nonaggression treaties, and ententes.
[58] For examples of this logic, see Bosco 2014a; Tiemessen 2014.
[59] Charanie 2021.   [60] Kelley 2007; Nooruddin and Payton 2010.

attack tactics when attempting to protect American troops from the ICC. For example, the Bush administration withheld foreign aid from states that supported the ICC and threatened to invade The Hague, and the Trump administration imposed sanctions on ICC personnel. The Democratic presidents employed more subtle forms of American influence – what I called velvet gloved tactics – to oppose investigations that threatened US troops or American foreign policy interests. For instance, the Obama and Biden administrations withheld evidence, exerted behind-the-scenes pressure, and used the presidential "bully pulpit" to thwart ICC investigations. These differences across the four presidential administrations might influence the ICC's willingness to take on the daunting task of investigating the US military. Specifically, the prosecutor may be more hesitant to open an investigation implicating American troops when a Republican occupies the White House because the Court can anticipate a relatively harsher American response. To address this over-time variation in the degree of aggression in the US–ICC relationship, I control for each president's tenure.[61]

Findings

In this section, I employ a variety of statistical tests to evaluate the empirical record: Does the ICC target the US? More specifically, are ICC investigations disproportionately likely in situations involving the American military? I start with the regression estimates, then analyze the substantive size of the effects, and finally evaluate the robustness of the results.

Regression Results

Since the opening of an ICC investigation is a dichotomous outcome, I estimate discrete duration models in Table 5.2. These models use logistic regression and, in addition to the covariates described in the previous section, include cubic time polynomials measuring how long each country has been at risk of an ICC investigation. I start with a simple model that includes only the variables for America's military

---

[61] Biden is the omitted category. Including a dummy variable for whether a Republican or Democrat occupies the White House produces nearly identical results.

Findings

Table 5.2 *Correlates of ICC investigations*

	(1)	(2)	(3)	(4)	(5)
US Military Presence	0.007	0.064	−0.064	−0.066	−0.042
	(0.601)	(0.608)	(0.680)	(0.671)	(0.656)
Rome Ratifier	0.771	0.505	0.302	0.349	0.352
	(0.624)	(0.660)	(0.794)	(0.812)	(0.865)
Gravity of Violence	0.026**	0.026**	0.027**	0.027*	0.026*
	(0.013)	(0.013)	(0.014)	(0.014)	(0.014)
Rule of Law	−1.495	−0.926	−0.920	−0.973	−1.055
	(1.394)	(1.565)	(1.653)	(1.657)	(1.757)
Africa		0.771	1.105	1.148	1.167
		(0.669)	(0.808)	(0.845)	(0.856)
P5 Alliance			0.789	0.793	0.816
			(1.025)	(1.011)	(1.052)
Article 98				−0.151	−0.155
				(0.661)	(0.638)
Bush					−0.260
					(1.783)
Obama					−0.324
					(1.482)
Trump					0.197
					(1.242)
Time	−0.771**	−0.773**	−0.778**	−0.768**	−0.749**
	(0.347)	(0.340)	(0.331)	(0.333)	(0.353)
Time^2	0.076	0.079*	0.080*	0.080*	0.074*
	(0.047)	(0.044)	(0.044)	(0.044)	(0.042)
Time^3	−0.002	−0.002	−0.002	−0.002	−0.002
	(0.002)	(0.001)	(0.001)	(0.001)	(0.001)
N	855	855	855	855	855
AIC	129.83	130.53	131.51	133.47	139.17
BIC	167.84	173.29	179.02	185.73	205.69

Standard errors clustered by country in parentheses.
* $p < 0.10$, ** $p < 0.05$ (two-tailed).

presence, ratification of the Rome Statute, and the proxies for gravity and complementarity. I then add the political covariates individually to assuage concerns about "garbage can" regressions.[62]

---

[62] Achen 2005.

The crucial issue in the regression models is whether there is a statistically significant correlation between American troop presence and ICC investigations. Statistical significance can be a confusing concept. At its most basic, however, it describes the likelihood that an observed correlation between two variables is due to chance alone (as opposed to some kind of "real" relationship). Regression tests capture this likelihood with a p-value, a number that ranges from 0 to 1. The lower the p-value, the more confident we can be that the results are not due to luck or randomness. The standard convention in the social sciences is to treat p-values of 0.05 or less as statistically significant, although other thresholds are sometimes used. The key takeaway is that a statistically significant result means we are reasonably confident that a real relationship between the variables exists.[63]

If the sort of anti-American bias that US policymakers frequently discuss actually exists at the ICC, then the US military presence variable should be statistically significant and positive.[64] The results, however, do not support the allegations of bias. Across all five models in Table 5.2, the regression estimates are consistent: The relationship between ICC investigations and the presence of American troops in a country is statistically insignificant at conventional levels. In fact, the p-value for the US military presence variable is never less than 0.91, far beyond any plausible threshold of statistical significance. In plain English, the ICC is no more or less likely to investigate situations where the US military is present.

The regression estimates for the legal variables are generally consistent with the theoretical expectations. To start, investigations are more likely in countries that have ratified the Rome Statute. This is an intuitive finding since the ICC automatically has jurisdiction to investigate atrocity crimes in these countries. Yet, the Rome Statute ratification variable is never statistically significant in any of the models. The insignificant result for the ratification of the ICC's founding treaty validates my decision to include all countries with one-sided violence against civilians, not just those that joined the Court, in the sample of cases for the analysis. As described earlier, the ICC has opened

---

[63] Even a statistically significant correlation, however, does not necessarily mean that the relationship is causal.

[64] With logit models, the regression results only allow a determination of whether the effect is positive or negative. To understand the magnitude of the effect, it is necessary to calculate substantive effects, which I do later in the chapter.

investigations into possible crimes committed in five countries – Sudan, Libya, the Ivory Coast, Myanmar, and Ukraine – that did not ratify the Rome Statute. Hence, ICC membership increases the odds of an investigation, but perhaps not as dramatically as one might imagine. The results for the rule of law index, which serves as a proxy the complementarity principle, are similar in the sense that the coefficients are signed in the expected direction but are not statistically significant. Specifically, the negative coefficient indicates that the ICC is somewhat less likely to open investigations in countries where the domestic rule of law is strong, a result consistent with the complementarity principle.

The final legal covariate – the gravity of violence – is the only variable that is statistically significant across all five models. The significant and positive coefficients indicate that the likelihood of an ICC investigation increases in tandem with the number of civilians killed. In other words, the ICC appears to be doing a good job following its legal mandate to focus on the worst of the worst. This may come as a surprise to some observers of the Court. The ICC is often attacked for failing to follow the gravity principle – not necessarily because the situations it investigates are insufficiently grave but because plenty of other grave situations never get investigated. For instance, William Schabas describes the gravity principle as an "inchoate notion" and insists that it "strikes the observer as little more than obfuscation, a labored attempt to make the determinations look more judicial than they really are."[65] But the results from my analysis suggest that the ICC's decisions about when and where to open investigations do, in fact, appear to follow an impartial judicial logic.

None of the political variables in Table 5.2 are statistically significant. One of them – Africa – deserves closer scrutiny. As described earlier, accusations of anti-Africa bias have frequently been lodged against the ICC. If this sort of bias exists at the investigation stage, then we should see a significant and positive relationship between one-sided violence located in Africa and ICC investigations. But that is not the case: the Africa variable is positive but never statistically significant. Why? There are three possible explanations. First, a large share of civil conflicts and grave human rights abuses have taken place in Africa, so a large number of investigations there is not necessarily evidence of ICC bias.[66] Second, Africa represents the largest regional

---

[65] Schabas 2012, 89. [66] Smeulers, Weerdesteijn, and Hola 2015.

block of votes in the ICC's Assembly of State Parties, the organ of the ICC responsible for selecting the Court's prosecutor and judges.[67] Since each member of the Assembly gets one vote (i.e., votes from wealthy or powerful countries do not get extra weight like in many other international institutions), it would be difficult for anti-African interests to capture the ICC.[68] Third, several African regimes invited the ICC to open investigations in their countries – that is, they strategically self-referred to the Court in the hopes of marginalizing domestic political opponents – during the ICC's early years.[69] Hence, the substantial number of investigations in Africa may not reflect some desire to "pick on" Africa and but instead may be indicative of the ICC's desire to prioritize investigations in situations where it has a cooperative government.

Overall, this discussion of the covariates is meant to highlight some notable and surprising findings on patterns of ICC investigations. However, it should not distract from the main result in this section: the relationship between ICC investigations and the presence of American troops in a country is statistically insignificant in all five models. Rather than target the US military, the results suggest that the ICC is following its mandate to investigate the world's gravest abuses.

Substantive Effects

The regression estimates in Table 5.2 demonstrate that the relationship between ICC investigations and the presence of American troops in a country is statistically insignificant. These null results are consistent with a finding of "no effect" for the US military presence variable, but they do not necessarily mean the data are *inconsistent with meaningful effects*. As research on negligible effects and equivalence testing illustrates, a large confidence interval (perhaps due to a relatively small sample size like the one in my study) could include both negligible effects and meaningful effects.[70] To address this issue, I follow Carlisle Rainey's approach that calls for explicitly defining what counts as the

---

[67] The ICC classifies its regional membership as follows: thirty-three African states, nineteen Asia-Pacific states, twenty Eastern European states, twenty-eight Latin American and Caribbean states, and twenty-five Western European states.
[68] Austin and Thieme 2016, 345.   [69] Ba 2020.
[70] Rainey 2014; Hartman and Hidalgo 2018.

Findings   221

smallest substantively meaningful effect (or, *m*).[71] Only if the estimated substantive effect and its 90 percent confidence interval fall entirely within the range of −*m* to *m*, can one conclude that a variable's effect is negligible. If any part of the confidence interval exceeds this range, I cannot rule out meaningful effects.

Defining *m* is challenging. The choice of a value for *m* is unique to each particular piece of scholarship and inevitably is at least somewhat arbitrary. One option for defining *m* is to benchmark against the effect sizes for a particular variable in previously published studies on the topic. However, this is only possible in well-developed empirical literatures with a reasonable degree of consensus on what counts as a "meaningful" effect size. The literature on the determinants of ICC investigations, which is still relatively underdeveloped, lacks the sort of consensus required to implement this approach.

An alternative option is for scholars to choose and justify *m* based on their substantive knowledge of the topic and the data at hand. While some might balk at the idea of allowing scholars to define *m* themselves, Rainey makes a compelling case for doing so: "Choosing *m* and explicitly testing the hypothesis drives the researcher to make a clearer and more compelling argument for a negligible effect than any apparent alternative."[72] I therefore choose *m* by letting the data speak for itself. Specifically, I define *m* as 2.6 percentage points, which is the predicted change in the probability of an ICC investigation when the cumulative number of civilian killings in a country increases from 500 to 5,000. By the unfortunate standards of atrocity crimes, this represents a moderate increase in the death toll. In fact, these numbers approximate the levels of one-sided violence in Kenya and the Central Africa Republic, respectively, before the ICC opened investigations. Using this value as *m*, I conclude an effect size is negligible only if its confidence interval falls entirely between −2.6 and 2.6 percentage points.

The results, which are reported in Figure 5.2, show that it is possible to rule out effect sizes larger than 2.6 percentage points because the confidence intervals for the average marginal effects consistently fall entirely within the negligible effects range (the dashed lines). Despite this, readers might still doubt my conclusion that the effect of American troops on ICC investigations is negligible because they are

[71] Rainey 2014.   [72] Rainey 2014, 1085.

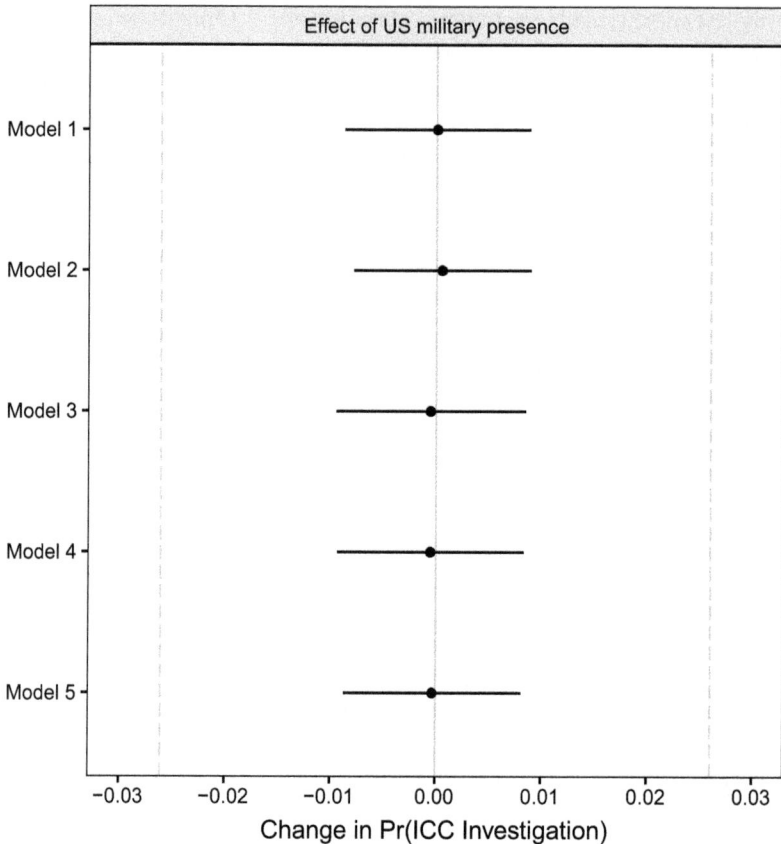

Figure 5.2 The negligible effects of US military presence on ICC investigations

wary of the choice of m. Fortunately, it is easy to inspect the results in Figure 5.2 and visually assess the robustness of my choice of m. If, for example, the confidence intervals come very close to exceeding the negligible effects range, then skepticism may be warranted. But if the confidence intervals fall well within the negligible effects range, then faith in the results should increase. The latter scenario describes my results. Even though I argued that 2.6 percentage points represents an appropriate value for m, all five models allow me to make a stronger claim: effect sizes larger than just 1 percentage point are implausible. Therefore, even if one quibbles with the choice of m, skeptical readers can rest assured that all plausible effect sizes are considerably smaller

Findings

than the negligible effects range. Even if *m* was cut in half, my conclusions would be the same. The bottom line is that the effect of American military presence on ICC investigations is either nonexistent or extremely small.

Robustness Checks

The preceding results – both the regression estimates and the substantive effects – support the conclusion that the ICC does not target the American military. But how robust are the results? The models in Table 5.2 provide arguably the most effective way to explore potential anti-American bias in the ICC's investigations, but there are reasonable alternatives as well. To the extent that different statistical techniques and variable definitions yield similar results, confidence in the core finding should increase. I therefore subject my results to several different robustness checks.

First, I assess whether rare events bias might drive my results. Rare events bias can occur for dichotomous outcomes – such as whether or not the ICC initiates an investigation – and is especially acute when "events" (i.e., an investigation is opened) are far less common than "nonevents" (i.e., an investigation is not opened). This sort of bias causes standard regression models to underestimate the probably of the rare events and can lead to misleading inferences. Given that the ICC has opened only seventeen investigations to date, rare events bias is a legitimate concern. Fortunately, statisticians have developed techniques to account for the possibility of rare events bias. This allows scholars to confirm that their analyses of rare but important outcomes in international politics – not just ICC investigations but also wars, revolutions, coups, and the like – are not the product of rare events bias. When I reestimate the models using a rare events modeling technique, I find that the results are virtually identical.[73]

Second, I consider preliminary examinations as an alternative dependent variable.[74] Recall that in the main analysis I deliberately choose to focus on the ICC's investigations rather than its preliminary examinations for a pair of reasons. To start, the ICC has a lower level

---

[73] Specifically, I use a penalized maximum likelihood regression technique to account for possible rare events bias. See Firth 1993.

[74] For another analysis of preliminary examinations, see Prorok, Appel, and Minhas 2024.

of discretion over preliminary examinations, making them a less than ideal place to judge the degree of ICC bias. Additionally, the ICC sometimes keeps secret the date on which it opens preliminary examinations. In these cases, the ICC merely shares when preliminary examinations are "made public." This leaves some ambiguity about when preliminary examinations started and makes statistical modeling difficult. Despite these issues, it is a useful robustness check to verify that my results are similar when the dependent variable is the opening of an ICC preliminary examination.[75] In these models, my conclusions are unchanged.

Third, I examine an alternative measure of the independent variable of interest: US military presence. The alternative measure shifts the focus from American military bases to American troops themselves. Specifically, I use Michael Allen, Michael Flynn, and Carla Martinez Machain's dataset that codes the number of active-duty American troops deployed in each country for every year between 1950 and 2020.[76] Relative to Vine's dataset on US military bases, an obvious advantage of this dataset is its time-series cross-sectional structure. For my purposes, however, the deployments data have some drawbacks as well. The original source for the numbers of American troops deployed in each country is the Defense Manpower Data Center, a part of the Department of Defense. As described above, the Pentagon's reporting on its overseas military presence is questionable. Additionally, the Pentagon's standards for reporting troop levels are not consistent over time.[77] Finally, the numbers only include active-duty troops that are publicly assigned to a host country. This means that special forces, reservists, and National Guard deployments are often not captured in the data. For these reasons, the precise numbers of troops should be interpreted with a healthy dose of caution. Nevertheless, the deployments dataset is useful for determining which countries do and do not have an American military presence. I therefore use Allen, Flynn, and

---

[75] For these models, I use the date that preliminary examinations were made public if the opening date was kept secret. Other than that, the basic structure of the tests is comparable to the main models. That is, the unit of analysis is the country year. A country enters my sample after its first instance of one-sided violence, putting it "at risk" of a preliminary examination. The country exits my sample if and when the ICC opens a preliminary examination.

[76] Allen, Flynn, and Martinez Machain 2022.

[77] Allen, Flynn, and Martinez Machain 2022, 357.

Martinez Machain's dataset to create a dummy variable indicating whether countries have any American troops deployed to their territory in a given year. This alternative measure produces results that are very similar to my main measure of US military presence.

Fourth, I address the concern that ICC investigations stemming from UN Security Council referrals could be different than other investigations. More specifically, investigations due to Security Council referrals are inherently politicized to at least some degree.[78] Referrals suggest that there is major power support for an investigation, so the opening of an investigation might reflect the preferences of the "P5" members of the Security Council as much as ICC decision-making. For example, the very fact that a Security Council referral occurred means that the US opted not to use its veto power to block ICC jurisdiction. One might be tempted to argue that the two investigations stemming from Security Council referrals – Sudan and Libya – are so unique that they ought to be excluded from the analysis. I did not pursue this strategy in the main analysis because the ICC still has agency after a referral: the Court can decide not to open an investigation even when the Security Council initiates a referral. I therefore kept Security Council referrals in the analysis and controlled for the dynamics linked to these situations (specifically, whether each country has an alliance with a P5 member). Nonetheless, it is possible that unique dynamics are at play in the Sudan and Libya cases. To ensure that these UN Security Council referral investigations do not drive or distort my results, I reestimate the models after excluding them from the sample. My results are consistent.

Fifth, I address a possible concern about selection effects relating to the fact that America's overseas military presence is not randomly distributed around the world. It would be problematic, for example, if US troops are stationed in places that are disproportionately more/less likely to experience factors that also make ICC involvement more/less likely. Fortunately, we can assess this concern empirically. Table 5.2 shows that the variable most robustly linked to ICC investigations is the gravity of violence in a country. I therefore check whether countries with an American military presence (using both definitions) tend to have disproportionately high or low levels of violence against civilians. I find that this is not the case. The gravity of violence in a

---

[78] Tiemessen 2014.

country does not have a statistically significant correlation with US military bases or US troop deployments. This suggests the American military does not end up in countries that have a systematically higher or lower underlying risk of ICC investigations, which assuages concerns about selection effects.

Extension: Does the ICC Target America's Friends?

As an extension of my main results, I assess whether ICC investigations target America's friends. Even if the ICC does not unfairly go after the US military – as already shown in this chapter – it is possible that the ICC still threatens American interests by disproportionately targeting American-aligned countries with its investigations. To date, this concern has been most prominent with the ICC investigation in Palestine. Even though this investigation encompasses atrocities committed on both the Israeli and Palestinian sides, the public discourse surrounding this situation – including reactions from the media and policymakers – has generally treated it as an investigation of Israel. Indeed, the ICC's Palestine investigation elicited harsh reactions from Israeli and American leadership. For example, Israeli Prime Minister Benjamin Netanyahu labeled the ICC investigation a case of "pure antisemitism" and vowed "to fight this perversion of justice with all our might!"[79] After the ICC issued arrest warrants for Netanyahu and his defense minister, Yoav Gallant, official Washington briefly set aside partisan differences as Congressional Republicans, Congressional Democrats, and the Biden White House all denounced the ICC.[80] The origin of American animosity to the Court's investigation in Palestine, as described in Chapter 4, was twofold. First, the US viewed the investigation through the lens of precedent setting. The ICC was exercising territorial jurisdiction over individuals from a nonmember state for acts committed on the territory of a member state – something Washington had opposed ever since negotiations in Rome. Second, Israel was America's staunchest ally in the Middle East. The US had no desire to see the conduct of one of its closest partners second-guessed in an ICC investigation.

---

[79] Israel Ministry of Foreign Affairs 2021.
[80] For details, see the discussion of the American reaction to the Palestine investigation in Chapter 4.

This example suggests a more general question: Do ICC investigations disproportionately target America's friends? To check, I reestimate the five models from Table 5.2 with one notable change: Instead of the US military presence variable, I include a variable that measures how similar each country's voting in the UN General Assembly is to that of the US, a standard proxy for the degree of foreign policy alignment between two countries.[81] I find no evidence to indicate that the ICC investigates America's friends at a higher rate than other countries. In particular, the UN voting similarity variable is never statistically significant (nor is it even close to significance: the *p*-value for this variable exceeds 0.77 in all five models). Thus, the ICC investigation in Palestine is not part of a broader trend in which ICC investigations systematically target America's partners and allies.

Conclusion

When diplomats gathered in Rome in 1998 and succeeded in creating the first permanent institution of international justice, most of the world celebrated their historic achievement. Human rights activists, international lawyers, NGOs, and foreign policy officials in many countries expressed high hopes that the new International Criminal Court could stay the hand of would-be mass murderers and establish a world in which the rule of law restrained the worst excesses of war. But the American foreign policy community saw it differently. Many in Washington became convinced the ICC was bound to initiate politicized investigations that targeted American troops stationed around the world. This fear has formed the backbone of US opposition to the ICC ever since the Court's creation.

But is America's fear justified? This chapter provided an answer. My goal was to avoid the pitfalls that come with cherry-picking just one or a handful of ICC investigations and instead conduct a systematic statistical analysis of the ICC's entire track record. I started with a global sample of civilian killings that approximates the universe of situations the ICC might plausibly investigate. I then used data on the locations of all US overseas military bases to examine how the presence of American troops in a country affects the likelihood of the ICC launching an investigation. Contrary to the common narrative of

---

[81] Bailey, Strezhnev, and Voeten 2017.

anti-American bias, the estimated effects of US military bases were statistically indistinguishable from zero. Moreover, the results were estimated precisely enough to rule out even relatively small substantive effects. A slew of robustness checks confirmed that the results hold regardless of which statistical techniques are used or how the key concepts are measured. Simply put, there is no evidence that ICC investigations target America's military.

6 | *The Future of US–ICC Relations*

This book started with a puzzle about American foreign policy. Despite its unprecedented dominance of global affairs, the US fears a group of prosecutors and judges sitting in a quiet Dutch town along the shores of the North Sea. This collection of international lawyers – the ICC – possesses none of the traditional markers of power in world politics. It has no army, no diplomatic corps, no currency, and so on. Yet American officials often are worried enough about the ICC to discuss the Court as if it were a dire foreign policy threat on par with a geopolitical rival, rogue state, or terrorist group. To make sense of the bizarre relationship between the world's superpower and one of its most prominent international institutions, I asked three questions in this book. First, why is the US afraid of the ICC? Second, when does the US actively oppose the ICC? Third, does the ICC's track record justify the hostility that it has faced from the US?

To answer the first question, I began by zooming out from the specifics of the US–ICC relationship to analyze America's broader relationship with international criminal tribunals. If the US has historically been opposed to international justice institutions, then its hostility to the ICC is not particularly surprising. However, as I demonstrated in Chapter 2, this is not the case. Against the wishes of its allies and adversaries alike, the US almost singlehandedly forged the tribunals at Nuremberg and Tokyo after World War II. The US then led the way in creating, funding, staffing, and supporting the tribunals for Yugoslavia and Rwanda in the early post–Cold War period. Even after the ICC was established, the US has continued to devote significant military, diplomatic, and financial support to other international tribunals. Against this backdrop of steady American support for international justice, the ICC stands out as the only tribunal that routinely sparks the wrath of official Washington.

What exactly is it about the ICC that makes the American foreign policy community – presidents and members of Congress, diplomats and military officers, Republicans and Democrats – so worried? Their overarching fear, I explained in Chapter 3, is that the ICC might initiate politically biased investigations and prosecutions that target American troops scattered across the globe. This fear is the result of the US losing two key negotiating battles over the Court's institutional design at the Rome Conference, the 1998 diplomatic gathering that established the ICC. The first is that the ICC has jurisdiction over all individuals – including those from states that, like the US, never joined the Court – when they are on the territory of an ICC member. The other is that the ICC has an independent prosecutor who can select his or her own situations to investigate without needing the permission of states or the UN Security Council. The combination of these two factors – the Court's territorial jurisdiction and the broad discretion afforded to its prosecutor – alarmed Clinton administration officials. Given America's global military presence, its troops would be uniquely exposed to the ICC's jurisdiction *and* might face an ICC prosecutor who was free to inject anti-American biases into the Court's work. From the US perspective, the Rome Conference spawned to a new threat to America's global military.

When answering the second question, I shifted my focus toward US policy in the post-Rome period. Even though American wariness about the ICC's potential to target its troops is a constant, I showed that US policy toward the ICC is a variable. To explain variation in American policy toward the Court, I introduced a typology in Chapter 4 that identifies three strategies the US might pursue in response to ICC investigations: opposition, assistance, and neglect. I then considered why the US might pick one strategy over the others. My theory focused on the interaction of two variables: whether the ICC investigation threatens American troops and whether the ICC investigation advances broader American foreign policy goals. I finally documented US policy toward the ICC during the Bush, Obama, Trump, and Biden administrations. Despite their many differences, all four presidents tended to behave in a manner consistent with my theoretical expectations.

Answering the third question required a careful probe into the ICC's track record over the past two decades. Specifically, do the allegations of bias that American officials often hurl at the ICC stand up to social scientific scrutiny? The central idea motivating my analysis of ICC investigations in Chapter 5 was that US officials are mistaken when they quickly jump to conclusions about ICC bias by cherry-picking just one or perhaps a small handful of investigations that they do not like. In fact, it is impossible to draw legitimate inferences about the extent of anti-American bias at the ICC by examining only the Court's investigations – a valid analysis must include all ICC investigations as well as the situations the ICC decided *not* to investigate. I therefore created a global sample of civilian killings that approximates the universe of situations the ICC might plausibly investigate and employed geolocated data on all US overseas military bases to examine how the presence of American troops in a country affects the likelihood of the ICC opening an investigation. My results were clear and consistent: There is no evidence to suggest that ICC investigations unfairly target the American military.

Is a Better Relationship Possible?

My book's findings question the very basis of America's wariness of the ICC. The critique – now more than two decades old – that the ICC *would* inject anti-American biases into its investigations has not come to pass. That said, some in Washington oppose the ICC simply because it *could* theoretically target Americans. This distinction – would versus could – is crucial for thinking systematically about whether a better US–ICC relationship is possible.

Documenting the absence of ICC bias to date will do nothing to sway the "could" camp because they insist that the Court should not be able to exercise jurisdiction over American personnel under any circumstance. This perspective goes all the way back to the Rome Conference and is most closely associated with the Department of Defense and its allies in Congress. For example, during the negotiations that produced the Court, Pentagon officials "insisted on sealtight ways to immunize all soldiers from the reach of the International Criminal Court."[1] Likewise, Senator Jesse Helms and other hardliners in Congress insisted that it would be unacceptable if American troops had anything less than "100% protection" from the ICC.[2] This perspective continues to the present day. Most notably, the Pentagon sought to undermine American efforts to aid the ICC's investigation in Ukraine – even as the rest of the US foreign policy community

---

[1] Scheffer 2012a, 181.   [2] Wedgwood 1998, 21.

wanted to support the investigation – because the Pentagon worried about setting a precedent that could make it easier for the ICC to exercise jurisdiction over Americans in the future. As Secretary of Defense Llyod Austin put it, "I will always prioritize the protection of U.S. military personnel."[3] According to this mindset, other foreign policy goals – even high-level priorities such as punishing Vladimir Putin for Russia's invasion of Ukraine – are secondary to shielding American forces from ICC scrutiny.

For the "would" crowd, the ICC's track record matters. According to this perspective, the fact that the ICC has jurisdiction over Americans (at least while they are on the territory of ICC members) matters less than what the ICC actually does with that jurisdiction. If the Court injects anti-American biases into its work and unfairly targets American troops, then the US should do everything it can to protect its soldiers. But if the Court refrains from doing so, there is little reason for the US to exhibit hostility toward the ICC. Bill Clinton was an early adopter of this perspective. As documented in Chapter 3, the Clinton administration was deeply concerned about the possibility of ICC bias, fearing that the Court's prosecutor would become an "international Kenneth Starr" who cast harsh judgment on American military actions around the world.[4] These fears were significant enough for Clinton to instruct the US delegation to vote against the ICC's creation in Rome. At the same time, however, Clinton was not inherently opposed to ICC jurisdiction over American personnel. When Clinton made his last-minute decision to sign the Rome Statute but not seek Senate ratification of the treaty, he noted that the US might support the ICC – and might even join it someday – but only after evaluating the ICC's track record: "The United States should have the chance to observe and assess the functioning of the court, over time, before choosing to become subject to its jurisdiction."[5]

The US has now had more than two decades to do what Clinton wanted: observe and assess the functioning of the ICC.[6] The results

---

[3] Phil Stewart and Idrees Ali, "US Senators Accuse Pentagon of Hindering War Crimes Prosecution of Russia," *Reuters*, May 11, 2023.
[4] Weschler 2000, 95.   [5] Clinton 2000.
[6] Scholars have also observed and assessed the functioning of the ICC. For example, the *Journal of Human Rights* published a special issue in 2023 that judged the ICC's performance in the twenty-five years since the Rome Conference. See Broache et al. 2023.

should be encouraging to American officials who were once concerned that the ICC prosecutor would morph into some sort of anti-American Ken Starr on the global stage. While US officials have certainly disagreed with some ICC actions – such as the investigations in Afghanistan and Palestine – there is no evidence of systematic anti-American bias at the Court. In contradiction to the American fears expressed in Rome and beyond, the likelihood of the ICC opening an investigation into a given situation is no higher when American troops are present. Moreover, no American has ever faced an ICC arrest warrant, let alone a trial at The Hague. Instead of demonstrating political bias, my results suggest that the Court has done a reasonably good job following its legal mandate by investigating the world's gravest atrocity crimes.

This may not be surprising to those who have closely followed the ICC's track record. There is ample evidence that at least some American policymakers have updated their assessment of the threat that the Court poses to US troops in particular and US foreign policy interests more broadly. A notable example is David Scheffer, the leader of the American delegation in Rome. Scheffer was a harsh critic of the ICC that emerged from the negotiations in Rome, where he repeatedly pushed for some kind of exemption that would place American soldiers beyond the ICC's reach. But a quarter of a century later, Scheffer is now an ardent ICC supporter who urges the US to join the Court. Scheffer's evolution from critic to supporter follows the logic of the "would" perspective – that is, the US should judge the ICC based on what it actually has done, not on what it hypothetically could do. In his words, "While there are some imperfections in the workings of the ICC, as there are with every legal system, the ICC's professionalism and track record merit Washington's respect."[7]

The challenge for US–ICC relations, however, is that not everyone in Washington follows the ICC's track record so closely. ICC critics in the US, ranging from members of Congress to Pentagon officials, routinely describe the rules governing how the ICC works in misleading or erroneous terms.[8] It remains an open question whether these mistakes are genuine or whether American officials are strategically

---

[7] Scheffer 2023.
[8] For example, several prominent senators signed an open letter that criticized the ICC for failing to investigate foreign leaders such as China's Xi Jinping and Syria's Bashar Assad – even though the ICC unambiguously does not have jurisdiction over crimes committed in China or Syria. See Cotton 2024.

misrepresenting the ICC to advance their criticisms of the Court. But some scholars, after combing through Congressional statements on the ICC, have concluded that several members of the House and the Senate "lack even an elementary understanding of the International Criminal Court."[9]

Looking ahead, there are reasons for both pessimism and optimism about the future of US–ICC relations. The case for pessimism focuses on American political elites. Put simply, it matters who controls the levers of power in Washington. If the pragmatic "would" camp holds sway, a better US–ICC relationship becomes a more realistic prospect. Indeed, ICC proponents in the US can now point to the Court's track record, including the evidence documented in this book. But when the absolutist "could" camp has the upper hand in the halls of power, US–ICC relations are likely to take a turn for the worse regardless of anything that the ICC does (or does not do). The crucial barrier to better US–ICC relations is that the balance of power in Washington has typically favored the "could" camp, a group that includes nearly all Republicans and many Democrats as well. This distribution of power appears unlikely to change anytime soon.

Moreover, Donald Trump's return to the White House poses a unique risk to the US–ICC relationship. To be clear, what makes Trump different is *not* his eagerness to oppose ICC investigations that might implicate American troops or harm American foreign policy interests. As I demonstrated in Chapter 4, opposing this sort of ICC investigation is a rare area of bipartisanship in Washington. With Trump, the unique risk is that the US might conceivably return to blanket opposition toward the ICC (similar to Bush's first term) rather than a case-by-case assessment of whether to assist, oppose, or neglect specific ICC investigations. In other words, the Trump administration's antagonism toward the Court might be so great that it throws the entire US–ICC relationship into disarray and jeopardizes the ability of the US to support even the investigations that are consistent with American interests such as those in Ukraine, Libya, and Sudan.

This risk is real because of how far Trump is willing to go when attacking the Court.[10] One of Trump's earliest actions upon retaking

---

[9] Trahan and Fairlie 2020.
[10] On Trump's general disregard for international humanitarian law, see Ford 2021; Gift 2025.

the White House for his second term was to sign Executive Order 14203, which imposed new sanctions on ICC personnel as retaliation for the Court's investigation of Israeli conduct in Palestine. While the executive order only explicitly named ICC Prosecutor Karim Khan,[11] it included vague language stating that any person, institution, or company providing "services" to Khan could face "tangible and significant consequences."[12] This clause has already undermined the ICC's capacity to conduct basic work in all its investigations, not just the one in Palestine. For instance, Trump's sanctions have chilled the willingness of third parties to cooperate with the ICC. Microsoft, which provides data and cloud services to the Court, cancelled Khan's email after he was named in the sanctions.[13] Nongovernmental organizations, who often work closely with the ICC on tasks such as evidence collection, have halted collaboration with the Court out of fear that their assistance might pique the Trump administration's ire.[14] Within the Court, the effects of Trump's sanctions are being felt beyond just Khan. For example, the executive order appears to block the ICC's lead prosecutor in the Sudan investigation from doing his job since it could be interpreted as providing services to Khan – despite the fact that successive American presidents have supported the Sudan investigation.[15] In other words, Trump's second term may shift the US away from selective engagement with ICC investigations and toward blanket opposition to the Court as a whole.

This situation will not be easy to defuse. The tactics that the Trump administration has used against the ICC are so aggressive and indiscriminate that the ICC may feel compelled to push back.[16] Some have even speculated that the ICC might issue an arrest warrant for Trump for using American sanctions to obstruct justice in places such as

---

[11] In June 2025, the Trump administration expanded the sanctions to include four ICC judges connected to the Afghanistan and Palestine investigations.
[12] Office of the President 2025.
[13] Molly Quell, "Trump's Sanctions on ICC Prosecutor Have Halted Tribunal's Work," *Associated Press*, May 15, 2025.
[14] Ibid.   [15] Ibid.
[16] Some of America's traditional adversaries have cheered on Trump's assault on the ICC. For example, one Russian diplomat described American sanctions on the ICC as "a gift to Moscow." See Pyotr Kozlov, "Kremlin Gloats as Trump Sanctions International Criminal Court," *Moscow Times*, February 7, 2025.

Afghanistan and Palestine.[17] The basis for such a charge would be Article 70 of the Rome Statute, which authorizes the ICC to pursue the arrest of those responsible for "offenses against the administration of justice." As much as the Court's supporters may feel justified in targeting Trump, this is an area where the ICC needs to tread carefully. Trump would likely view an arrest warrant with his name on it as both a threat and an insult, which in turn would provide an easy justification for him to escalate America's war on the ICC to new heights.

The case for optimism about future US–ICC relations focuses on the American public rather than American political elites. One of the more remarkable aspects of US hostility to the ICC is the degree to which it is confined to "inside the beltway" circles: politicians, policymakers, lobbyists, think tanks, and the like. The average American citizen takes a much brighter view of the ICC. Public opinion surveys conducted on behalf of the American Bar Association offer some notable findings in this regard.[18] First, American public opinion about the ICC is mostly positive – more Americans favor joining the ICC than staying out – and is slowly but surely improving over time. Second, the American public is far more open to the possibility of the ICC investigating US troops than are government officials and other DC insiders. When asked specifically about an ICC investigation examining of the conduct of US servicemembers in Afghanistan, the number of Americans who supported the investigation (45 percent) more than doubled the number who opposed it (21 percent).[19] Third, there is plenty of room for US public opinion about the ICC to improve even further, particularly if the ICC can engage in effective outreach efforts to the American public. Most Americans know very little about the Court, but approval of the ICC moves in tandem with knowledge about it: Americans who know more about the ICC are more likely to support the Court.[20] All three of these public opinion trends bode well for the future of US–ICC relations. To the extent that public opinion plays a role in shaping American foreign policy, it will be increasingly difficult for government

---

[17] Kenneth Roth, "Trump's Sanctions Against the ICC Are Disgraceful," *The Guardian*, February 9, 2025.

[18] American Bar Association 2018.

[19] The remaining 34 percent were unsure whether they would support or oppose the investigation.

[20] Framing American engagement with the ICC as a human rights issue also increases support for the Court among the US public. See Zvobgo 2019.

officials to find support for aggressive policies designed to destroy the ICC.

Policy Recommendations

Having made the case that a better US–ICC relationship is at least possible – though far from guaranteed, especially in the short term – it is worth considering what a better relationship would look like in practice. In doing so, I limit myself to options that are politically feasible in the US. For example, I do not advocate for the US to ratify the Rome Statute and formally join the ICC as a state party. To be sure, there are some compelling reasons for the US to consider joining the ICC at some point in the future. Academic studies show that powerful states, such as the US, are often able to advance their own foreign policy interests when they work within the structure of international institutions.[21] In the context of the ICC, joining would give the US a vote in the Assembly of State Parties, meaning that it could play a role in selecting the ICC's personnel. Even more importantly, joining would allow the US to nominate its nationals for positions at the ICC. Using its substantial diplomatic clout, it is not difficult to imagine the US placing an American judge on the bench or inserting an American into the all-important prosecutor position. With Americans in positions of influence at the ICC, Washington's ongoing concerns about anti-American bias at the Court presumably would be assuaged.

At the same time, however, it is unrealistic to expect the US to ratify the Rome Statute in the foreseeable future. Joining the Court would automatically expose all American troops everywhere in the world to the ICC's jurisdiction. Given long-standing US objections to the ICC exercising jurisdiction over American servicemembers in a more limited set of circumstances – that is, only when they are on the territory of an ICC member – joining the Court appears to be a nonstarter for many American officials. Even if an American president was willing to risk his or her political career by advocating for ICC membership, it is inconceivable that two-thirds of the Senate would be willing to ratify the Rome Statute in the current climate. To be fair, American politicians occasionally express support for the idea of joining the ICC, such as when Senator Bernie Sanders called on the

[21] Ikenberry 2000; Stone 2011.

US to become an ICC member in 2024 as part of his "revolution in American foreign policy" proposal.[22] But this remains a fringe perspective. As documented throughout this book, American concerns about the ICC targeting US military personnel is one area where bipartisanship is still alive and well.

In what follows, I outline some simple steps that Washington can take to improve the US–ICC relationship – without undermining the security of American troops – even if the US never joins the Court.[23]

Recognize the ICC's Territorial Jurisdiction

Every American president since the late 1990s has insisted the Court should never have jurisdiction over Americans because the US has not joined the ICC. This long-standing position is absolute: American officials even reject ICC jurisdiction when Americans are physically in ICC member states. To most of the world, particularly the ICC's 125 member states, this is a politically toxic position. From their perspective, American nationals on foreign soil have always been subject to the laws of the host country.[24] The ICC's territorial jurisdiction therefore should be uncontroversial because states merely are choosing to delegate the right to prosecute a limited set of heinous crimes – genocide, war crimes, and crimes against humanity – to the ICC instead of prosecuting those crimes in their own courts. Consequently, in the eyes of much of the world, the American rejection of the ICC's territorial jurisdiction is tantamount to insisting that other countries are not free to make their own decisions about how to address crimes that occur within their borders.

The US should stop insisting that the ICC does not have jurisdiction over American nationals when they are on the territory of ICC members. The US should drop this position not because it is an unpopular viewpoint in foreign capitals but rather because it is counterproductive for American foreign policy. No matter how many times American officials insist that they do not recognize the ICC's territorial

---

[22] Sanders 2024.
[23] I focus on policy recommendations for Washington rather than The Hague because the friction in the US–ICC relationship has generally come from the American side.
[24] Status of forces agreements between the US and the states hosting American troops represent a partial exception.

jurisdiction, it does nothing to protect US troops deployed abroad. The reason is simple: the ICC's judges and prosecutors do not – and cannot – agree with the US. The Rome Statute unambiguously gives the Court the authority to investigate and prosecute individuals from nonmember states while they are on the territory of member states. The ICC has proved that it is unwilling to backtrack on matters of jurisdiction even in the face of tremendous American pressure, such as the Trump administration's belligerent reaction to the Afghanistan investigation. Hence, American bluster on the Court's territorial jurisdiction not only alienates the ICC's supporters but it also fails to shield American soldiers from ICC jurisdiction while they are deployed to an ICC member state.

Objecting to the ICC's territorial jurisdiction comes with another cost for American foreign policy: it exposes the US to charges of double standards. To be sure, accusations of hypocrisy and victor's justice have plagued the international justice movement ever since Nuremberg. But US policy on the ICC's territorial jurisdiction – especially during the Biden administration – took American double standards to an unprecedented level. In just a few years, the American view on the ICC's territorial jurisdiction seesawed in tandem with Washington's geopolitical interests. When the issue was ICC jurisdiction over Americans in Afghanistan, the US clung to its traditional position that the Court should never have jurisdiction over individuals from nonmember states. But when the issue was the Court's jurisdiction over Russians in Ukraine, the US suddenly decided that it was acceptable for the ICC to exert jurisdiction over the armed forces of a nonmember state. Finally, when the issue was ICC jurisdiction over Israelis in Palestine, the US once again reverted to its position that individuals from nonmember states were above the law. This hypocrisy in American policy sounded the death knell for any principled American legal objection to the ICC's territorial jurisdiction – which was dubious from the beginning – and instead revealed that America's objection was a crude political calculation. The rest of the world noticed.

Embrace the Complementarity Defense

Recognizing that the ICC has jurisdiction over Americans while they are on the territory of ICC members does not mean that the US must give up on protecting its soldiers around the world from unwanted ICC scrutiny. In fact, there is a far more effective way for the US to shield its troops from ICC investigations and prosecutions: the complementarity principle. The ICC was intentionally designed as a "court of last resort" that must back off whenever national courts make genuine attempts to investigate and prosecute abuses on their own. This means that even if American forces were to commit atrocity crimes on the territory of an ICC member state, they would not face an ICC investigation or prosecution – as long as the US does, in fact, address such abuses domestically. Since the US is already committed to prosecuting these crimes under federal criminal law and the Uniform Code of Military Justice, the US merely needs to follow its own laws to stop ICC investigations or prosecutions that implicate American servicemembers.

In practice, embracing complementarity as the primary American defense against ICC scrutiny means two things for US policy. First, the US must recommit to domestic accountability for its armed forces. The US has a distinguished history as a leader in regulating the horrors of warfare going all the way back to the Abraham Lincoln administration's adoption of the Leiber Code during the American Civil War. Indeed, the Leiber Code – which governed the conduct of the Union army – later served as a template for other national militaries and internationally recognized laws of war, such as the Geneva Conventions. But there is a widespread perception that the US commitment to holding its own troops accountable for violations of the laws of war has waned since the start of the global war on terror.[25] For example, the US – under Bush, Obama, Trump, and Biden combined – only brought criminal charges against a small number of servicemembers for their conduct in Afghanistan and Iraq despite numerous accusations of war crimes. On top of that, American politicians sometimes see a political advantage in perpetuating impunity for American forces. Most notably, Trump pardoned two of the soldiers that the US military justice system had, in fact, charged with war crimes in Afghanistan. Trump then brought the pardoned soldiers onstage at a political fundraiser and bragged at a campaign rally that he had "stuck up for [these] great warriors against the deep state."[26] This sort of behavior – which occurred right before the ICC opened its Afghanistan

---

[25] See, for example, Moreno-Ocampo 2022.
[26] Maggie Haberman, "Trump Brings 2 Officers He Cleared of War Crimes Onstage at Fund-Raiser," *New York Times*, December 8, 2019.

investigation – undermined the credibility of American claims that an ICC investigation was unwarranted on the grounds that the US was already making genuine efforts to address war crimes at the domestic level.

Second, the US should be more transparent about how it addresses atrocity crimes at home. The ICC can only defer to national legal proceedings if it knows something about those proceedings. All too often, the US shrouds its investigations into the conduct of its military and intelligence personnel in secrecy. For example, in response to public outcry over CIA torture at "black sites" around the world, the Department of Justice appointed John Durham to lead a special inquiry.[27] Durham ultimately recommended against pressing criminal charges – even in cases that resulted in the deaths of detainees – and the Obama administration accepted his recommendation. This decision prompted a great deal of international skepticism about Durham's investigation and America's commitment to accountability more broadly.[28] The skepticism was compounded by the fact that the US government released almost no information about the investigation, making it impossible for outsiders to judge whether the US was correct in its assessment that criminal charges against CIA personnel were unwarranted. Even some American officials found this silence frustrating. Attorney General Eric Holder proclaimed, "I'd love to be able to just throw on the table all the work that was done by John Durham, and let people see how seriously we took [allegations of torture]."[29] At the same time, however, Holder's Department of Justice insisted that every page of the report remain secret.[30] This obsession with secrecy undermines the ability of the US to protect its troops under the complementarity principle because the lack of transparency makes it hard for the ICC to determine whether genuine investigations are underway in the US.

---

[27] The same John Durham was later tasked with investigating the original FBI investigation into potential collusion between Russia and Donald Trump's campaign during the 2016 election.
[28] Charlie Savage, "U.N. Commission Presses U.S. on Torture," *New York Times*, November 13, 2014.
[29] Dan Froomkin, "Holder, Too Late, Calls for Transparency on DOJ Torture Investigation," *The Intercept*, October 15, 2015.
[30] Charlie Savage, "U.S. Tells Court That Documents from Torture Investigation Should Remain Secret," *New York Times*, December 10, 2014.

If the US can do these two things – follow through on its own laws concerning military justice and increase the transparency of its accountability efforts – American troops have little to fear from the ICC. The reason is simple: Unlike American attempts to dispute the Court's territorial jurisdiction, complementarity is a defense that the ICC readily accepts. The ICC has a documented track record of backing off when national courts conduct legitimate investigations on their own, such as when the Court terminated its preliminary examination in Colombia because it recognized that genuine accountability processes were occurring there. A situation involving the US would be no different. In fact, during the height of American attacks on the ICC over the Afghanistan investigation, ICC President Chile Eboe-Osuji offered the US an easy way out of the crisis, promising, "All it takes [for the ICC to defer to the US under the complementarity principle] is for American authorities to submit individuals suspected of violations in Afghanistan to America's own very effective system of justice. Doing so should effectively address the Afghan victims' demand for justice. The ICC would fully welcome that."[31] Looking ahead, embracing the complementarity defense is the best way for the US to avoid another Afghanistan-style standoff with the ICC.

Repeal the ASPA

Congress should repeal the American Servicemembers' Protection Act. This piece of 2002 legislation – a holdover from Bush's initial round of attacks on the ICC – continues to impose restrictions on the US government's ability to take basic steps to aid the Court. While Congress has already added some carve-outs to this general prohibition on assistance to the ICC, the end result is a nebulous patchwork of rules and regulations. Even American policymakers themselves are often unsure what they are legally permitted to do to help the ICC in cases where the US decides to pursue an assistance strategy. As described in Chapter 4, when the Biden administration opted to support the Ukraine investigation, White House lawyers were uncertain how much "wiggle room" they had as the administration weighed its options for aiding the ICC's efforts to hold Russians accountable for

---

[31] Chile Eboe-Osuji, "All We Want Is Justice for Victims, Says the ICC," *New York Times*, June 18, 2020.

war crimes in Ukraine.³² It is time to remove all legal restrictions on American assistance to the Court.

Repealing the ASPA should be palatable to Congress even though many members remain deeply skeptical of the ICC. Why? Repealing the ASPA does not commit the US to anything. The practical effect of repealing the ASPA would merely make it easier for the US to support the ICC in situations where the US already wants to assist the Court. For example, in future crises like the one in Ukraine – where ICC involvement is a "win-win" for both the US and the Court – the US would be able to marshal support for an investigation without first needing new Congressional legislation (as it did in Ukraine). On the flipside, the US would still be able to oppose ICC investigations that it deems threatening or frivolous even if it repeals the ASPA. As a result, repealing the ASPA has no downside risk for the US. But it would have an upside: the US would gain some goodwill from ICC member states who uniformly deplore this legislation and its antagonistic threats to invade The Hague.

Enforce ICC Arrest Warrants

All too often, the perpetrators of atrocity crimes live with impunity. The ICC's fundamental weakness is enforcement: it does not have a police force to make arrests. The Court must rely on states to apprehend suspects and send them to The Hague. This occasionally works, but it often is problematic. For example, former Sudanese leader Omar Bashir traveled widely across Africa and the Middle East for a decade despite facing an ICC arrest warrant connected to his regime's atrocities in Darfur. Even ICC state parties, the very countries that accepted a legal obligation to arrest wanted individuals who enter their territory, sometimes fall short. ICC member Mongolia, for instance, warmly welcomed ICC fugitive Vladimir Putin for an official visit in 2024. Instead of following through on its obligation to arrest Putin, Mongolia – part of Russia's historical sphere of influence in Central Asia – decided to prioritize maintaining a good relationship with its more powerful neighbor.³³ The unfortunate moral of this story is that

---

³² Charlie Savage, "U.S. Weighs Shift to Support Hague Court as It Investigates Russian Atrocities," *New York Times*, April 11, 2022.
³³ Valerie Hopkins, "Putin Gets a Red-Carpet Welcome in Mongolia Despite Arrest Warrant," *New York Times*, September 3, 2024.

even when the ICC has the jurisdiction to prosecute war criminals, getting them to The Hague is another matter.

The US is uniquely positioned to help enforce ICC arrest warrants given its unrivaled military, economic, and diplomatic clout. To be clear, this does not mean that the US needs to engage in military interventions that risk the lives of American soldiers for the sake of getting ICC suspects to The Hague. Rather, the US could make a big difference to the ICC's enforcement efforts simply by focusing on the "low-hanging fruit." Most notably, the context for arresting oppressive government officials or rebel group leaders is far more favorable after they have fallen from power.[34] For instance, the Obama administration learned that it was relatively costless for the US to help transfer two African warlords to the ICC who were on the run after falling out with their own rebel groups. The US does not necessarily even need to carry out arrests itself to make a difference. The discussion of American support for other international tribunals in Chapter 2 demonstrated that American pressure is often enough to get other countries to arrest the architects of atrocities. American economic and diplomatic incentives were enough to convince Serbia to send Slobodan Milosevic to the ICTY and to persuade Nigeria to transfer Charles Taylor to the SCSL. The lesson from all of these cases is that the US was able to play a constructive role in bringing perpetrators to trial without any adverse consequences for the US. If punishing war criminals and preventing future atrocities is in the American national interest – as several presidents have said – then the US would benefit from assisting the ICC in this regard.

There is, however, one potential downside for the ICC if it comes to rely too heavily on the US for enforcement. To the extent that the US is willing to help enforce ICC arrest warrants, Washington presumably will limit its assistance to cases where apprehending suspects is consistent with America's geopolitical interests. There is no realistic prospect of American support for, say, arresting and transferring Israeli officials or soldiers to The Hague. This selectivity in America's willingness to fill the ICC's enforcement gap would risk entrenching two tiers of justice into the ICC's operations: suspects who are friendly with the US would be more likely to escape punishment than those who are adversarial with the US. The ICC, in turn, would face a difficult decision: accept

[34] For more on this point, see Krcmaric 2020.

American assistance with strings attached or reject it all together. In other words, the ICC would have to grapple with the issue of whether uneven justice is better than no justice at all.[35]

Reconceptualize the Protection of American Troops

As a final recommendation, American officials ought to step back and rethink what it means to protect US troops. American servicemembers are routinely exposed to extraordinary risks in the course of their duties. Since the ICC's founding, for example, the US has fought major wars in Afghanistan and Iraq. The US military has also been ordered to participate in other conflicts – by providing airstrikes, counterterrorism raids, evacuations of American civilians, and so forth – in dozens of countries such as Syria, Yemen, Pakistan, Libya, Mali, Somalia, and Haiti. When US politicians deploy American troops to war zones, failed states, or terrorism hotspots, it is treated as run-of-the-mill foreign policy. But when there is even a tiny risk that the ICC might prosecute an American solider – something that still has never happened – it is treated as an existential threat. If American politicians are serious about protecting their soldiers, they should recognize that the current mode of thinking is out of proportion to the risks involved. Scaling back the use of military force abroad would be a far more effective strategy for protecting the lives and liberty of American servicemembers than demonizing the ICC.

---

[35] On how the ICC handled a similar issue in the context of atypically high state support for its Ukraine investigation, see Vasiliev 2022.

References

Abbott, Kenneth W., and Duncan Snidal. 1998. "Why States Act through Formal International Organizations." *Journal of Conflict Resolution* 42 (1): 3–32.

Achen, Christopher H. 2005. "Let's Put Garbage-Can Regressions and Garbage-Can Probits Where They Belong." *Conflict Management and Peace Science* 22 (4): 327–339.

Akhavan, Payam. 2001. "Beyond Impunity: Can International Criminal Justice Prevent Future Atrocities?" *American Journal of International Law* 95 (1): 7–31.

Al Hussein, Zeid Raad, Bruno Stagno Ugarte, Christian Wenaweser, and Tiina Intelman. 2019. "The International Criminal Court Needs Fixing." *New Atlanticist*, April 24, 2019. Available at www.atlanticcouncil.org/blogs/new-atlanticist/the-international-criminal-court-needs-fixing/.

Allee, Todd L., and Paul K. Huth. 2006. "Legitimizing Dispute Settlement: International Legal Rulings as Domestic Political Cover." *American Political Science Review* 100 (2): 219–234.

Allen, Michael A., Michael E. Flynn, Carla Martinez Machain, and Andrew Stravers. 2020. "Outside the Wire: U.S. Military Deployments and Public Opinion in Host States." *American Political Science Review* 114 (2): 326–341.

Allen, Michael A., Michael E. Flynn, and Carla Martinez Machain. 2022. "US Global Military Deployments, 1950–2020." *Conflict Management and Peace Science* 39 (3): 351–370.

Alter, Karen J. 2008. "Delegating to International Courts: Self-Binding vs. Other-Binding Delegation." *Law and Contemporary Problems* 71 (1): 37–76.

  2014. *The New Terrain of International Law: Courts, Politics, Rights*. Princeton, NJ: Princeton University Press.

Alter, Karen J., and Sophie Meunier. 2009. "The Politics of International Regime Complexity." *Perspectives on Politics* 7 (1): 13–24.

Amanpour, Christiane. 2024. "Interview with ICC Chief Prosecutor Karim Khan." *CNN News*, May 20, 2024. Available at https://transcripts.cnn.com/show/ampr/date/2024-05-20/segment/01.

American Bar Association. 2018. *April 2018 Ipsos Poll Results*. Available at www.ipsos.com/en-us/news-polls/ABA-International-Criminal-Court-Study-2018-04-11.
Amnesty International. 2019. "Afghanistan: ICC Refuses to Authorize Investigation, Caving into USA Threats." *Amnesty International Press Release*, April 12, 2019. Available at www.amnesty.org/en/latest/press-release/2019/04/afghanistan-icc-refuses-to-authorize-investigation-caving-into-usa-threats/.
Anderson, Jon Lee. 2014. "The Mission: A Last Defense against Genocide." *The New Yorker*, October 20, 2014. Available at www.newyorker.com/magazine/2014/10/20/mission-3.
Anderson, Kenneth. 2009. "The Rise of International Criminal Law: Intended and Unintended Consequences." *European Journal of International Law* 20 (2): 331–358.
Andreas, Peter, and Kelly M. Greenhill, eds. 2010. *Sex, Drugs, and Body Counts: The Politics of Numbers in Global Crime and Conflict*. Ithaca, NY: Cornell University Press.
Appel, Benjamin J. 2018. "In the Shadow of the International Criminal Court: Does the ICC Deter Human Rights Violations?" *Journal of Conflict Resolution* 62 (1): 3–28.
Arendt, Hannah. 1977. *Eichmann in Jerusalem: A Report on the Banality of Evil*. New York: Penguin.
Asada, Sadao. 1998. "The Shock of the Atomic Bomb and Japan's Decision to Surrender: A Reconsideration." *Pacific Historical Review* 67 (4): 477–512.
Austin, W. Chadwick, and Michael Thieme. 2016. "Is the International Criminal Court Anti-African?" *Peace Review* 28 (3): 342–350.
Ba, Oumar. 2020. *States of Justice: The Politics of the International Criminal Court*. Cambridge: Cambridge University Press.
Bailey, Michael A., Anton Strezhnev, and Erik Voeten. 2017. "Estimating Dynamic State Preferences from United Nations Voting Data." *Journal of Conflict Resolution* 61 (2): 430–456.
Baker, Anni. 2004. *American Soldiers Overseas: The Global Military Presence*. Westport, CT: Praeger.
Baker, Peter, and Susan Glasser. 2020. *The Man Who Ran Washington: The Life and Times of James A. Baker III*. New York: Knopf.
Barnett, Michael. 2002. *Eyewitness to a Genocide: The United Nations and Rwanda*. Ithaca, NY: Cornell University Press.
Barriga, Stefan, Wolfgang Danspeckgruber, and Christian Wenaweser. 2009. *The Princeton Process on the Crime of Aggression: Materials of the Special Working Group on the Crime of Aggression, 2003–2009*. Boulder, CO: Lynne Rienner Publishers.

Bass, Gary J. 2000. *Stay the Hand of Vengeance: The Politics of War Crimes Tribunals*. Princeton, NJ: Princeton University Press.
   2023. *Judgment at Tokyo: World War II on Trial and the Making of Modern Asia*. New York: Knopf.
Bell, Andrew. 2022. "Combatant Socialization and Norms of Restraint: Examining Officer Training at the US Military Academy and Army ROTC." *Journal of Peace Research* 59 (2): 180–196.
Benedetti, Fanny, and John L. Washburn. 1999. "Drafting the International Criminal Court Treaty: Two Years to Rome and an Afterword on the Rome Diplomatic Conference." *Global Governance* 5 (1): 1–37.
Berlin, Mark S. 2016. "Why (Not) Arrest? Third-Party State Compliance and Noncompliance with International Criminal Tribunals." *Journal of Human Rights* 15 (4): 509–532.
Bing, Dai. 2020. "Statement by the Deputy Permanent Representative of China to the United Nations." United Nations Security Council Document S/2020/1108, November 10, 2020. Available at www.securitycouncilreport.org/atf/cf/%7B65BFCF9B-6D27-4E9C-8CD3-CF6E4FF96FF9%7D/s_2020_1108.pdf.
Bix, Herbert P. 2000. *Hirohito and the Making of Modern Japan*. New York: Harper Collins.
Blaker, James R. 1990. *United States Overseas Basing: An Anatomy of the Dilemma*. New York: Praeger.
Blinken, Anthony J. 2021a. "The United States Opposes the ICC Investigation into the Palestinian Situation." Washington, DC: Department of State, March 3, 2021. Available at https://2021-2025.state.gov/the-united-states-opposes-the-icc-investigation-into-the-palestinian-situation/.
   2021b. "Ending Sanctions and Visa Restrictions against Personnel of the International Criminal Court." Washington, DC: Department of State, April 2, 2021. Available at https://2021-2025.state.gov/ending-sanctions-and-visa-restrictions-against-personnel-of-the-international-criminal-court/.
Bolton, John. 2007. *Surrender Is Not an Option: Defending America at the United Nations and Abroad*. New York: Simon & Schuster.
Bolton, John R. 1998. "Courting Danger: What's Wrong with the International Criminal Court." *The National Interest* 54: 60–71.
   2018. "Address to the Federalist Society." Washington, DC, September 10, 2018. Available at www.americanrhetoric.com/speeches/johnboltonfederalistsociety2018.htm.
Borger, Julian. 2016. *The Butcher's Trail: How the Search for Balkan War Criminals Became the World's Most Successful Manhunt*. New York: Other Press.

Borrell, Josep. 2020. "International Criminal Court: Statement by the High Representative/Vice-President Josep Borrell on US Sanctions." Brussels: European Union, September 3, 2020. Available at www.eeas.europa.eu/eeas/international-criminal-court-statement-high-representativevice-president-josep-borrell-us-sanctions_en.

Bosco, David. 2013. "The War over U.S. War Crimes in Afghanistan Is Heating Up." *Foreign Policy*, December 3, 2013. Available at https://foreignpolicy.com/2014/12/03/the-war-over-u-s-war-crimes-in-afghanistan-is-heating-up-icc-hague/.

2014a. *Rough Justice: The International Criminal Court in a World of Power Politics*. Oxford: Oxford University Press.

2014b. "Is the ICC Investigating Crimes by U.S. Forces in Afghanistan?" *Foreign Policy*, May 15, 2014. Available at https://foreignpolicy.com/2014/05/15/is-the-icc-investigating-crimes-by-u-s-forces-in-afghanistan/.

2016. "Palestine in The Hague: Justice, Geopolitics, and the International Criminal Court." *Global Governance* 22 (1): 155–171.

2017. "Discretion and State Influence at the International Criminal Court: The Prosecutor's Preliminary Examinations." *American Journal of International Law* 111 (2): 395–414.

Boucher, Richard. 2002. "International Criminal Court: Letter to UN Secretary General Kofi Annan." Washington, DC: Department of State, May 6, 2002. Available at https://2001-2009.state.gov/r/pa/prs/ps/2002/9968.htm.

Brackman, Arnold C. 1987. *The Other Nuremberg: The Untold Story of the Tokyo War Crimes Trials*. New York: William Morrow.

Breedlove, Philip, Wesley Clark, and Ben Hodges. 2023. "Why Isn't the Pentagon Helping the International Court Prosecute Putin?" *Defense One*, May 23, 2023. Available at www.defenseone.com/ideas/2023/05/why-isnt-pentagon-helping-international-court-prosecute-putin/386681/.

Briza, Jan. 2005. "Serbia's US Dilemma." Institute for War and Peace Reporting, September 6, 2005. Available at https://iwpr.net/global-voices/serbias-us-dilemma.

Broache, M. P., Kate Cronin-Furman, David Mendeloff, and Jacqueline R. McAllister. 2023. "The International Criminal Court at 25." *Journal of Human Rights* 22 (1): 1–3.

Broache, M. P., and Kyle Reed. 2023. "Who Stands Up for the ICC? Explaining Variation in State Party Responses to US Sanctions." *Foreign Policy Analysis* 19 (1): 1–21.

Brookings Institution. 2013. "How The Hague Courts and Tribunals Protect Human Rights." Washington, DC, April 4, 2013. Available at www.brookings.edu/wp-content/uploads/2013/03/20130404_hague_human_rights_tribunals_transcript.pdf.

Brooks, Stephen G., G. John Ikenberry, and William C. Wohlforth. 2012. "Don't Come Home, America: The Case against Retrenchment." *International Security* 37 (3): 7–51.

Brutger, Ryan, and Richard Clark. 2023. "At What Cost? Power, Payments, and Public Support of International Organizations." *Review of International Organizations* 18 (3): 431–465.

Buchwald, Todd. 2020. "What Kinds of Situations and Cases Should the ICC Pursue? The Independent Expert Review of the ICC and the Question of Aperture." *Just Security*, November 30, 2020. Available at www.justsecurity.org/73530/part-i-what-kinds-of-situations-and-cases-should-the-icc-pursue-the-independent-expert-review-of-the-icc-and-the-question-of-aperture/.

Buchwald, Todd, David M. Crane, Stephen J. Rapp, David Scheffer, and Clint Williamson. 2020. "Former Officials Challenge Pompeo's Threats to the International Criminal Court." *Just Security*, March 18, 2020. Available at www.justsecurity.org/69255/former-officials-challenge-pompeos-threats-to-the-international-criminal-court/.

Buchwald, Todd, and Beth Van Schaack. 2021. *ASIL Task Force on Policy Options for U.S. Engagement with the ICC*. Washington, DC: American Society of International Law. Available at www.asil-us-icc-task-force.org/.

Bureau of Political-Military Affairs. 2003. "American Servicemembers' Protection Act." Washington, DC: Department of State. Available at https://2001-2009.state.gov/t/pm/rls/othr/misc/23425.htm.

Burke-White, Willaim W. 2021. "Trump's Sanctions on the International Criminal Court: Inappropriate, Ineffective, and Dangerous." *ICC Forum*, January 1, 2021. Available at https://iccforum.com/sanctions.

Busby, Joshua W., and Jonathan Monten. 2012. "Republican Elites and Foreign Policy Attitudes." *Political Science Quarterly* 127 (1): 105–142.

Bush, George W. 2004. "Presidential Debate between George W. Bush and John Kerry." Carol Gables, Florida, September 20, 2004. Available at www.presidency.ucsb.edu/documents/presidential-debate-coral-gables-florida.

Butow, Robert J. C. 1954. *Japan's Decision to Surrender*. Stanford, CA: Stanford University Press.

Calder, Kent E. 2007. *Embattled Garrisons: Comparative Base Politics and American Globalism*. Princeton, NJ: Princeton University Press.

Cardin, Benjamin L., and Rob Portman. 2020. "Letter to Secretary of State Michael R. Pompeo." May 13, 2020. Available at www.cardin.senate.gov/press-releases/cardin-portman-lead-bipartisan-senate-call-for-pompeo-to-defend-israel-against-politically-motivated-investigations-by-the-international-criminal-court/.

Carnegie, Allison, and Austin Carson. 2020. *Secrets in Global Governance: Disclosure Dilemmas and the Challenge of International Cooperation*. New York: Cambridge University Press.

Cassese, Antonio. 2008. *International Criminal Law*. 2nd ed. New York: Oxford University Press.

Casto, William R. 2012. "Advising Presidents: Robert Jackson and the Destroyers-For-Bases Deal." *American Journal of Legal History* 52 (1): 1–135.

Chapman, Terrence L., and Stephen Chaudoin. 2013. "Ratification Patterns and the International Criminal Court." *International Studies Quarterly* 57 (2): 400–409.

2020. "Public Reactions to International Legal Institutions: The International Criminal Court in a Developing Democracy." *Journal of Politics* 82 (4): 1305–1320.

Charanie, Shehzad. 2021. "Delivering the ICC Vision through Deeds Not Words: An Interview with Karim Khan QC." *Opinio Juris*, May 21, 2021. Available at http://opiniojuris.org/2021/05/21/selling-the-icc-vision-through-deeds-not-words-an-interview-with-karim-khan-qc/.

Chayes, Abram, and Antonia Handler Chayes. 1993. "On Compliance." *International Organization* 47 (2): 175–205.

Clements, Richard. 2024. *The Justice Factory: Management Practices at the International Criminal Court*. Cambridge: Cambridge University Press.

Clinton, Bill. 2000. "Statement on Signature of the International Criminal Court Treaty." Washington, DC: Department of State, December 31, 2000. Available at https://1997-2001.state.gov/global/swci/001231_clinton_icc.html.

2004. *My Life*. New York: Random House.

Cobban, Helena. 2006. "International Courts." *Foreign Policy* 153 (1): 22–28.

Cohen, David, and Yuma Totani. 2018. *The Tokyo War Crimes Tribunal: Law, History, Jurisprudence*. Cambridge: Cambridge University Press.

Cohen, Elliot A. 2024. "Cancel the Foreign-Policy Apocalypse." *The Atlantic*, July 17, 2024. Available at www.theatlantic.com/politics/archive/2024/07/cancel-foreign-policy-apocalypse-donald-trump-ukraine/679038/.

Collier, David, Jody LaPorte, and Jason Seawright. 2012. "Putting Typologies to Work: Concept Formation, Measurement, and Analytic Rigor." *Political Research Quarterly* 65 (1): 217–232.

Congress of the United States of America. 2022. "Consolidated Appropriations Act, 2023." Washington, DC. Available at www.congress.gov/117/bills/hr2617/BILLS-117hr2617enr.pdf.

Congressional Record – Senate. 2002. "Supplemental Appropriations Act for Fiscal Year 2002." Washington, DC. Available at www.congress.gov/crec/2002/06/06/CREC-2002-06-06-pt1-PgS5132.pdf.

Cooley, Alexander. 2008. *Base Politics: Democratic Change and the U.S. Military Overseas*. Ithaca, NY: Cornell University Press.

Coppedge, Michael, John Gerring, Carl Hendrik Knutsen, and Staffan I. Lindberg. 2024. "V-Dem Country-Year Dataset Version 14." *Varieties of Democracy Project*. Available at www.v-dem.net/data/the-v-dem-dataset/.

Cotton, Tom. 2024. "Letter to Karim Khan." April 24, 2024. Available at www.politico.com/f/?id=0000018f-4e0e-d759-a9ff-ff4ee9420000.

Craddock, Bantz. 2005. "Fiscal Year 2006 National Defense Authorization Budget Request." Hearing before the House Armed Services Committee. Washington, DC, March 9, 2005. Available at https://adamisacson.com/files/old_cip_colombia/050309crad.pdf.

Crawford, Neta C. 2022. *The Pentagon, Climate Change, and War: Charting the Rise and Fall of U.S. Military Emissions*. Cambridge, MA: MIT Press.

Cronin-Furman, Kate. 2013. "Managing Expectations: International Criminal Trials and the Prospects for Deterrence of Mass Atrocity." *International Journal of Transitional Justice* 7 (3): 434–454.

Cruvellier, Thierry. 2006. *Court of Remorse: Inside the International Criminal Tribunal for Rwanda*. Madison: University of Wisconsin Press.

Cruvellier, Thierry, and Mustapha K. Darboe. 2019. "Will Fatou Bensouda Face the Truth Commission in Gambia?" *Justice Info*, July 11, 2019. Available at www.justiceinfo.net/en/41906-will-fatou-bensouda-face-the-truth-commission-trrc-gambia.html.

Cuéllar, Mariano-Florentino. 2003. "The International Criminal Court and the Political Economy of Antitreaty Discourse." *Stanford Law Review* 55 (5): 1597–1632.

Dancy, Geoff. 2017. "Searching for Deterrence at the International Criminal Court." *International Criminal Law Review* 17 (4): 625–655.

Dancy, Geoff, Yvonne Marie Dutton, Tessa Alleblas, and Eamon Aloyo. 2020. "What Determines Perceptions of Bias toward the International Criminal Court? Evidence from Kenya." *Journal of Conflict Resolution* 64 (7–8): 1443–1469.

Danforth, John C. 2005. "Peace and Accountability: A Way Forward." New York: US Mission to the UN, January 7, 2005. Available at https://nsarchive2.gwu.edu/NSAEBB/NSAEBB335/Document4.PDF.

Dannenbaum, Tom. 2018. *The Crime of Aggression, Humanity, and the Soldier*. Cambridge: Cambridge University Press.

Danner, Allison Marston. 2003. "Navigating Law and Politics: The Prosecutor of the International Criminal Court and the Independent Counsel." *Stanford Law Review* 55 (5): 1633–1665.

deGuzman, Margaret M. 2012. "How Serious Are International Crimes? The Gravity Problem in International Criminal Law." *Columbia Journal of Transnational Law* 51 (1): 18–68.

2020. *Shocking the Conscience of Humanity: Gravity and the Legitimacy of International Criminal Law*. Oxford: Oxford University Press.

DeLay, Thomas. 2005. "Statement at the House of Representatives Debate on the Henry J. Hyde United Nations Reform Act." Washington, DC: House of Representatives, June 16, 2005. Available at www.congress.gov/congressional-record/volume-151/issue-80/house-section/article/H4615-2?q=%7B%22search%22%3A%22Europe%22%7D&s=1&r=52.

Department of Defense. 2023. "Base Structure Report." Washington, DC. Available at www.acq.osd.mil/eie/Downloads/BSI/Base%20Structure%20Report%20FY23.xlsx.

Department of State. 2020. "Secretary Michael R. Pompeo at a Press Availability with Secretary of Defense Mark Esper, Attorney General William Barr, and National Security Advisor Robert O'Brien." Washington, DC, June 11, 2020. Available at https://2017-2021.state.gov/secretary-michael-r-pompeo-at-a-press-availability-with-secretary-of-defense-mark-esper-attorney-general-william-barr-and-national-security-advisor-robert-obrien/index.html.

Department of State. 2022. "Department Press Briefing." Washington, DC, March 23, 2022. Available at https://2021-2025.state.gov/briefings/department-press-briefing-march-23-2022/.

Des Forges, Alison. 1999. *Leave None to Tell the Story: Genocide in Rwanda*. New York: Human Rights Watch.

Dobson, Jillian, and Sofia Stolk. 2020. "The Prosecutor's Important Announcements; the Communication of Moral Authority at the International Criminal Court." *Law, Culture and the Humanities* 16 (3): 391–410.

Doshi, Rush. 2021. *The Long Game: China's Grand Strategy to Displace American Order*. Oxford: Oxford University Press.

Dower, John W. 1986. *War without Mercy: Race and Power in the Pacific War*. New York: Pantheon.

1999. *Embracing Defeat: Japan in the Wake of World War II*. New York: Norton.

Downes, Alexander B. 2008. *Targeting Civilians in War*. Ithaca, NY: Cornell University Press.

Drumbl, Mark A. 2005. "Collective Violence and Individual Punishment: The Criminality of Mass Atrocity." *Northwestern University Law Review* 99 (2): 539–610.

Dunlap, Charles J. Jr. 2008. "Lawfare Today: A Perspective." *Yale Journal of International Affairs* 3 (1): 146–154.

Eck, Kristine, and Lisa Hultman. 2007. "One-Sided Violence against Civilians in War: Insights from New Fatality Data." *Journal of Peace Research* 44 (2): 233–246.

Efrat, Asif. 2023. "How to Handle Offending Troops Overseas: The U.S. Military's Legal Strategy during the Cold War." *Armed Forces & Society* 49 (2): 489–506.

Ehrenfreund, Norbert. 2007. *The Nuremberg Legacy: How the Nazi War Crimes Trials Changed the Course of History*. New York: Palgrave MacMillan.

Eilstrup-Sangiovanni, Mette, and J. C. Sharman. 2022. *Vigilantes beyond Borders: NGOs as Enforcers of International Law*. Princeton, NJ: Princeton University Press.

El Zeidy, Mohamed M. 2002. "The Principle of Complementarity: A New Machinery to Implement International Criminal Law." *Michigan Journal of International Law* 23 (4): 869–976.

Elman, Colin. 2005. "Explanatory Typologies in Qualitative Studies of International Politics." *International Organization* 59 (2): 293–326.

Escriba-Folch, Abel, and Daniel Krcmaric. 2017. "Dictators in Exile: Explaining the Destinations of Ex-Rulers." *Journal of Politics* 79 (2): 560–575.

Escriba-Folch, Abel, and Joseph Wright. 2015. *Foreign Pressure and the Politics of Autocratic Survival*. Oxford: Oxford University Press.

Feil, Scott R. 1998. *Preventing Genocide: How the Early Use of Force Might Have Succeeded in Rwanda*. New York: Carnegie Corporation. Available at www.carnegie.org/publications/preventing-genocide-how-the-early-use-of-force-might-have-succeeded-in-rwanda/.

Feis, Herbert. 1966. *The Atomic Bomb and the End of World War II*. Princeton, NJ: Princeton University Press.

Ferencz, Benjamin B. 1998. "International Criminal Courts: The Legacy of Nuremberg." *Pace International Law Review* 10 (1): 203–235.

Ferguson, Niall. 2005. *Colossus: The Rise and Fall of the American Empire*. New York: Penguin.

Firth, David. 1993. "Bias Reduction of Maximum Likelihood Estimates." *Biometrika* 80 (1): 27–38.

Ford, Stuart. 2011. "How Leadership in International Criminal Law Is Shifting from the United States to Europe and Asia: An Analysis of Spending on and Contributions to International Criminal Courts." *Saint Louis University Law Journal* 55 (3): 953–999.

2021. "Don Quixote or Darth Vader? President Trump's Views on International Humanitarian Law." *Washington University Global Studies Law Review* 20 (1): 45–98.

Foreign and Commonwealth Office. 2018. "UK Statement to the ICC Assembly of States Parties 17th Session." The Hague, Netherlands,

December 5, 2018. Available at www.gov.uk/government/speeches/uk-statement-to-icc-assembly-of-states-parties-17th-session.
Friedman, Hal M. 2000. *Creating an American Lake: United States Imperialism and Strategic Security in the Pacific Basin, 1945–1947.* Westport, CT: Praeger.
Gberie, Lansana. 2005. *A Dirty War in West Africa: The RUF and the Destruction of Sierra Leone.* Bloomington: Indiana University Press.
Gent, Stephen E., and Megan Shannon. 2010. "The Effectiveness of International Arbitration and Adjudication: Getting Into a Bind." *Journal of Politics* 72 (2): 366–380.
Gholz, Eugene, Daryl G. Press, and Harvey M. Sapolsky. 1997. "Come Home, America: The Strategy of Restraint in the Face of Temptation." *International Security* 21 (4): 5–48.
Gibler, Douglas M. 2009. *International Military Alliances, 1648–2008.* Washington, DC: CQ Press.
Gift, Thomas. 2025. *Killing Machines: Trump, the Law of War, and the Future of Military Impunity.* Cambridge: Cambridge University Press.
Gilbert, G. M. 1947. *Nuremberg Diary.* New York: Farrar, Straus, and Giroux.
Gillem, Mark L. 2007. *America Town: Building the Outposts of Empire.* Minneapolis: University of Minnesota Press.
Gilligan, Michael J. 2006. "Is Enforcement Necessary for Effectiveness? A Model of the International Criminal Regime." *International Organization* 60 (4): 935–967.
Ginsburg, Tom. 2009. "The Clash of Commitments at the International Criminal Court." *Chicago Journal of International Law* 9 (2): 499–514.
Glennon, Michael. 2010. "The Blank-Prose Crime of Aggression." *Yale Journal of International Law* 35: 71–114.
Goldsmith, Jack. 2003. "The Self-Defeating International Criminal Court." *University of Chicago Law Review* 70 (1): 89–104.
Goldsmith, Jack, and Stephen D. Krasner. 2003. "The Limits of Idealism." *Daedalus* 132 (1): 47–63.
Goldsmith, Jack L., and Eric A. Posner. 2005. *The Limits of International Law.* New York: Oxford University Press.
Goldstone, Richard. 2000. *For Humanity: Reflections of a War Crimes Investigator.* New Haven, CT: Yale University Press.
  2007. "Historical Evolution: From Nuremberg to the International Criminal Court." *Penn State International Law Review* 25 (4): 763–777.
Goodliffe, Jay, and Darren Hawkins. 2009. "A Funny Thing Happened on the Way to Rome: Explaining International Criminal Court Negotiations." *Journal of Politics* 71 (3): 977–997.

Gordon, Philip H. 2003. "Bridging the Atlantic Divide." *Foreign Affairs* 82 (1): 70–83.

Gries, Peter. 2014. *The Politics of American Foreign Policy: How Ideology Divides Liberals and Conservatives over Foreign Affairs*. Stanford, CA: Stanford University Press.

Grossman, Marc. 2002. "American Foreign Policy and the International Criminal Court." Washington, DC: Center for Strategic and International Studies, May 6, 2002. Available at https://2001-2009.state.gov/p/us/rm/9949.htm.

Guest, Iain. 1995. *On Trial: The United Nations, War Crimes, and the Former Yugoslavia*. Washington, DC: Refugee Policy Group.

Guzman, Andrew T. 2008. *How International Law Works: A Rational Choice Theory*. Oxford: Oxford University Press.

Hagan, John. 2003. *Justice in the Balkans: Prosecuting War Crimes in the Hague Tribunal*. Chicago: University of Chicago Press.

Hamilton, Rebecca. 2011. *Fighting for Darfur: Public Action and the Struggle to Stop Genocide*. New York: Palgrave MacMillan.

Harff, Barbara. 2003. "No Lessons Learned from the Holocaust? Assessing Risks of Genocide and Political Mass Murder since 1955." *American Political Science Review* 97 (1): 57–73.

Hartman, Erin, and F. Daniel Hidalgo. 2018. "An Equivalence Approach to Balance and Placebo Tests." *American Journal of Political Science* 62 (4): 1000–1013.

Hashimoto, Barry. 2020. "Autocratic Consent to International Law: The Case of the International Criminal Court's Jurisdiction, 1998–2017." *International Organization* 74 (2): 331–362.

Hathaway, Oona A. 2022. "A Crime in Search of a Court: How to Hold Russia Accountable." *Foreign Affairs*, May 19, 2022. Available at www.foreignaffairs.com/articles/ukraine/2022-05-19/crime-search-court.

Hathaway, Oona A., Paul K. Stauch, Beatrice A. Walton, and Zoe A. Weinberg. 2019. "What Is a War Crime?" *Yale Journal of International Law* 44 (1): 53–113.

Hazan, Pierre. 2004. *Justice in a Time of War: The True Story behind the International Criminal Tribunal for the Former Yugoslavia*. College Station: Texas A&M University Press.

Helfer, Laurence R., and Anne-Marie Slaughter. 2005. "Why States Create International Tribunals: A Response to Professors Posner and Yoo." *California Law Review* 93 (3): 899–956.

Heller, Kevin Jon. 2011. *The Nuremberg Military Tribunals and the Origins of International Criminal Law*. New York: Oxford University Press.

Henningsen, Troels Burchall, and Line Engbo Gissel. 2020. "Non-cooperation with the International Criminal Court in Gatekeeper States:

Regime Security in Deby's Chad." *Cambridge Review of International Affairs* 35 (6): 826–845.

Hillebrecht, Courtney. 2016. "The Deterrent Effects of the International Criminal Court: Evidence from Libya." *International Interactions* 42 (4): 616–643.

    2021. *Saving the International Justice Regime: Beyond Backlash against International Courts*. New York: Cambridge University Press.

Hillebrecht, Courtney, and Scott Straus. 2017. "Who Prosecutes the Perpetrators? State Cooperation with ICC Indictments." *Human Rights Quarterly* 39 (1): 162–188.

Holbrooke, Richard C. 1999. *To End a War*. New York: Modern Library.

Holt, Victoria K., and Elisabeth W. Dallas. 2006. *On Trial: The US Military and the International Criminal Court*. Washington, DC: Henry L. Stimson Center.

Hopgood, Stephen. 2013. *The Endtimes of Human Rights*. Ithaca, NY: Cornell University Press.

Human Rights First. 2023. "Commending US Policy on ICC's Ukraine Investigation." July 27, 2023. Available at https://humanrightsfirst.org/library/commending-u-s-policy-on-iccs-ukraine-investigation/.

Human Rights Watch. 2002. "US: 'Hague Invasion Act' Becomes Law." August 3, 2002. Available at www.hrw.org/news/2002/08/03/us-hague-invasion-act-becomes-law.

    2020. "Oppose Trump Administration Measures against the International Criminal Court." June 11, 2020. Available at www.hrw.org/news/2020/06/11/oppose-trump-administration-measures-against-international-criminal-court.

Hurd, Ian. 2017. *How to Do Things with International Law*. Princeton, NJ: Princeton University Press.

Ignatieff, Michael. 2005. *American Exceptionalism and Human Rights*. Princeton, NJ: Princeton University Press.

Ikenberry, G. John. 2000. *After Victory: Institutions, Strategic Restraint, and the Rebuilding of Order after Major Wars*. Princeton, NJ: Princeton University Press.

    2004. "Illusions of Empire: Defining the New American Order." *Foreign Affairs* 83 (2): 144–154.

Immerwahr, Daniel. 2019. *How to Hide an Empire: A History of the Greater United States*. New York: Farrar, Straus and Giroux.

International Crisis Group. 2002. *Liberia: The Key to Ending Regional Instability*. Brussels: International Crisis Group.

International Military Tribunal. 1947. *Trial of the Major War Criminals before the International Military Tribunal*. Vol. 1. Nuremberg: International Military Tribunal.

Ireland, Kiel, and Julian Bava. 2016. "The American Servicemembers' Protection Act: Pathways to, and Constraints on, U.S. Cooperation with the International Criminal Court." *Stanford Law and Policy Lab*, June 1, 2016. Available at https://law.stanford.edu/publications/the-american-servicemembers-protection-act-pathways-to-and-constraints-on-u-s-cooperation-with-the-international-criminal-court/.

Israel Ministry of Foreign Affairs. 2021. "Prime Minister Netanyahu's Statement Regarding the ICC Decision." February 6, 2021. Available at https://mfa.gov.il/MFA/PressRoom/2021/Pages/Statement-by-PM-Netanyahu-regarding-the-ICC-decision-6-February-2021.aspx.

Jain, Neha. 2013. "Individual Responsibility for Mass Atrocity: In Search of a Concept of Perpetration." *American Journal of Comparative Law* 61 (4): 831–871.

Jentleson, Bruce W. 2023. "Beyond the Rhetoric: A Globally Credible US Role for a Rules-Based Order." *The Washington Quarterly* 46 (3): 83–102.

Jentleson, Bruce W., and Christopher A. Whytock. 2005. "Who Won Libya? The Force-Diplomacy Debate and Its Implications for Theory and Policy." *International Security* 30 (3): 47–86.

Jo, Hyeran, and Beth Simmons. 2016. "Can the International Criminal Court Deter Atrocity?" *International Organization* 70 (3): 443–475.

Joffe, Josef. 2003. "Continental Divides." *The National Interest* 71 (1): 157–160.

Johansen, Robert C. 2006. "The Impact of US Policy toward the International Criminal Court on the Prevention of Genocide, War Crimes, and Crimes against Humanity." *Human Rights Quarterly* 28 (2): 301–331.

Johns, Leslie, and Francesca Parente. 2024. "The Politics of Punishment: Why Dictators Join the International Criminal Court." *International Studies Quarterly* 68 (3): 1–15.

Johnson, Chalmers. 2000. *Blowback: The Costs and Consequences of American Empire*. New York: Henry Holt.

2004. *The Sorrows of Empire: Militarism, Secrecy, and the End of the Republic*. New York: Metropolitan Books.

Johnson-Sirleaf, Ellen. 2006. "Johnson-Sirleaf Describes Attempts to Come to Terms with Liberia's Violent Past." *Newshour with Jim Lehrer*, March 23, 2006. Available at www.pbs.org/newshour/show/johnson-sirleaf-describes-attempts-to-come-to-terms-with-liberias-violent-past.

Kaplan, Robert D. 2008. *Hog Pilots, Blue Water Grunts: The American Military in the Air, at Sea, and on the Ground*. New York: Knopf.

Kaye, David. 2013. "America's Honeymoon with the ICC." *Foreign Affairs*, April 16, 2013. Available at www.foreignaffairs.com/articles/139170/david-kaye/americas-honeymoon-with-the-icc?page=show.

Kelley, Judith. 2007. "Who Keeps International Commitments and Why? The International Criminal Court and Bilateral Nonsurrender Agreements." *American Political Science Review* 101 (3): 573–589.

Keohane, Robert O. 1984. *After Hegemony: Cooperation and Discord in the World Political Economy*. Princeton, NJ: Princeton University Press.

Kersten, Mark. 2016. *Justice in Conflict: The Effects of the International Criminal Court's Interventions on Ending Wars and Building Peace*. Oxford: Oxford University Press.

Kim, Hunjoon, and Kathryn Sikkink. 2010. "Explaining the Deterrence Effect of Human Rights Prosecutions for Transitional Countries." *International Studies Quarterly* 54 (4): 939–963.

Kissinger, Henry A. 2001. "The Pitfalls of Universal Jurisdiction." *Foreign Affairs* 80 (4): 86–96.

Koh, Harold. 2010. "The Obama Administration and International Law." Washington, DC: American Society of International Law, March 25, 2010. Available at https://2009-2017.state.gov/s/l/releases/remarks/139119.htm.

Koh, Harold Hongju, and Todd F. Buchwald. 2015. "The Crime of Aggression: The United States Perspective." *American Journal of International Law* 109 (2): 257–295.

Koremenos, Barbara, Charles Lipson, and Duncan Snidal. 2001. "The Rational Design of International Institutions." *International Organization* 55 (4): 761–799.

Krauthammer, Charles. 1990. "The Unipolar Moment." *Foreign Affairs* 70 (1): 23–33.

Krcmaric, Daniel. 2014. "Refugee Flows, Ethnic Power Relations, and the Spread of Conflict." *Security Studies* 23 (1): 182–216.

  2018. "Should I Stay or Should I Go? Leaders, Exile, and the Dilemmas of International Justice." *American Journal of Political Science* 62 (2): 486–498.

  2020. *The Justice Dilemma: Leaders and Exile in an Era of Accountability*. Ithaca, NY: Cornell University Press.

  2022. "Nowhere to Hide? Global Policing and the Politics of Extradition." *International Security* 47 (2): 7–47.

  2023. "Does the International Criminal Court Target the American Military?" *American Political Science Review* 117 (1): 325–331.

Krcmaric, Daniel, Stephen C. Nelson, and Andrew Roberts. 2020. "Studying Leaders and Elites: The Personal Biography Approach." *Annual Review of Political Science* 23: 133–151.

Kreps, Sarah. 2009. "American Grand Strategy after Iraq." *Orbis* 53 (4): 629–645.

Ku, Julian, and Jide Nzelibe. 2006. "Do International Criminal Tribunals Deter or Exacerbate Humanitarian Atrocities?" *Washington University Law Review* 84: 777.

Kuperman, Alan. 2001. *The Limits of Humanitarian Intervention: Genocide in Rwanda*. Washington, DC: Brookings Institution Press.

Leigh, Monroe. 2001. "The United States and the Statute of Rome." *American Journal of International Law* 95 (1): 124–131.

Lichtblau, Eric. 2014. *The Nazis Next Door: How America Became a Safe Haven for Hitler's Men*. Boston: Mariner Books.

Lietzau, William K. 2001. "International Criminal Law after Rome: Concerns from a U.S. Military Perspective." *Law and Contemporary Problems* 64 (1): 119–140.

Lischer, Sarah Kenyon. 2005. *Dangerous Sanctuaries: Refugee Camps, Civil War, and the Dilemmas of Humanitarian Aid*. Ithaca, NY: Cornell University Press.

Luce, Henry R. 1941. "The American Century." *Life*, February 17, 1941.

Luria, Elaine, and Mike Gallagher. 2020. "Letter to Secretary of State Michael R. Pompeo." May 12, 2020. Available at https://web.archive.org/web/20200924215418/https://luria.house.gov/sites/luria.house.gov/files/wysiwyg_uploaded/2020.05.12%20Luria%20Gallagher%20letter%20to%20Sec%20Pompeo%20on%20ICC.pdf.

MacArthur, Douglas. 1964. *Reminiscences*. New York: McGraw-Hill.

Macedo, Stephen. 2004. *Universal Jurisdiction: National Courts and the Prosecution of Serious Crimes under International Law*. Philadelphia: University of Pennsylvania Press.

McAllister, Jacqueline R. 2020. "Deterring Wartime Atrocities: Hard Lessons from the Yugoslav Tribunal." *International Security* 44 (3): 84–128.

———. 2023. "Casting a Shadow over War Zones? Hard Truths about the ICC's Efforts to Deter Wartime Atrocities." *Journal of Human Rights* 22 (1): 94–108.

Mearsheimer, John J. 1994. "The False Promise of International Institutions." *International Security* 19 (3): 5–49.

Meernik, James. 2008. "It's Time to Stop Running: A Model of the Apprehension of Suspected War Criminals." *International Studies Perspectives* 9 (2): 165–182.

———. 2015. "The International Criminal Court and the Deterrence of Human Rights Atrocities." *Civil Wars* 17 (3): 318–339.

Minear, Richard H. 1971. *Victor's Justice: The Tokyo War Crimes Trial*. Princeton, NJ: Princeton University Press.

Mitchell, Sara McLaughlin, and Emilia Justyna Powell. 2011. *Domestic Law Goes Global: Legal Traditions and International Courts*. New York: Cambridge University Press.

Moravcsik, Andrew. 2000. "The Origins of Human Rights Regimes: Democratic Delegation in Postwar Europe." *International Organization* 54 (2): 217–252.

2002. "The Human Rights Blame Game." *Newsweek International*, April 22, 2002. Available at www.princeton.edu/~amoravcs/library/blame.pdf.

Moreno-Ocampo, Luis. 2005. "Statement at the Informal Meeting of Legal Advisors of Ministries of Foreign Affairs." New York, October 24, 2005. Available at www.icc-cpi.int/NR/rdonlyres/9D70039E-4BEC-4F32-9D4A-CEA8B6799E37/143836/LMO_20051024_English.pdf.

2009. "The International Criminal Court in Motion." In Carsten Stahn and Goran Sluiter (eds.), *The Emerging Practice of the International Criminal Court*, 13–19. Leiden: Brill Nijhoff.

2010. "Pursuing International Justice: A Conversation with Luis Moreno-Ocampo." New York: Council on Foreign Relations, February 4, 2010. Available at www.cfr.org/event/pursuing-international-justice-conversation-luis-moreno-ocampo-0.

2022. *War and Justice in the 21st Century: A Case Study on the International Criminal Court and Its Interaction with the War on Terror*. Oxford: Oxford University Press.

Morgenthau Jr., Henry. 1944. *Morgenthau Diaries*. Vol. 768. Hyde Park, NY: Franklin D. Roosevelt Presidential Library Digitized Collections. Available at www.fdrlibrary.org/morgenthau.

Morris, Madeline. 2000. "The Jurisdiction of the International Criminal Court over Nationals of Non-Party States." *ILSA Journal of International & Comparative Law* 6 (1): 363–369.

Morton, Jeffrey S. 2000. *The International Law Commission of the United Nations*. Columbia: University of South Carolina Press.

Mueller, John. 2000. "The Banality of 'Ethnic War'." *International Security* 25 (1): 42–70.

Nalepa, Monika, and Emilia Justyna Powell. 2016. "The Role of Domestic Opposition and International Justice Regimes in Peaceful Transitions of Power." *Journal of Conflict Resolution* 60 (7): 1191–1218.

Nash, William L. 2000. "The ICC and the Deployment of U.S. Armed Forces." In Sarah B. Sewall and Carl Kaysen (eds.), *The United States and the International Criminal Court: National Security and International Law*, 153–175. Lanham, MD: Rowman and Littlefield.

Neier, Aryeh. 2019. "Indicting the International Criminal Court." *Project Syndicate*, May 8, 2019. Available at www.project-syndicate.org/commentary/icc-criticism-afghanistan-investigation-by-aryeh-neier-2019-05.

Nexon, Daniel H., and Thomas Wright. 2007. "What's at Stake in the American Empire Debate." *American Political Science Review* 101 (2): 253–271.

No Peace without Justice International. 1998. "India Blasts Special Treatment for Security Council." *Terra Viva*, June 17, 1998. Available at www.legal-tools.org/doc/f83fcc/pdf/.

Nooruddin, Irfan, and Autumn Lockwood Payton. 2010. "Dynamics of Influence in International Politics: The ICC, BIAs, and Economic Sanctions." *Journal of Peace Research* 47 (6): 711–721.

Nouwen, Sarah M. H. 2014. *Complementarity in the Line of Fire: The Catalyzing Effect of the International Criminal Court in Uganda and Sudan*. Cambridge: Cambridge University Press.

Nouwen, Sarah M. H., and Wouter G. Werner. 2010. "Doing Justice to the Political: The International Criminal Court in Uganda and Sudan." *European Journal of International Law* 21 (4): 941–965.

Nuland, Victoria. 2013. "Daily Press Briefing." Washington, DC: Department of State, March 18, 2013. Available at https://2009-2017.state.gov/r/pa/prs/dpb/2013/03/206377.htm.

Office of the Historian. 1943. "Bohlen Minutes." *Foreign Relations of the United States: The Conferences at Cairo and Tehran*. Washington, DC: Department of State. Available at https://history.state.gov/historicaldocuments/frus1943CairoTehran.

Office of the President. 2020. "Executive Order 13928: Blocking Property of Certain Persons Associated with the International Criminal Court." Washington, DC: The White House. June 11, 2020. Available at www.federalregister.gov/documents/2020/06/15/2020-12953/blocking-property-of-certain-persons-associated-with-the-international-criminal-court.

Office of the President. 2021a. "Remarks by President Biden on America's Place in the World." Washington, DC: The White House, February 4, 2021. Available at www.whitehouse.gov/briefing-room/speeches-remarks/2021/02/04/remarks-by-president-biden-on-americas-place-in-the-world/.

Office of the President. 2021b. "Executive Order 14022: Termination of Emergency with Respect to the International Criminal Court." Washington, DC: The White House, April 1, 2021. Available at www.federalregister.gov/documents/2021/04/07/2021-07239/termination-of-emergency-with-respect-to-the-international-criminal-court.

Office of the President. 2025. "Executive Order 14203: Imposing Sanctions on the International Criminal Court." Washington, DC: The White House, February 6, 2025. Available at www.federalregister.gov/documents/2025/02/12/2025-02612/imposing-sanctions-on-the-international-criminal-court.

Office of the Prosecutor. 2013. "Policy Paper on Preliminary Examinations." The Hague, Netherlands: International Criminal Court, November 1, 2013. Available at www.icc-cpi.int/iccdocs/otp/OTP-Policy_Paper_Preliminary_Examinations_2013-ENG.pdf.

2014. "Report on Preliminary Examination Activities 2014." The Hague, Netherlands: International Criminal Court, December 2, 2014. Available at www.icc-cpi.int/sites/default/files/iccdocs/otp/OTP-Pre-Exam-2014.pdf.

2015. "Report on Preliminary Examination Activities 2015." The Hague, Netherlands: International Criminal Court, November 12, 2015. Available at www.icc-cpi.int/sites/default/files/iccdocs/otp/OTP-PE-rep-2015-Eng.pdf.

2016. "Report on Preliminary Examination Activities 2016." The Hague, Netherlands: International Criminal Court, November 14, 2016. Available at www.icc-cpi.int/sites/default/files/iccdocs/otp/161114-otp-rep-PE_ENG.pdf.

2017. "Situation in the Islamic Republic of Afghanistan: Request for Authorization of an Investigation Pursuant to Article 15." The Hague, Netherlands: International Criminal Court, November 20, 2017. Available at www.icc-cpi.int/sites/default/files/CourtRecords/CR2017_06891.PDF.

2021. "Statement of the Prosecutor of the International Criminal Court, Karim A. A. Khan QC, Following the Application for an Expedited Order Under Article 18(2) Seeking Authorization to Resume Investigations in the Situation in Afghanistan." The Hague, Netherlands: International Criminal Court, September 27, 2021. Available at www.icc-cpi.int/news/statement-prosecutor-international-criminal-court-karim-khan-qc-following-application.

Office of Representative Elaine Luria. 2020. "Representatives Elaine Luria and Mike Gallagher Lead 262 Colleagues to Send Letter to Secretary Pompeo Regarding the International Criminal Court." Washington, DC, May 14, 2020. Available at https://web.archive.org/web/20200922172125/https:/luria.house.gov/media/press-releases/representatives-elaine-luria-and-mike-gallagher-lead-262-colleagues-send-letter.

Office of Senator Chris Coons. 2022. "Senators Coons and Portman Statement on Congressional Delegation to The Hague." Washington, DC, November 5, 2022. Available at www.coons.senate.gov/news/press-releases/senators-coons-and-portman-statement-on-congressional-delegation-to-the-hague.

O'Hanlon, Michael. 2008. *Unfinished Business: U.S. Overseas Military Presence in the 21st Century*. Washington, DC: Center for a New American Security.

Olsen, Tricia D., Leigh A. Payne, and Andrew G. Reiter. 2010. "The Justice Balance: When Transitional Justice Improves Human Rights and Democracy." *Human Rights Quarterly* 32 (4): 980–1007.

O'Mahony, Angela, Miranda Priebe, Bryan Frederick et al. 2018. *U.S. Presence and the Incidence of Conflict*. Santa Monica, CA: RAND Corporation.

Orentlicher, Diane F. 1991. "Settling Accounts: The Duty to Prosecute Human Rights Violations of a Prior Regime." *Yale Law Journal* 100 (8): 2537.

2004. "Unilateral Multilateralism: United States Policy toward the International Criminal Court." *Cornell International Law Journal* 36 (3): 415–433.

Overy, Richard. 2001. *Interrogations: The Nazi Elite in Allied Hands, 1945.* New York: Viking.

Pape, Robert A. 1993. "Why Japan Surrendered." *International Security* 18 (2): 154–201.

Parenti, Michael. 2000. *To Kill a Nation: The Attack on Yugoslavia.* London: Verso.

Perriello, Tom, and Marieke Wierda. 2006. *The Special Court for Sierra Leone under Scrutiny.* New York: International Center for Transitional Justice.

Persico, Joseph E. 1994. *Nuremberg: Infamy on Trial.* New York: Viking.

Peskin, Victor. 2008. *International Justice in Rwanda and the Balkans: Virtual Trials and the Struggle for State Cooperation.* Cambridge: Cambridge University Press.

Pompeo, Michael R. 2020a. "ICC Decision on Afghanistan." Washington, DC: Department of State, March 5, 2020. Available at https://2017-2021.state.gov/icc-decision-on-afghanistan/index.html.

2020b. "The International Criminal Court's Illegitimate Prosecutions." Washington, DC: Department of State, May 15, 2020. Available at https://2017-2021.state.gov/the-international-criminal-courts-illegitimate-prosecutions/.

Posen, Barry R. 2014. *Restraint: A New Foundation for U.S. Grand Strategy.* Ithaca, NY: Cornell University Press.

Posner, Eric. 2004. "The Decline of the International Court of Justice." *John M. Olin Program in Law and Economics Working Paper 233.* Available at https://chicagounbound.uchicago.edu/law_and_economics/500.

Posner, Eric, and John Yoo. 2005. "Judicial Independence in International Tribunals." *California Law Review* 93 (1): 1–74.

Powell, Emilia Justyna, and Krista E. Wiegand. 2014. "Strategic Selection: Political and Legal Mechanisms of Territorial Dispute Resolution." *Journal of Peace Research* 51 (3): 361–374.

2023. *The Peaceful Resolution of Territorial and Maritime Disputes.* New York: Oxford University Press.

Power, Samantha. 2001. "Bystanders to Genocide." *The Atlantic* 288 (2): 84–108.

2003. *A Problem from Hell: America and the Age of Genocide.* New York: Perennial.

Pre-Trial Chamber. 2019. "Decision Pursuant to Article 15 of the Rome Statute on the Authorization of an Investigation into the Situation in the Islamic Republic of Afghanistan." The Hague, Netherlands:

International Criminal Court, April 12, 2019. Available at www.icc-cpi.int/sites/default/files/CourtRecords/CR2019_02068.PDF.
Prorok, Alyssa K. 2017. "The (In)compatibility of Peace and Justice? The International Criminal Court and Civil Conflict Termination." *International Organization* 71 (2): 213–243.
Prorok, Alyssa K., Benjamin Appel, and Shahryar Minhas. 2024. "Understanding the Determinants of ICC Involvement: Legal Mandate and Power Politics." *International Studies Quarterly* 68 (2): 1–15.
Prunier, Gerard. 2008. *Africa's World War: Congo, the Rwandan Genocide, and the Making of a Continental Catastrophe*. Oxford: Oxford University Press.
Putnam, Tonya L. 2020. "Mingling and Strategic Augmentation of International Legal Obligations." *International Organization* 74 (1): 31–64.
Rabkin, Jeremy. 2000. "The International Criminal Court: Protecting American Servicemen and Officials from the Threat of International Prosecution." Hearing before the Senate Committee on Foreign Relations, Washington, DC, June 14, 2020. Available at www.govinfo.gov/content/pkg/CHRG-106shrg67980/pdf/CHRG-106shrg67980.pdf.
  2007. "No Substitute for Sovereignty: Why International Criminal Justice Has a Bleak Future – And Deserves It." In Edel Hughes, William A. Schabas, and Ramesh Thakur (eds.), *Atrocities and International Accountability: Beyond Transitional Justice*, 98–132. Tokyo: United Nations University Press.
Rainey, Carlisle. 2014. "Arguing for a Negligible Effect." *American Journal of Political Science* 58 (4): 1083–1091.
Rapp, Stephen J. 2012. "The State Department's Rewards Programs: Performance and Potential." Statement before the House Foreign Affairs Subcommittee on Terrorism, Nonproliferation, and Trade. Washington, DC, March 7, 2012. Available at www.govinfo.gov/content/pkg/CHRG-112hhrg73278/html/CHRG-112hhrg73278.htm.
Rathke, Jeff. 2015. "Statement on ICC Prosecutor's Decision." Washington, DC: Department of State, January 16, 2015. Available at https://2009-2017.state.gov/r/pa/prs/ps/2015/01/236082.htm.
Reichler, Paul. 2001. "Holding America to Its Own Best Standards: Abe Chayes and Nicaragua in the World Court." *Harvard International Law Journal* 42 (1): 15–46.
Rice, Susan. 2011. "Remarks in an Explanation of Vote on Resolution 1970 on Libya Sanctions." New York: US Mission to the UN, February 26, 2011. Available at https://2009-2017.state.gov/p/io/rm/2011/157390.htm.
Richardson, Bill. 1998. "Statement at the United Nations Plenipotentiaries Conference on the Establishment of an International Criminal Court."

Rome, Italy, June 17, 1998. Available at www.legal-tools.org/doc/c2766e/pdf/.

Rivkin Jr., David, and Lee Casey. 1999. "The International Criminal Court vs. the American People." Washington, DC: The Heritage Foundation, February 5, 1999. Available at www.heritage.org/report/the-international-criminal-court-vs-the-american-people#pgfId=1018109.

Roach, Steven C. 2013. "How Political Is the ICC? Pressing Challenges and the Need for Diplomatic Efficacy." *Global Governance* 19 (4): 507–523.

Robertson, Geoffrey. 2012. *Crimes against Humanity: The Struggle for Global Justice*. New York: New Press.

Roth, Kenneth. 2025. *Righting Wrongs: Three Decades on the Front Lines Battling Abusive Governments*. New York: Knopf.

Rubio, Marco, and Jacky Rosen. 2024. "Letter to President Joe Biden." May 9, 2024. Available at www.rubio.senate.gov/wp-content/uploads/2024/05/05.09.24-Rubio-Rosen-letter-to-POTUS-re-ICC.pdf.

Rudolph, Christopher. 2017. *Power and Principle: The Politics of International Criminal Courts*. Ithaca, NY: Cornell University Press.

Ruggie, John Gerard. 2005. "American Exceptionalism, Exemptionalism, and Global Governance." In Michael Ignatieff (ed.), *American Exceptionalism and Human Rights*, 304–338. Princeton, NJ: Princeton University Press.

Sadat, Leila Nadya. 2004. "Summer in Rome, Spring in the Hague, Winter in Washington? U.S. Policy towards the International Criminal Court." *Wisconsin International Law Journal* 21 (1): 557–597.

Sadat, Leila Nadya, and S. Richard Carden. 2000. "The New International Criminal Court: An Uneasy Revolution." *Georgetown Law Journal* 88 (3): 381–474.

Sandars, Christopher T. 2000. *America's Overseas Garrisons: The Leasehold Empire*. Oxford: Oxford University Press.

Sanders, Bernie. 2024. "A Revolution in American Foreign Policy." *Foreign Affairs*, March 18, 2024. Available at www.foreignaffairs.com/united-states/revolution-american-foreign-policy-bernie-sanders.

Sands, Philippe. 2005. *Lawless World: America and the Making and Breaking of Global Rules*. New York: Penguin.

2021. *The Ratline: The Exalted Life and Mysterious Death of a Nazi Fugitive*. New York: Knopf.

2022. *The Last Colony: A Tale of Exile, Justice, and Courage*. New York: Knopf.

Schabas, William A. 2004. "United States Hostility to the International Criminal Court: It's All about the Security Council." *European Journal of International Law* 15 (4): 701–720.

2010. "Victor's Justice: Selecting Situations at the International Criminal Court." *The John Marshall Law Review* 43 (3): 535–552.

2012. *Unimaginable Atrocities: Justice, Politics, and Rights at the War Crimes Tribunals*. Oxford: Oxford University Press.

Schake, Kori. 2016. "Trump Is an Outlier, and the Data Prove It." *Foreign Policy*, October 14, 2016. Available at https://foreignpolicy.com/2016/10/14/trump-is-an-outlier-and-the-data-prove-it-trade-united-states-immigration-clinton-election/.

Scharf, Michael P. 1997. *Balkan Justice: The Story behind the First International War Crimes Trial since Nuremberg*. Durham, NC: Carolina Academic Press.

2001. "The ICC's Jurisdiction over the Nationals of Non-Party States: A Critique of the U.S. Position." *Law and Contemporary Problems* 64 (1): 67.

Scheffer, David. 2012a. *All the Missing Souls: A Personal History of the War Crimes Tribunals*. Princeton, NJ: Princeton University Press.

2012b. "America's Embrace of the International Criminal Court." *Jurist*, July 2, 2012. Available at www.jurist.org/commentary/2012/07/dan-scheffer-us-icc/.

2023. "Why the United States Should Ratify the Rome Statute." *Articles of War*, July 17, 2023. Available at https://lieber.westpoint.edu/united-states-should-ratify-rome-statute/.

Scheffer, David J. 1999. "The United States and the International Criminal Court." *American Journal of International Law* 93 (1): 12–22.

Schelling, Thomas C. 1966. *Arms and Influence*. New Haven, CT: Yale University Press.

Schiff, Benjamin N. 2008. *Building the International Criminal Court*. New York: Cambridge University Press.

Schomerus, Mareike, Tim Allen, and Koen Vlassenroot. 2012. "KONY 2012 and the Prospects for Change." *Foreign Affairs*, March 13, 2012. Available at www.foreignaffairs.com/articles/africa/2012-03-13/kony-2012-and-prospects-change.

Senate Committee on Foreign Relations. 1998. "Is a U.N. International Criminal Court in the U.S. National Interest?" Hearing before the Subcommittee on International Operations of the Senate Committee on Foreign Relations. Washington, DC, July 23, 1998. Available at www.govinfo.gov/content/pkg/CHRG-105shrg50976/html/CHRG-105shrg50976.htm.

2021. "Nomination of Hon. Linda Thomas-Greenfield to Be United States Representative to the United Nations." Washington, DC, January 27, 2021. Available at www.govinfo.gov/content/pkg/CHRG-117shrg45209/html/CHRG-117shrg45209.htm.

2014. "Committee Study of the Central Intelligence Agency's Detention and Interrogation Program." Washington, DC, December 9, 2014. Available at www.intelligence.senate.gov/sites/default/files/publications/CRPT-113srpt288.pdf.

Sewall, Sarah B., Carl Kaysen, and Michael P. Scharf. 2000. "The United States and the International Criminal Court: An Overview." In Sarah B. Sewall and Carl Kaysen (eds.), *The United States and the International Criminal Court: National Security and International Law*, 1–27. Lanham, MD: Rowman and Littlefield.

Shattuck, John. 2003. *Freedom on Fire: Human Rights Wars and America's Response*. Cambridge, MA: Harvard University Press.

Shaw, Martin. 2015. *What Is Genocide?* 2nd ed. Cambridge: Polity.

Shawcross, Hartley. 1995. *Life Sentence: The Memoirs of Lord Shawcross*. London: Constable.

Shklar, Judith N. 1964. *Legalism: Law, Morals, and Political Trials*. Cambridge, MA: Harvard University Press.

Sigal, Leon V. 1988. *Fighting to a Finish: The Politics of War Termination in the United States and Japan, 1945*. Ithaca, NY: Cornell University Press.

Sikkink, Kathryn. 2011. *The Justice Cascade: How Human Rights Prosecutions Are Changing World Politics*. New York: Norton.

Simmons, Beth A., and Allison Danner. 2010. "Credible Commitments and the International Criminal Court." *International Organization* 64 (2): 225–256.

Slaughter, Anne-Marie. 1997. "The Real New World Order." *Foreign Affairs* 76 (5): 183–197.

Smeulers, Alette, Maartje Weerdesteijn, and Barbora Hola. 2015. "The Selection of Situations by the ICC: An Empirically Based Evaluation of the OPT's Performance." *International Criminal Law Review* 15 (1): 1–39.

Smith, Bradley F. 1981. *The Road to Nuremberg*. New York: Basic Books.

1982. *The American Road to Nuremberg: The Documentary Record, 1944–1945*. Stanford, CA: Hoover Institution Press.

Snyder, Jack, and Leslie Vinjamuri. 2003. "Trials and Errors: Principle and Pragmatism in Strategies of International Justice." *International Security* 28 (3): 5–44.

Snyder, Timothy. 2010. *Bloodlands: Europe between Hitler and Stalin*. New York: Basic Books.

Spruyt, Hendrik. 2008. "American Empire as an Analytic Question or a Rhetorical Move?" *International Studies Perspectives* 9 (3): 290–299.

Steinacher, Gerald. 2011. *Nazis on the Run: How Hitler's Henchmen Fled Justice*. New York: Oxford University Press.

Steinberg, Richard H. 2024. "Politics and Justice at the International Criminal Court." *Israel Law Review* 57 (2): 308–350.

Stone, Randall W. 2011. *Controlling Institutions: International Organizations and the Global Economy*. Cambridge: Cambridge University Press.

Stover, Eric, Victor Peskin, and Alexa Koenig. 2016. *Hiding in Plain Sight: The Pursuit of War Criminals from Nuremberg to the War on Terror*. Oakland: University of California Press.

Straus, Scott. 2005. "Darfur and the Genocide Debate." *Foreign Affairs* 84 (1): 123–133.

2006. *The Order of Genocide: Race, Power, and War in Rwanda*. Ithaca, NY: Cornell University Press.

2007. "What Is the Relationship between Hate Radio and Violence? Rethinking Rwanda's 'Radio Machete'." *Politics & Society* 35 (4): 609–637.

Struett, Michael J. 2012. "Why the International Criminal Court Must Pretend to Ignore Politics." *Ethics & International Affairs* 26 (1): 83–92.

Sundberg, Ralph, and Erik Melander. 2013. "Introducing the UCDP Georeferenced Event Dataset." *Journal of Peace Research* 50 (4): 523–532.

Taylor, Telford. 1992. *The Anatomy of the Nuremberg Trials: A Personal Memoir*. New York: Knopf.

Teitel, Ruti G. 2003. "Transitional Justice Genealogy." *Harvard Human Rights Journal* 16 (1): 69–94.

Tejan-Cole, Abdul. 2009. "A Big Man in a Small Cell: Charles Taylor and the Special Court for Sierra Leone." In Ellen L. Lutz and Caitlin Reiger (eds.), *Prosecuting Heads of State*, 205–232. New York: Cambridge University Press.

Tiemessen, Alana. 2014. "The International Criminal Court and the Politics of Prosecutions." *International Journal of Human Rights* 18 (4–5): 444–461.

Trahan, Jennifer. 2012. "A Meaningful Definition of the Crime of Aggression: A Response to Michael Glennon." *University of Pennsylvania Journal of International Law* 33 (4): 907–969.

Trahan, Jennifer, and Megan Fairlie. 2020. "At Best, Some U.S. House and Senate Members Lack Even an Elementary Understanding of the International Criminal Court." *Opinio Juris*, May 18, 2020. Available at http://opiniojuris.org/2020/05/18/at-best-some-u-s-house-and-senate-members-lack-even-an-elementary-understanding-of-the-international-criminal-court/.

United Nations. 1998. "United Nations Diplomatic Conference of Plenipotentiaries on the Establishment of an International Criminal Court." Vol. 2. Rome. Available at https://legal.un.org/icc/rome/proceedings/e/rome%20proceedings_v2_e.pdf.

United States House of Representatives. 2024. "Illegitimate Court Counteraction Act." Washington, DC, June 4, 2024. Available at www.congress.gov/bill/118th-congress/house-bill/8282/text.

United States Senate. 2022. "Senate Resolution 546." Washington, DC, March 15, 2022. Available at www.congress.gov/bill/117th-congress/senate-resolution/546/text?r=3&s=5.

Uzonyi, Gary, Nam Kyu Kim, Nakissa Jahanbani, and Victor Asal. 2021. "Genocide, Politicide, and the Prospects of Democratization since 1900." *Journal of Conflict Resolution* 65 (9): 1521–1550.

Valentino, Benjamin A. 2004. *Final Solutions: Mass Killing and Genocide in the Twentieth Century*. Ithaca, NY: Cornell University Press.

Van Schaack, Beth. 1998. "The Definition of Crimes against Humanity: Resolving the Incoherence." *Columbia Journal of Transnational Law* 37 (1): 787–850.

Van Schaack, Beth, and Ronald C. Slye. 2021. *International Criminal Law: Intersections and Contradictions*. St. Paul, MN: Foundation Press.

Vandewalle, Dirk J. 2012. *A History of Modern Libya*. 2nd ed. New York: Cambridge University Press.

Vasiliev, Sergey. 2022. "Watershed Moment or Same Old?: Ukraine and the Future of International Criminal Justice." *Journal of International Criminal Justice* 20 (4): 893–909.

Vine, David. 2015. *Base Nation: How U.S. Military Bases Abroad Harm America and the World*. New York: Metropolitan Books.

———. 2019. "Lists of U.S. Military Bases Abroad, 1776–2019." *American University Digital Research Archive*. Available at https://doi.org/10.17606/vfyb-nc07.

Vinjamuri, Leslie. 2016. "The International Criminal Court and the Paradox of Authority." *Law and Contemporary Problems* 79 (1): 275–287.

Voeten, Erik. 2008. "The Impartiality of International Judges: Evidence from the European Court of Human Rights." *American Political Science Review* 102 (4): 417–433.

———. 2013. "Public Opinion and the Legitimacy of International Courts." *Theoretical Inquiries in Law* 14 (2): 411–436.

———. 2021. *Ideology and International Institutions*. Princeton, NJ: Princeton University Press.

Wald, Patricia M. 2001. "The International Criminal Tribunal for the Former Yugoslavia Comes of Age: Some Observations on Day-to-Day Dilemmas of an International Court." *Washington University Journal of Law and Policy* 5 (1): 87–118.

Walt, Stephen M. 1985. "Alliance Formation and the Balance of World Power." *International Security* 9 (4): 3–43.

Walters, Guy. 2009. *Hunting Evil: The Nazi War Criminals Who Escaped and the Quest to Bring Them to Justice*. New York: Broadway Books.
Waugh, Colin M. 2011. *Charles Taylor and Liberia: Ambition and Atrocity in Africa's Lone Star State*. New York: Zed Books.
Wedgwood, Ruth. 1998. "Fiddling in Rome: America and the International Criminal Court." *Foreign Affairs* 77 (6): 20–24.
　1999. "Improve the International Criminal Court." Presentation at the 'Toward an International Criminal Court?' Conference. New York: Council on Foreign Relations, July 1, 1999. Available at https://cdn.cfr.org/sites/default/files/pdf/1999/07/International_Criminal_Court.pdf.
　2000. "The Constitution and the ICC." In Sarah B. Sewall and Carl Kaysen (eds.), *The United States and the International Criminal Court: National Security and International Law*, 119–136. Lanham, MD: Rowman and Littlefield.
Weisbord, Noah. 2019. *The Crime of Aggression: The Quest for Justice in an Age of Drones, Cyberattacks, Insurgents, and Autocrats*. Princeton, NJ: Princeton University Press.
Wertheim, Stephen. 2020. *Tomorrow, the World: The Birth of U.S. Global Supremacy*. Cambridge, MA: Harvard University Press.
Weschler, Lawrence. 2000. "Exceptional Cases in Rome: The United States and the Struggle for an ICC." In Sarah B. Sewall and Carl Kaysen (eds.), *The United States and the International Criminal Court: National Security and International Law*, 85–111. Lanham, MD: Rowman and Littlefield.
The White House. 2010. "National Security Strategy." Washington, DC. Available at https://obamawhitehouse.archives.gov/sites/default/files/rss_viewer/national_security_strategy.pdf.
　2015. "National Security Strategy." Washington, DC. Available at https://obamawhitehouse.archives.gov/sites/default/files/docs/2015_national_security_strategy_2.pdf.
　2022. "Press Briefing by Press Secretary Jen Psaki and National Security Advisor Jake Sullivan." Washington, DC, April 4, 2022. Available at https://bidenwhitehouse.archives.gov/briefing-room/press-briefings/2022/04/04/press-briefing-by-press-secretary-jen-psaki-and-national-security-advisor-jake-sullivan/.
　2023. "Remarks by President Biden before Marine One Departure." Washington, DC, March 17, 2023. Available at https://bidenwhitehouse.archives.gov/briefing-room/speeches-remarks/2023/03/17/remarks-by-president-biden-before-marine-one-departure-32/.
　2024. "Statement from President Joe Biden on the Warrant Applications by the International Criminal Court." Washington, DC, May 20, 2024.

Available at https://bidenwhitehouse.archives.gov/briefing-room/statements-releases/2024/05/20/statement-from-president-joe-biden-on-the-warrant-applications-by-the-international-criminal-court/.

Whiting, Alex. 2019. "The ICC's Afghanistan Decision: Bending to U.S. or Focusing Court on Successful Investigations?" *Just Security*, April 12, 2019. Available at www.justsecurity.org/63613/the-iccs-afghanistan-decision-bending-to-u-s-or-focusing-court-on-successful-investigations/.

Wippman, David. 1999. "Atrocities, Deterrence, and the Limits of International Justice." *Fordham International Law Journal* 23: 473–488.

Witt, John Fabian. 2012. *Lincoln's Code: The Laws of War in American History*. New York: Free Press.

Woods, Chris. 2011. "CIA Drones Quit One Pakistan Site – But US Keeps Access to Other Airbases." *Bureau of Investigative Journalism*, December 15, 2011. Available at www.thebureauinvestigates.com/stories/2011-12-15/cia-drones-quit-one-pakistan-site-but-us-keeps-access-to-other-airbases.

Woodward, Bob. 1996. *The Choice*. New York: Simon & Schuster.

Yeo, Andrew. 2011. *Activists, Alliances, and Anti-U.S. Base Protests*. Cambridge: Cambridge University Press.

Zvobgo, Kelebogile. 2019. "Human Rights versus National Interests: Shifting US Public Attitudes on the International Criminal Court." *International Studies Quarterly* 63 (4): 1065–1078.

2021a. "Stay the Hand of Justice? US Resistance to the International Criminal Court." *International Studies Perspectives* 22 (4): 483–486.

2021b. "The ICC's Flawed Afghan Investigation." *Foreign Affairs*, November 3, 2021. Available at www.foreignaffairs.com/articles/afghanistan/2021-11-03/iccs-flawed-afghan-investigation.

2023. "It's Time for America to Join the International Criminal Court." *Foreign Affairs*, October 19, 2023. Available at www.foreignaffairs.com/ukraine/time-america-join-international-criminal-court-vladimir-putin.

Zvobgo, Kelebogile, and Stephen Chaudoin. 2025. "Complementarity and Public Views on Overlapping International and Domestic Courts." *Journal of Politics*, 87 (3): 1028–1044.

Index

Aideed, Mohammed Farah, 65
Al Hassan, Ag Abdoul Aziz, 99
Al Hussein, Zeid Raad, 2
Albright, Madeleine, 55, 57
Allen, Michael, 224
al-Mahdi, Ahmad, 99
American military bases
  American empire debate, 108
  Base Structure Report, 207
  Camp Humphreys, 106
  Camp Lemonnier, 109
  costs and benefits, 15–17
  Diego Garcia, 17
  exposure to ICC jurisdiction, 103–115
  Fort Leavenworth, 103
  global military presence, 206–211
  Guantanamo Bay, 104
  lily pads, 209
  Pearl Harbor, 104
  Ramstein, 106, 209
  Soto Cano, 207
  Subic Bay, 106
American Servicemembers' Protection Act, 144–148, 150, 175, 178, 242
Amnesty International, 82, 85
Anatomy of the Nuremberg Trials, The, 37
Annan, Kofi, 2, 81, 143
Antibalaka, 11
arap Moi, Daniel, 75
Arbour, Louise, 58, 65, 73
Arendt, Hannah, 33, 203
Armitage, Richard, 207
Arms and Influence, 106
Article 98 agreements, 146–147, 215
Arusha Accords, 68
Assad, Bashar, 155
Austin, Llyod, 184, 232
Axworthy, Lloyd, 131

Baker, James, 54
Barr, William, 171
Bashir, Omar, 9, 51, 91, 97, 148, 243
Bass, Gary, 40
Bellinger, John, 149, 151
Bemba, Jean-Pierre, 9
Bensouda, Fatou, 88, 154, 162, 165, 172
Berger, Sandy, 63
Bernays, Murray, 32
Biddle, Francis, 36
Biden, Joe, 127, 176–194
Bix, Herbert, 46
Black Hawk Down incident, 65, 68
Blewitt, Graham, 62
Blinken, Anthony, 2, 178, 190
Bolton, John, 1, 8, 121, 142, 167–168, 171
Bosco, David, 87, 132, 212
Boutros-Ghali, Boutros, 57
Brackman, Arnold, 43
Brookings Institution, 154
Buchwald, Todd, 159, 167
Burke-White, William, 15
Bush, George H.W., 52
Bush, George W., 133, 142–151

Cambodian Genocide Justice Act, 78, 134
Carden, Richard, 2
Carter Doctrine, 107
Cassese, Antonio, 62
Central Registry of War Criminals and Security Suspects, 38
Chartier, Christian, 62
Chayes, Abram, 111
Chayes, Antonia, 111
Christopher, Warren, 61
Churchill, Winston, 31–32
Clark, Wesley, 68
Clinton, Bill, 55, 69, 101, 127–130, 232

Clinton, Hillary, 127, 156, 175
Coalition for the International Criminal Court, 11, 117
Corell, Hans, 2
Cotton, Tom, 175, 192
Counter Intelligence Corps, 38
Craddock, Bantz, 150
Crane, David, 80

Dallaire, Romeo, 69
Danforth, John, 149
Dayton Accords, 59, 64
Defense Intelligence Agency, 74
deGuzman, Margaret, 212
Deif, Mohammed, 191
DeLay, Tom, 120
destroyers-for-bases deal, 104
Deutch, John, 63
Dicker, Richard, 123
Djindjic, Zoran, 67
Dodd, Christopher, 145
Dokmanovic, Slavko, 66
Donovan, William, 37
Dower, John, 47
Durham, John, 241
Duterte, Rodrigo, 13, 51

Eagleburger, Lawrence, 54
Eboe-Osuji, Chile, 170, 242
Eden, Anthony, 31
Einsatzgruppen trial, 39
Eisenhower, Dwight D., 30
Emperor Hirohito, 42, 45
extradition, 76, 147
Extraordinary African Chambers, 78
Extraordinary Chambers in the Courts of Cambodia, 78

Federalist Society, 167
Feinstein, Dianne, 127
Ferencz, Benjamin, 39, 129, 146
Ferguson, Niall, 108
Fetterman, John, 192
Fleischer, Ari, 143, 147
Flynn, Michael, 224

Gaddafi, Muammar, 51, 91, 140, 153, 155
Gallagher, Edward, 170
Gallant, Yoav, 190–191, 226
Garland, Merrick, 184

Gbagbo, Laurent, 51, 99
Geneva Conventions, 27, 202, 240
Genocide Convention, 52, 201
Gerasimov, Valery, 187
Gillem, Mark, 108
Goering, Hermann, 29, 39
Goldsmith, Jack, 97, 110
Goldstone, Richard, 51, 58, 60, 63, 65, 71, 77
Golsteyn, Matthew, 170
Graham, Lindsey, 5, 183, 194
Grams, Rod, 127
Grossman, Marc, 143
Gutman, Roy, 54

Habyarimana, Juvenal, 67
Hagan, John, 52
Haniyeh, Ismail, 191
Harris, Kamala, 190
Hathaway, Oona, 202
Hebert, F. Edward, 105
Helms, Jesse, 13, 111, 120, 124, 127, 231
Hillebrecht, Courtney, 88
Hiroshima, 41
Hitler, Adolf, 29
Holbrooke, Richard, 59, 65
Holder, Eric, 241
Hollis, Brenda, 62, 81
Holocaust, 28–30
Hull, Cordell, 30
Human Rights Watch, 82, 99, 123
Hussein, Saddam, 52

Illegitimate Court Counteraction Act, 191
Indian Removal Act, 103
International Court of Justice, 21
International Criminal Court
  Afghanistan investigation, 141, 161–174, 177–179
  Africa bias, 214, 219
  American public opinion toward, 236
  American sanctions on, 14, 172–173, 177–179, 235
  American strategies toward, 132–142
  American unsigning, 143
  arrests, 95–98
  Assembly of State Parties, 86, 237
  Bangladesh/Myanmar investigation, 176

Index

Burundi investigation, 176
Central African Republic
  investigation, 10, 140, 151, 157
complementarity, 94, 213, 240
crimes, 91–93, 200–206
Democratic Republic of the Congo
  investigation, 151
Georgia investigation, 157
gravity, 94, 212
interests of justice, 94, 170–171
investigations, 93–95, 197–200
Ivory Coast investigation, 157
judges, 88
jurisdiction, 89–93
Kenya investigation, 157
Libya investigation, 140, 153, 155
Mali investigation, 157
measuring anti-American bias of,
  196–201
offenses against the administration of
  justice, 236
Office of the Prosecutor, 87
organization, 86–88
Palestine investigation, 188–193
Philippines investigation, 193
preliminary examinations, 94, 198, 223
proprio motu authority, 94, 117,
  163, 166, 197
prosecutor's discretion, 115–124
Russian spy, 13
Sudan investigation, 148–151
Syria referral, 153, 214
trials, 99–101
Uganda investigation, 151
Ukraine investigation, 5, 92, 141,
  180–188
Venezuela investigation, 193
International Criminal Tribunal for
  Rwanda, 71–77
International Criminal Tribunal for
  Yugoslavia, 10, 56–67
International Law Commission, 101, 116
International Military Education and
  Training program, 150
International Monetary Fund, 18
International Tribunal for the Law of
  the Sea, 22

Jackson, Robert, 28, 36, 50–51
Jammeh, Yahya, 88
Jean-Pierre, Karine, 192
Joffe, Josef, 19
Johnson, Mike, 193
justice cascade, 20
Justice for Victims of War Crimes Act, 138

Kabbah, Ahmed Tejan, 79
Kagame, Paul, 69–70
Kaltenbrunner, Ernst, 29
Kampala Conference, 158–161
Karadzic, Radovan, 53, 67
Katanga, Germain, 99
Keenan, Joseph B., 45
Kellogg-Briand Pact, 10
Kenyatta, Uhuru, 51
Khan, Karim, 22, 88, 92, 179, 190, 215
Kido, Koichi, 48
Kirsch, Philippe, 11, 102, 125
Kissinger, Henry, 38, 121
Klein, Jacques, 66
Kobylash, Sergei, 187
Koh, Harold, 152, 159–160
Kony, Joseph, 91, 157
Kosovo Specialist Chambers, 78
Ku, Julian, 11

Lake, Anthony, 58, 63
Last Days of Hitler, The, 33
Law of the Sea Convention, 22
League of Nations, 9
Leiber Code, 27, 240
LeMay, Curtis, 39
Lemkin, Raphael, 201
Lewinsky, Monica, 120, 127
Lewis, Anthony, 126
Lietzau, William, 125
like-minded group, 112, 123
Lippman, Thomas, 126
Lorance, Clint, 170
Lord's Resistance Army, 154, 157
Lubanga, Thomas, 99
Luce, Henry, 106
Luria, Elaine, 175
Lvova-Belova, Maria, 187

M23 rebel group, 154
MacArthur, Douglas, 43–48
Mandela, Nelson, 61
Martinez Machain, Carla, 224
McDonald, Gabrielle, 62

McNamara, Robert, 129
Meron, Theodor, 3, 125
Milley, Mark, 211
Milosevic, Slobodan, 10, 14, 53, 66–67
Mladic, Ratko, 53, 67
Mochochoko, Phakiso, 172
Moreno-Ocampo, Luis, 2, 23, 87, 118, 144, 204
Morgenthau Jr., Henry, 30
Morgenthau Plan, 30–32

Nagasaki, 41
National Patriotic Front of Liberia, 81
Neier, Aryeh, 99
Netanyahu, Benjamin, 9, 51, 191, 226
No Peace Without Justice, 82
North Atlantic Treaty Organization, 13, 59, 64
Ntaganda, Bosco, 99, 154
Ntaryamira, Cyprien, 67
Nuremberg Tribunal, 28–41
Nzelibe, Jide, 11

Obama, Barack, 151–164
Obasanjo, Olusegun, 81
Office of Global Criminal Justice, 165, 167
Ongwen, Dominic, 99, 154, 156
Operation Paperclip, 38, 46

Pace, William, 11, 117
Pal, Radhabinod, 48
peace versus justice debate, 24, 56
Pearl Harbor, 45
Pocan, Mark, 191
Pompeo, Mike, 1, 7, 168, 171, 189
Potsdam Conference, 105
Powell, Colin, 67
Power, Samantha, 68, 152
Princeton process on the crime of aggression, 158
Prosper, Pierre-Richard, 73, 147, 149
Psaki, Jen, 189
Putin, Vladimir, 5, 18, 51, 93, 141, 180–187, 243
Pye, Lucien, 45

Quebec Conference, 32

Rabkin, Jeremy, 50
Rademaker, Stephen, 145

Radio Television Libre des Mille Collines, 75
Rainey, Carlisle, 220
Rapp, Stephen, 73, 81, 84, 152, 154
Revolutionary Armed Forces of Colombia, 95
Revolutionary United Front, 79
Rice, Condoleezza, 82, 150
Rice, Susan, 153
Richardson, Bill, 116, 121
Robertson, Geoffrey, 29
Roosevelt, Franklin D., 30–35
Rosenbaum, Eli, 184
Rosenberg, Alfred, 37
Rough Justice, 132
Ruggie, John, 13
Rwandan Patriotic Front, 68

Sadat, Leila, 2
Sanders, Bernie, 237
Sankoh, Foday, 79, 81
Schabas, William, 84
Scheffer, David, 3, 76, 80, 102, 110, 155, 203, 233
Schelling, Thomas, 106
Scheveningen prison, 98
Shattuck, John, 70, 73
Shawcross, Hartley, 31
Shklar, Judith, 23
Shoigu, Sergei, 187
Sinwar, Yahya, 191
Sirleaf, Ellen Johnson, 82
Slaughter, Anne-Marie, 152
Sokolov, Viktor, 187
Soros Foundation, 82
Special Court for Sierra Leone, 78–84
Special Criminal Court in the Central African Republic, 78
Special Panels for Serious Crimes in East Timor, 78
Special Tribunal for Lebanon, 78
Srebrenica, 64
Stalin, Joseph, 31
Starr, Kenneth, 119, 151
status of forces agreements, 106, 147, 238
Stimson, Henry, 32–33
Sullivan, Jake, 181
Supreme Court, 29, 48

Index

Tan, Morse, 171, 173
Taylor, Charles, 81–83
Taylor, Telford, 37, 39
Tehran Conference, 31
Tejan-Cole, Abdul, 81
Thatcher, Margaret, 52
Thomas-Greenfield, Linda, 180
Tillerson, Rex, 165
Tito, Josip Broz, 53
Tojo, Hideki, 45, 47
Tokyo Tribunal, 41–49
Torres, Ritchie, 192
Trevor-Roper, Hugh, 33
Truman, Harry, 35, 42, 105
Trump, Donald, 1, 164–176, 234

unipolar moment, 18, 56
United Nations Security Council, 18, 21, 56, 93, 115, 149, 160, 214

Van Schaack, Beth, 73, 181, 185
victor's justice, 39, 48, 52, 113
Vienna Convention on the Law of Treaties, 111, 144
Vine, David, 108, 209
Vishinsky, Andrei, 34

War Crimes Rewards Program, 84
Watanabe, Mutsuhiro, 46
Wedgwood, Ruth, 101
Weisbord, Noah, 159
Whiting, Alex, 171
Williamson, Clint, 66
World Bank, 18

Zakaria, Fareed, 19
Zelensky, Volodymyr, 186

For EU product safety concerns, contact us at Calle de José Abascal, 56–1°,
28003 Madrid, Spain or eugpsr@cambridge.org.